W. S. GILBERT'S
THEATRICAL CRITICISM

W. S. Gilbert (1870s)

W. S. GILBERT'S THEATRICAL CRITICISM

Jane W. Stedman

The Society for Theatre Research
London

First Published 2000
by The Society for Theatre Research
c/o The Theatre Museum, 1e Tavistock Street, London WC2E 7PA

ISBN 0 85430 068 6

General Editor: Dr Richard Foulkes
Volume Editor: Dr John Russell Stephens

Set by Blot Publishing
8 Chanctonbury, ASHINGTON, West Sussex RH20 3QE
www.blot.co.uk

Printed by Plumridge & Co.
41 High Street, LINTON, Cambridgeshire

To my nieces, Jen and Sue,
whose mother and I danced
up and down my study, singing
'If Saphir I choose to marry'
to the music of an old wind-up
phonograph.

Table of Contents

List of Illustrations

Preface

This book is not intended to be an exhaustive account of W. S. Gilbert as a reviewer of plays, but rather a relatively brief discussion of the milieu in which he worked as a critic, an indication of the scope of his criticism (which, like his imaginative works, often emphasized and repeated certain themes), and a concentrated look at his reviews in the form of burlesque plays, published in *Fun*, as his most satiric, best, and funniest criticism.

Fortunately these plays began under the second editor of *Fun*, Tom Hood, and therefore can be identified, not only by style, but in the marked copies of the proprietor's file in the Henry E. Huntington Library, which annotate authorship of and payment made for each contribution beginning in 1865. Peter Joslin's marked copies of Gilbert's own run of *Fun* begin in 1862. Needless to say, I owe thanks to both these sources.

I have, however, made no attempt to list or discuss every Gilbert burlesque play, although I believe I have indicated his range and techniques. I have used the Bab Ballads as they originally appeared in *Fun*, but have also silently noted James Ellis's edition (Harvard University Press, 1970), which indicates a few non-substantive changes in subsequent editions.

The dates attached to the burlesques are those on which they were published unless otherwise noted. Almost always these dates were some two weeks after opening night, and indeed the play might, like *Oonagh*, have closed before Gilbert's review appeared. In quoting from other critics, I have emphasized those of the *Athenaeum* and the *Tomahawk* as presenting more or less opposite ends of the reviewer's spectrum.

Furthermore, I have italicised titles of all plays, whether they were published or not, in an effort to make them stand out clearly from other quoted material. I have not regularly preserved Victorian distinctions of the large and small capitals, but have made all large capitals. The compositors of *Fun* did not attempt consistency in setting Gilbert's reviews; so there are some variations in speaker designation; in double spacing between some lines, but not regularly, and so on. Double quotation marks are, I assume, Gilbert's. I have retained enough to give the effect of the original, but since this is not a facsimile edition, I have not attempted to reproduce the exact appearance of each physical page. Nor have I dealt with the material chronologically except in the distinction between the time he wrote his burlesque playlets and the times he wrote essays on theatre or gave interviews. Gilbert's style did not alter noticeably; chronology therefore does not seem to be a controlling factor.

While the ultimate purpose of this book is to further the reader's specific knowledge of an early aspect of Gilbert's work, I would like to think that its immediate effect will be to produce laughter – at a play written in the leading actress's mumbles, at a miscostumed female congregation bearing Little Nell's soul aloft, at dusty oceans and heroines who faint over every available piece of furniture.

As always, I owe my husband, George C. McElroy, a great debt of gratitude for suspending his own work to read, comment on, and laugh uproariously at Gilbert's works as exemplified in this book. My thanks, too, are owing to John Russell Stephens, a painstaking and eagle-eyed editor.

Jane W. Stedman
Chicago 1999

....

I should like to echo the author's thanks to John Russell Stephens for his invaluable contribution as volume editor and add a note of appreciation to Le Forbes (Blot Publishing) for preparing the book for printing.

Richard Foulkes
General Editor of Publications
Society for Theatre Research

1 The Stage and its Denizens: Forms, Standards and Givens

W. S. Gilbert wrote very little theoretical criticism; nevertheless, he worked from a well-thought-out set of critical principles, early arrived at and later modified in relatively minor details. These principles may be gathered from his journalism, his periodical articles and his occasional speeches, from interviews he gave the press and opinions he gave privately. Of course, the parodistic elements of many of his own libretti in themselves constitute criticism of a kind, and his most effective reviews took the form of parody.

In 1861 Gilbert began to contribute to a newly founded comic weekly, *Fun*, imitator and rival of *Punch*, which for some years it nearly equalled in circulation and surpassed in comicality. Here Gilbert began his career as a journalist and was soon writing about the London stage since *Fun*, like other comic periodicals of its day, was staffed largely by people who wrote or reviewed plays (sometimes both), among them Tom Robertson, E. L. Blanchard, Arthur Sketchley, Clement Scott and Henry S. Leigh. H. J. Byron, author of innumerable burlesques, *Our Boys*, and other comedies, was its first editor, followed in 1865 by Thomas Hood the younger, who was, however, not a dramatist. F. C. Burnand went from *Fun* to *Punch*. Although Gilbert did not limit himself to *Fun*, his best known, funniest, and most perceptive criticism appeared there over the next ten years, especially from 1865 to 1871.

Gilbert, of course, had been stage-struck from boyhood as his father Dr William Gilbert had been before him. Dr Gilbert had written many unplayable plays, including a version of Bellini's *Norma*, re-titled *Morna*, and had translated the libretto of Donizetti's *Lucia di Lammermoor*. These texts have disappeared, and Dr Gilbert evidently never had the excitement of seeing a play of his own creating staged by amateurs or professionals. He consoled himself by writing articles and novels, which usually dealt with hallucinations, obsessions, or madness; with magic or with what he called 'the social deposits', that is, the poorest of the poor, driven by no fault of their own to gin or prostitution. Dr Gilbert was never a leading novelist, but he was a success in his own particular line, even being compared by reviewers to Daniel Defoe.

1

From such a father W. S. Gilbert no doubt derived an interest in drama more intense than that of most Victorian boys. At school he wrote, directed and acted in plays, including an appearance as Guy Fawkes. He followed a clown, Tom Barry, along the Strand, not quite daring to speak to him, until Barry turned disappointingly into a public house. He left school to appeal to Charles Kean, whose prestigious company he hoped to join, but was sent back to the classroom. He helped turn the University of London's Engineering Society into a Shakespearean Reading and Dramatic Society.

Young Gilbert also wrote innumerable plays, and finally in 1863 one was accepted for production at the Lyceum Theatre, a curtain-raising comedietta, entitled *Uncle Baby*, not very amusing and no better than dozens of others. It was not well-reviewed, but improved during its run of approximately a month. Managers, however, did not hasten to suggest that Gilbert might write for them.

In the 1860s the musical theatre was declining in quality although not in quantity. Pantomime, burlesque, and extravaganza, all in pun-riddled couplets interspersed with songs set to popular tunes and boisterous dances, tended to merge into each other. For the most part pantomime retained its identity by virtue of its ever-shortening harlequinade, but borrowed the idea of a spectacular 'transformation scene' from extravaganza. In it the leading fairy changed the set to a brilliant, fantastically magic locale replete with fairies floated aloft on wires; 'oh, their bony, baggy knees!' exclaimed Gilbert in 'Pantomimic Presentiments' (*Fun*, 2 December 1865). Then followed the harlequinade itself with clown, pantaloon, columbine, and harlequin, often a sprite or two; this, in turn, usually concluded with a 'rally' in which everyone rushed on and threw things, mostly vegetables. When Gilbert later included 'rally' in the stage directions of a non-musical play he was parodying, he clearly intended it as a derogatory device.

Audiences for burlesque were adult unlike those for pantomime, which was supposedly a children's entertainment. There was no transformation scene, no rally, no harlequinade, although a burlesque might sometimes be turned into a pantomime by the addition of the latter. Burlesque subjects were drawn (often a long way) from plays, novels, even from long poems such as Scott's *The Lady of the Lake*, transmuted with a punning subtitle 'Plaid in a Tartan' by Robert Reece (1866). In 'What Is A Burlesque?' (*Belgravia Annual*, 1868), Gilbert described the essentials:

> Story confused,
> Frequently used;
> Sillified pun
> Clumsily done.
> > Dresses grotesque,
> > Girls statuesque,
> > Scene picturesque –
> > That's a burlesque!

Later in life, however, he did recall some neat puns with pleasure, such as that which Albert Smith put in the mouth of Orson, mourning his foster-mother, a she-bear: 'Behold me strewin' / With leaves this little *bier* of my own *bruin*.'[1]

Extravaganza had some claim to pictorial elegance when James Robinson Planché imported it from France; then it gave the effect of a Perrault or D'Aulnoy fairytale realized on stage in appropriate costumes and with a certain decorum. For Planché's *Island of Jewels* (1849) William Beverley designed a charming effect in which the leaves of a gigantic palm tree opened to show fairies with a coronet of gems, which stimulated pantomime to increasingly spectacular scenes. By the 1860s the texts of extravaganza became almost interchangeable with those of burlesque, as witness, for instance, the genre labels attached to some of Gilbert's own early works.

All these forms were heavily transvestite, girls in tights appearing as princes and their friends, and male low comedians as mothers, mantraps, and historical characters such as Joan of Arc or Queen Elizabeth I. Gilbert disliked these 'dames' very much: 'to my thinking, Mr. Clarke, or any other actor, in girl's clothes is not a pleasant sight,' he wrote in an *Illustrated Times* review (4 January 1868). Again:

> It is a disgrace to the stage that men are suffered to wear women's clothes and pad themselves in imitation of women's figures. To any person of taste there is something utterly repulsive in the appearance of a man dressed, padded, and painted in imitation of a woman, with pink silk stockings and embroidered underclothing. (15 May 1869)

He also objected that the press paid too much attention to pantomime and its ilk, attention out of proportion to their real importance (2 January 1869). Gilbert perforce dealt with these as the

3

Theatrical Lounger of the *Illustrated Times*, but they did not appear in his major reviews for *Fun*.[2]

Non-musical plays tended to be farcical or melodramatic, and can be roughly divided into comedy-dramas, domestic dramas, sensation dramas and historical dramas.

Although the Victorians inherited melodrama instead of inventing it, they found it extraordinarily congenial. Their playwrights set to work extending and sophisticating it, while repeating its motifs, until Victorian melodrama became an enchanted country in which plots and characters either did not grow old or were perpetually rejuvenated by continual re-embodiment and revival. Indeed, melodrama was, and is, a fundamentally conservative art form, although in its staging, great stress has always been placed upon technical and scenic innovation. So constant were its intrinsic elements that during the nineteenth century a parody not only hit the immediate play at which it aimed, but also pierced a whole line of indistinct older melodramas standing behind it. It was therefore easy to satirize the genre *qua* genre.

Furthermore, a Victorian audience required satisfactory endings for both moral comfort and emotional pleasure. The outcome of melodrama, therefore, is almost always as foregone as that of tragedy, but the melodramatic purgation arises not through pity and fear, but through a faster-than-life variety of passions during which the spectator's own feelings are vicariously and repeatedly stimulated and drained.

Even Matthew Arnold admitted that, although one would not want to write a melodrama, he himself felt a hundred times as excited at seeing *The Corsican Brothers* as at seeing *Lear*. Violent actions and physical dangers are therefore available in almost every variety of Victorian – or later – melodrama. Dialogue was exclamatory, as Gilbert's punctuation in his burlesque plays shows.

Gilbert's view, expressed in his *Illustrated Times* review of Dr Westland Marston's *Life for Life* (13 March 1869), was simply that people go to the theatre, not to think, but to be amused 'or to have their feelings worked upon by a succession of dramatic events, appealing principally to the eye and incidentally to the ear'. Plays which achieved neither of these effects did not succeed financially.

During the mid-nineteenth century, there were no real tragedies except for revivals of earlier works, primarily, of course, Shakespeare's. Even these, however, were liable to be re-organized to make the star's role star-ier, as Gilbert was to object in 'Unappreciated Shakespeare' (*Illustrated Sporting and Dramatic News*, Christmas Number, 1882). He estimated that approximately half of *Hamlet's* lines were deleted from its stage performance.

Nor was there real comedy in Sheridan's sense of the word. Critics approached old, that is, eighteenth-century, comedy with ready-made reverence and new comedy, what there was of it, with a ready-made sneer. Only a few wished for truly biting satire; instead, the unimpeachable comic ideal was a sentimental one in which laughter was caused by pleasure in and sympathy with innocent or benevolent goodness combined with eccentricity or absurdity as exemplified by Mr Pickwick or a Cheeryble Brother. Going further, reviewers asked for tears with laughter. An unidentified critic quoted in Edgar Pemberton's life of Tom Robertson praised that playwright for finding 'Like all genuine humorists ... the source of humour to be very near the fount of tears'.[3] In an article 'What is Comedy?' the *Tomahawk* (21 December 1867) defined it as 'a real picture of human Nature, lighted up with brilliant flashes of wit, and teaching under cover of genial satire, a true lesson from the book of life'.

Nor did this viewpoint cease in the early twentieth century, for Miss Lawrence Alma-Tadema explained in the *Academy* (1 July 1905) that 'the essence of all true comedy is sympathy. . . .With a weakness which we do not understand we cannot sympathise; and, if we do not sympathise, we are unable to gain from the manifestation of it the kindly amusement which comedy should give.' A satirist of whom geniality and kindliness were demanded was disarmed before he ever entered the arena, and this attitude meant that very little true comedy was available for Gilbert to review in the 1860s. (His own works in the next decade were often labelled 'cruel', 'cynical' and 'lacking in sympathy'.)

Instead of comedy in the strict sense, there was farce. Farcical characters were Jonsonian humours reduced to comic tics; they spoke in catchwords and their business was stage business. Their function was not to reveal human nature but to amuse by releasing energy, which, as long as it was neither political nor sexual, did not concern the Lord Chamberlain's licenser of plays. The comedy of manners had become the comedy of behaviour. 'To call the comedy farcical is, I presume, to remove it at once out of the region of common sense,' wrote the Theatrical Lounger (*Illustrated Times*, 24 July 1869), who was probably Gilbert. This removal freed it from the necessity of causing tears except tears of laughter and allied it with nonsense, in which, as Elizabeth Sewell says, 'The absence of sympathy and fellow-feeling is fundamental.'[4] Unfortunately, since farce is a short form, Gilbert rarely expended a paragraph on it, if that, when reviewing.

Mid-Victorian plays, as we know, were generally adapted from the French or sometimes the German or from the novels of Scott, Dickens, and lesser popular writers. The debate over adaptation was rancorous and on-going not only before the 1860s but for more than a decade afterward. On 18 June 1864, for instance, *Fun* published 'Adapted from the French / Respectfully Dedicated to the Dramatists Of Great Britain', verses urging British playwrights to be truly original and lamenting that 'Our dramas, like our bonnets, are / Adapted from the French.' In March 1879, to choose another example, the use of 'new' to mean 'adapted' occasioned a series in the *Theatre*, which would last for three months. Touched off by a 'new' 1877 play, *Hester Grey*, by Robert Reece and H. B. Farnie, 'written expressly for Miss Wallis', it had been taken directly but silently from a French melodrama, *La Mendiante*. The *Manchester Guardian*, however, attributed it to an English play of the 1850s, *Ruth Oakley*, whereupon the *Theatre* quoting the *Guardian*, described the absence of 'adapted' as unjustifiable, and 'through a little over-zeal in our office' advertised it as 'a serious charge'. Reece and Farnie sued for libel, although Farnie dropped out before the case came to court. Their defence was that neither had seen *Ruth Oakley*, that *Hester Grey* was founded on the French play, and that they had not understood that the theatre bills would describe it simply as 'new'. Mr Justice Lopez found the *Theatre's* criticism just, but the periodical expressed regret for its over-zealousness. Tom Taylor, Palgrave Simpson, and John Hollingshead had all testified to the practice of calling an unacknowledged adaptation 'new', but all deprecated it. Gilbert, Byron, the actor John Hare, and the *Daily News* critic, Moy Thomas, were ready to testify on behalf of the *Theatre*, but were not called. The *Theatre* patted itself on the back for taking a righteous stand.

In April, it ran a round table on '"New" and "Original" Plays' with Gilbert, Byron, Thomas and F. C. Burnand as participants. Byron admitted that theatre people would understand 'new' traditionally meant not original, but disapproved of the term. Gilbert and Thomas were firmly against it, Thomas asking why a word should be used in a way that contradicted its dictionary meaning, and Gilbert roundly declaring that it would deceive the general public. Peremptorily he asserted that an author who put a translation forward as a new work should be publicly denounced and his translation treated as a fraud. After a good deal of word juggling, Burnand came down in favour of tradition.

On 30 April, Gilbert wrote to Clement Scott that 'My view was and is, that to adapt a play without acknowledging the source from which it is taken is dishonest.'[5] But in May Scott, writing as Saville Rowe (his *nom de théâtre* for his adaptations and collaborations), addressed the editor to complain about the inability of the round table to agree on any moral point, about Gilbert's references to imposters and frauds, and about Thomas's laying down the law about honesty as if he were a self-appointed schoolmaster. 'For my own part,' wrote Scott sniffily, 'I resent such dictation, or such inferences,' since he was as capable of distinguishing between right and wrong as they were.

Theatre managers found adaptations safer at the box office, for the play had already proved its worth in Paris, but even adaptations had to be made acceptable to an English audience. So a great deal of mid-Victorian talent went to denaturing 'strong' (that is, sexual) situations in order to produce a not-too-French French plot. Farces and comedies bore this process better than serious plays, for flirtation could be made as comic as seduction – and if the intrigue were not utterly innocent, it need not be absolutely guilty. With native ingenuity thus spending itself on laundering plays rather than originating them, the danger came not from French looseness in morals, but British looseness in dramatic construction, to which Gilbert's reviews frequently objected.

As to the public for whom these plays were adapted or originated, Gilbert saw many faults of the stage arising from or perpetuated by uncritical audiences. He described them in the last chapter of his first Comic Physiognomist series (*Fun*, 5 March 1864) as

> a flock of sheep who go whither they are driven, who applaud that which they are told to applaud, and who hiss that which they are advised to hiss. As to presuming to judge for themselves, no British public was ever guilty of such an indecency except on the following occasions:– 1. The first night of a new English opera, when everybody is encored in everything, and all the *artistes* are called before the curtain at the end of each

act.... Nevertheless, the opera is usually withdrawn in about a fortnight. 2. The first night of a play, when they applaud everything, including jokes which the author himself never contemplated, and then afterwards (having been told by the critics that it is bad) hiss it off the stage, and won't hear of it at any price....

Five years later in 'The British Playgoer, and All That Is Expected of Him' (*Tinsley's Magazine*, January 1869), Gilbert still was sure that the ordinary audience applauded or hissed 'just as their leaders tell 'em to', although British theatres fortunately did not have organized claques. Most of this article, however, satirises the absurdities seriously set before the credulous audience by authors, managers, and actors. For example, the British Playgoer is asked to believe

> ...that guests at a supper shall only sit round three sides of the table; that four or five persons conversing in a room shall do so standing in a row; ... that the inside of a house is much bigger than the outside; that gentlemen of undoubted breeding shall wear their hats indoors in the presence of ladies of exceptional refinement; ... that a mortgagee can at any moment foreclose; ...that pieces of broken crockery shaken up in a basket represent the kind of noise that a comic gentleman would make in falling through a skylight: ... and that in the best-regulated establishment there is always one comic footman in an exaggerated livery and impossible whiskers, whose only duty it is to announce names wrongly and to fall down with a tray of ices and apples ....

The British Playgoer must not be surprised to learn that dumb persons 'possess powers of pantomimic narration (if you only give them room enough) which throw mere vocal eloquence altogether into the shade'; that blind persons are 'the best qualified to unravel the mysteries with which a complicated murder-case is surrounded'; and that idiots 'have a special faculty of expressing themselves in blank verse....'

If the scene is laid on a man-of-war, the Playgoer will find that the captain wears a moustache, long hair, and carries a telescope. He is afraid of nothing except the discharge of his own pistol, and

> there is always a marine on board who is a prominent coward .... Although a dreadful coward in times of peace, he

performs prodigies of valour when he engages the enemy, and indeed it is generally owing to his intrepid but, at the same time, judicious course of action that Great Britain is not eventually swept from the map of Europe. The British playgoer will also learn that the crew of a man-of-war is composed of hardy tars in blue-satin trousers, small waists, and diamond earrings, who dance hornpipes with two union jacks apiece . . . .

(Any devotee of 1940s motion pictures dealing with the Second World War will realize that the coward-turned-hero is not limited to mid-Victorian melodrama.)

It is, however, scenes set in law courts which require the willingest suspension of disbelief. Assertions form the principal evidence against the accused; a husband's or wife's evidence is conclusive proof of the prisoner's innocence; a judge may disbelieve the most conclusive evidence of guilt on the grounds that no one with such an eye as the prisoner's could possibly be guilty. In fact, the judge may lead cheers on the acquittal of a popular malefactor. Title-deeds of incredible complexity may be written on a single sheet of paper; illegitimate sons can inherit peerages, while 'the last utterances of a dying criminal are quite sufficient to vest an estate in anybody whom it may occur to him to mention.' And so on.

Great consequences may arise from trivial causes, and Gilbert instances, without naming it, a recent play in which a British chaplain was determined to convert 'the lovely daughter of an excitable Thug'. This starts the whole Indian Mutiny. 'Whether it was altogether worth while that British subjects should undergo all the horrors of that mutiny in order that the Thuggess in question should be converted to Christianity' is something the British playgoer must never ask himself. Gilbert admits that honourable exceptions may be found, but until the stage is made 'a fair reflex of the outside world' managers will expect audiences' complaisance.

Although in his prose reviews for a variety of periodicals Gilbert attended most of the London theatres, his longest notices dealt with productions at the Adelphi, Olympic, Haymarket, Queen's and Holborn, but he went to others as well, including the Surrey, Prince of Wales's, St James's, and Lyceum. The first of these was managed by Benjamin Webster and was dirty on both sides of the curtain. Unventilated, with a horrid smell, the Adelphi made one sick to sit in it, according to the *Tomahawk* (27 July 1867). The mainstay of its dramatic bills was melodrama with a good deal of comic relief, and its supers, whom Gilbert christened 'the Adelphi guests', were badly costumed and badly drilled. Webster also managed the Olympic for one season in 1868, preceded by Horace Wigan in 1864 and followed by W. H. Liston.

The Queen's Theatre was under the management of Alfred Wigan, although the actual lessee was the politician Henry Labouchere, whose mistress, Henrietta Hodson, was its leading lady. The *Building News* (18 October 1867) described its grand staircase as one of the finest in London, and the artist Albert Moore painted a scene of Greek figures watching a play above the proscenium.

J. B. Buckstone managed the Haymarket from 1853 to 1878 with a company of ageing comedians, probably the most stable in London except for that of Marie Wilton and her husband, Squire Bancroft, at the Prince of Wales's. All but one of Gilbert's fairy verse plays, as well as three of his prose plays, were first performed at the Haymarket. During the 1860s Alfred Wigan and Webster turned up again in brief periods of management at the St James's Theatre, which was also in the successive hands of F. B. Chatterton, George Vining, Frank Matthews, Miss Herbert, W. S. Emden and Mrs John Wood. Sefton Perry was the manager during some of Gilbert's reviewing days. Gilbert reviewed the successive plays by Tom Robertson at the Prince of Wales's except for the first one, *Society* (1865); he also occasionally reviewed Robertson at other theatres, but did not find those plays so satisfactory. To a certain extent Gilbert was more personally involved with the innovative little house, which Marie Wilton had reclaimed from what was earlier known as 'the dust hole'. The Bancrofts were personal friends as was Robertson, from whose rehearsals he learned stagecraft and with whom he attended plays they were both reviewing. This friendly connection, however, did not keep Gilbert from objecting when he felt Robertson had written a play unworthy of himself, such as *The Nightingale*.

Of the dramatic critics who sat in these dirty, renovated, or new seats, John Oxenford was the doyen. In his early days as a reviewer for *The Times* he had been fairly strict until his editor told him that 'Whether a play is good or bad, whether a man acts well or ill, is of very little consequence to the great body of our readers ....'[6] In short, Oxenford was to ameliorate his reviews. Thereafter he made a habit of 'letting down easily a faulty artist or a crude dramatist ....'[7] He was still doing so in the 1860s, reserving any better hits for the *Saturday Review*, of which he was also critic. Thomas Purnell ('Q') described him as not unfair, only inadequate, never malicious, but having a bad effect on drama since his criticism did not show the public why one play was good and another bad.[8]

Purnell objected that in England theatrical criticism was not properly honoured and too often consisted of synopsising the plot and discussing the actors. Even then the reviewer was not always safe. In 1866, for example, when the *Glowworm's* critic remarked that in *The Watch-Cry* (Lyceum, November 1865) Sam Emery's part was spoken by the prompter, the outraged actor sued for libel and was awarded five guineas damages. In fact, the prompter had not spoken Emery's lines: Emery had simply made them up as he went along, having frequently forgotten the words the author (Palgrave Simpson) wrote. In a half-column prose comment (*Fun*, 27 January 1866) Gilbert observed that the fact that

> the dramatic critic of the *Glowworm* had the unparalleled audacity to say what he thought about a dramatic performance will probably bring that journal's criticism into favour with those playgoers who are not influenced by the petty considerations of advertisements and press admissions.
>
> The contemptible character of most of the press criticisms on dramatic performances is almost proverbial, and when we take into consideration the external influences which are brought to bear upon a dramatic critic as he sits down to write his article, it is difficult to see how his criticism can be otherwise than contemptible. In the first place he must take care not to offend the management, or his press admission will be stopped, and the theatre's advertisement be withdrawn from his paper. In the second place, he is probably on intimate terms with all the leading actors, who are a tetchy race of men, taking unqualified praise as their due, and regarding as a personal insult the slightest reflection on their performance .... In the third place as all the principal dramatic critics are dramatic authors also, they are on friendly terms with all the other dramatic authors, and they are naturally unwilling to write one word which may tend to disturb a friendship .... And now, to all these powerful influences is added the fact that if a dramatic critic dares to write what he thinks, in slightly hyperbolical terms, he is subject to a verdict of 'guilty of libel,' and its consequences.[9]

11

Nevertheless, in the 1860s, critics were becoming more independent. In 1867, Dutton Cook began to write forthright reviews for the *Pall Mall Gazette*. Joseph Knight, who had written for the *Literary Gazette* and for the *Sunday Times* since 1865, took over the *Athenaeum* dramatic reviews from J. A. Heraud in 1869; eminently frank, fair, and learned (he became editor of *Notes and Queries* in the 1880s), he was 'On the whole ... the fairest Knight that ever stars had to do with,' punned *Judy* (28 October 1891).

At the first night of Charles Reade's *It's Never Too Late to Mend* (1865), F. G. Tomlins, long of the *Morning Advertiser*, rose to protest at the highly realistic prison scene, which ended with the death of a pitiful adolescent, already on the verge of hanging himself to escape the sadistic prison governor. Other critics joined in as did most of the audience. Although to modern theatre-goers the objection may seem quixotic, it does indicate an unusual independence. Gilbert thereupon wrote two prose comments: 'In Re the Reade-er' (11 November 1865) and 'Fun and Fact' (25 November) as well as a parody review (see pp.53-54 below), all three in *Fun*. The first dealt with the angry letter which Charles Reade wrote to the *Reader* denouncing the 'venom and drivel', as he described it, of Tomlins's criticism, which he said was anonymous. Gilbert pointed out that the review was signed 'F. G. T.', well-known as the initials of one of the oldest and best dramatic critics, and therefore not anonymous. He also said that a critic was, in one sense, a reporter, so it was his duty to report that Tomlins and others addressed George Vining, the theatre manager, indignantly and that he replied to them. Finally, he remarked that the *Reader's* dramatic editor who published Reade's intemperate letter was – none other than – Reade's nephew. In the second comment, Gilbert treated satirically Vining's 'confused advertisement' in the *Standard*, pretending to quote from Gilbert's first article; Vining ended each of his sentences with 'See FUN.' A month later, Tom Hood, the editor of *Fun*, stopped the controversy, 'which is being craftily twisted into an advertisement of a bad piece'. Hood, however, stated very decidedly that it believed in Gilbert's accuracy (although, of course, it did not name him). The 'bad piece' nevertheless enjoyed a considerable run.

Although Tomlins was not a practising dramatist,[10] the problem of conflict of interest when a reviewer was simultaneously a playwright arose recurrently during the nineteenth century. In 1849, for instance, the *Stage Manager* (30 June) objected to 'The truckling, venal, tergiversating character' of most reviewers, who saw merit only in their own pieces, but were afraid to be hard on other authors for fear the others would be hard on them in return. Nearly forty years later a letter from 'A Young Author' to the *Era* (17 April 1886) asked whether such critics as Clement Scott of the *Daily Telegraph* and F. C. Burnand of *Punch* could tell us they never let thoughts of their own work bias their judgement of others. Certainly Burnand's jealousy of Gilbert as Sullivan's librettist weighted his reviews of the Savoy Operas, while the thin-skinned Scott took out his spites and lavished his enthusiasms on the works he reviewed.

Although in the 1860s Scott was not yet an influence, in time to come he would wield enormous power as the critic of the *Daily Telegraph* and other periodicals. G. A. Sala, who disliked him, told a fellow-journalist that Scott wrote 'a sugary, young-ladylike style that "took" with a large section of the public. It was a chocolate-creamy style, and "went down" – like chocolate creams.'[11] Scott's answer to 'A Young Author' was made anonymously in the *Theatre*, which Scott edited. 'No charge,' wrote Scott (June 1886), 'affecting the personal honour of any living critic has ever been justified in any degree whatsoever ...' He conveniently forgot that in an action for libel which he brought against the *Hornet* in 1873, he had himself been forced to admit that he had written libellous articles and therefore found it necessary to withdraw. Scott began writing and adapting plays in 1871 just as Gilbert left off reviewing them because he had become an established dramatist in his own right. Like William Archer, Gilbert believed one should not do both. Furthermore, there was a certain Pooh-Bah-ish flavour to Victorian reviewing in that a critic might substantiate his own views in one periodical by agreeing with them in another. For example, John Hollingshead, manager of the Gaiety Theatre, wrote to Clement Scott on 14 January 1879:

> I am not accustomed to 'brawl' anywhere, and certainly not in a club or theatre. What I said was that I should tell you that I thought it unfair of you – a practised journalist with a command of many 'organs' to be constantly pegging away at an opponent who had not your advantages. I know nothing of the merits of the quarrel between you & Mayer, but you cannot think ill of me for helping a man to the slight extent I have helped him, who has always served me well. I never do a back-handed thing ....[12]

There was also, as always, the merely mechanical question of timing the appearance of a review. Hollingshead, when the critic for the *Daily News*, believed himself unusual in writing his notices on the first night of performance and insisting that they appear the next morning. This was possible because the *News* went to press very late, a full hour after the *Telegraph*, for instance.[13] E. L. Blanchard, who wrote for the latter, rarely stayed through the entire evening: 'Wonderful to say I stop out the entire performance [of *Amy Robsart*] . . . .'[14] Gilbert's parodistic reviews usually appeared two weeks after opening night; so he was under no pressure to leave early and could take time to be amusing – if he needed time.

By 1871 some tightening of critical standards might be observed: 'a certain freedom of censure to which we have long been unaccustomed', as the *Illustrated London News* put it (4 November). Now 'the old extreme indulgence' was no longer the rule, and both plays and actors might be described as bad. Rather cynically, however, it wondered if this were a reaction in favour of higher-class drama or if managers were simply giving 'a patient public' unendurable things. Perhaps it was a bit of both. Nevertheless, the basic assumptions of most reviewers continued to be well-established 'givens', often of a virtuous nature: 'There is a healthy moral tone in the new drama which ought to secure it permanent success,' the *Illustrated London News* concluded in its review of Watts Phillips's play *Lost in London* (23 March 1867).

In the 1860s theatre critics were by no means well-paid. Oxenford was said to make £100 a year from *The Times*;[15] Scott was paid £2 a week by the *Sunday Times*. Gilbert received the usual 'measure pay' from *Fun*: £1 a column, adjusted downward for shorter pieces. Sometimes he may have had a few extra shillings in 1870-71, perhaps even a salary in 1871.[16] Drawings were paid for separately. Thus for his review of Robertson's *The Nightingale*, Gilbert received £1 14s. for the prose text and £1 5s. for the accompanying illustrations, not quite £3 in all. A review of *Ecarté* brought him £1 7s. 6d., and unillustrated full page texts did not go above £2.

This is the immediate milieu, its conditions and some of its inhabitants in, under, and among which and whom Gilbert worked. Now it is time to look more specifically at his work.

2 Gilbert's Early Theatrical Work for *Fun*

When Gilbert began to to write for *Fun* shortly after its inception in 1861, he seems to have contributed miscellaneous drawings frequently accompanied by some comic text. As yet he did not deal particularly with the theatre.[17] On 11 January 1862, however, a cartoon signed W. G. showed a stage villain kneeling, with the caption:

> *Hardened Ruffian is allowed five minutes to make his peace with 'Even. He does so in an earnest whisper to third wing, as follows:–*
>
> 'Here, Bill! If you can't get tick at the "George," run down to the "Ship Aground," and get half a pint of fourpenny ale, with two of gin in it; – and here – look sharp!'

He wears a plumed hat, cloak, doublet and boots; his broken sword lies near him and a very wooden lover and peasant girl stand in embrace in the background.

The next week another W. G. drawing, entitled 'GETTING UP THE COMIC BUSINESS', depicts Columbine, Clown, and Harlequin backstage, the latter holding a frothing tankard, with the dialogue:

'Now it's no use you a-jawing at me, Marier. I haint a-going to have my business dictated by any one, let alone the likes of you!'

'Why, I haint a-jawing, nor yet a-dictatin'. Only what I says is this, Ned, – after you has killed the old woman, I must have time to finish off my *pas* properly before the perlice comes in.'

Alcohol and theatre were combined in a W. S. G. drawing of 1863

15

In 1863 and 1864 Gilbert continued to write on and draw a variety of subjects including 'Sketches in Court'; short satiric reactions to printed news or advertisements; occasional verse; short pieces, some dealing with the theatre; as well as a fairly regular column (to which other members of the *Fun* staff might have occasionally contributed) titled 'Gossip of the Week' or occasionally 'Fashionable Intelligence' and composed of punning one- or two-liners, such as 'The artist who threw up his foreground is better'; 'The public lecturer who dwelt upon a topic has changed his residence' ; and 'A well-known low comedian the other night took the stage. The perplexity of the manager and other performers may be imagined' (1 August 1863).

Early in 1863, Gilbert contributed a series on 'The People of Pantomime', beginning with the Pantomime Demon and including the Pantomime Monarch, Prince, Giant, Servant and the Comic Business (4 February–14 March). The illustrations which accompany them are intricately grotesque – Gilbert was especially good at demons. The letter press is amusing if somewhat wordy. For example:

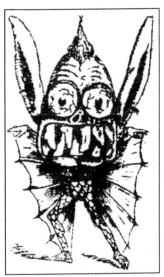

The Pantomime Dragon

When we were younger, that is to say, some ten or fifteen years ago, pantomime, as a rule, knew but one species of demon, and he was invariably typical of intoxication. The demon monarch was usually King Alcohol, while his domestic retinue consisted of Djin, Wiski, Wrunab, Brandi, Skiddam and Oiluns. But, of late years, the alcoholic demon has gone very much out of pantomimic fashion, and this may be fairly attributed to the fact, that the total abstinence party have lately overdone their work to such a degree, that they have gone far to render temperance ridiculous, and the consequence is, that the demons in question, instead of conveying a demoniacal and generally repulsive impression, would rather be hailed by the lightly disposed among the audience as a convivial sort of fellows, eminently typical of good fellowship and keeping it up. The modern demon appeals rather to the passions than the external senses, and the people that monopolize the opening scene of a pantomime are usually the representatives of Envy, Hatred, Malice, and All Uncharitableness.

It is a curious fact in the physiology of the stage demon, that his solo mission in this world is to open a pantomime. He is born for the opening scene, he passes a merry, though malicious existence during that scene, and, at its conclusion, he vanishes, never to reappear until the comic business requires his presence in the metempsychosed condition of an errand boy. And, if the stage holds up the mirror to nature, the antecedenta of the youth who brings our morning paper suggest a really alarming subject of consideration. Struck with this idea, we lately inquired of our publisher's boy whether he had any recollection of a former existence; our hopes, however, fell when he informed us that he never remembered having been a demon. They rose again on learning that his brother was a devil, but then again subsided when we ascertained that he meant a printer's, not a pantomime, devil.

The personal appearance of a demon is striking. His fiendish head is never connected with his infernal body through the medium of a neck, but fits inconveniently into his unholy stomach. His complexion, scorched and crackled by the infernal fires in which he passes his time, is of a brilliant green and red hue, and highly metallic in its appearance. The most inconvenient feature of the pantomime demon is, we should say, the bat-like web which usually reaches from his hands to his heels. If a demon ever swears, we should imagine that he would swear roundly at this web, whenever he has occasion to go against the wind, to put on a great coat, or to waltz with a female demon–if female demons there be, which of course, we are bound to doubt. The many inconveniences to which a pantomime demon is subjected–the fact that they are all dumb until elevated to the infernal throne–their unattractive personal appearance–the sulphuric atmosphere of red and green fire which they breathe, are eminently calculated to teach such a terrible lesson as to the ultimate fate of people who tell stories, that their existence is as essential as Sir Joshua Jebb himself to the well-being of a civilized community.

The Pantomime Monarch

There is no disguising the fact that, exemplary as our pantomime writers may be in other respects, their loyalty is in a very shaky condition indeed. Monarchy, as they are pleased to represent it, is invariably characterized by capricious tyranny of the most objectionable description. Your ordinary melodramatic tyrant is a sufficiently unbearable individual, but his tyranny is dove-like amiability compared with that of your pantomimic monarch. The Victoria autocrat seldom pushes his power further than to confine a minion who has dared to cross his love—and it is an aggravating thing to find one's self cut out—beneath the castle moat; but the tyrant of pantomime incontinently beheads a lord-in-waiting, who had omitted to warm his royal master's slip-

pers. In his playful moods, he condescends to joke with his meek, uncomplaining nobles. The pantomime monarch has but one joke, and that is not a good one—it consists in battering in his courtier's heads with an exaggerated sceptre. And here we may observe that, whenever the reader remarks the presence of a noble of melancholy and generally lymphatic expression amid a crowd of pleasant and comfortable-looking courtiers, in the opening of a pantomime, he may make up his mind that that depressed peer is destined to be bullied and thrashed by the pantomime monarch in a manner that no nobleman, who respected himself, would think of submitting to. His unhappy aspect may, with some show of reason, be attributed to a presentiment of the bad luck in store for him; but, personally, we rather incline to the belief that the gentleman who modelled the masks, feeling pretty sure that one despondent noble would pass, without remark, amid a crowd of jolly ones, until brought under the notice of the audience by the ill-treatment he is to receive at the hands of his royal master, gave him a lachrymose expression of countenance in order that when so brought under their notice his appearance might be found to correspond, to some extent, with the probable feelings of a nobleman suffering from concussion of the brain; and so provoke a feeling of sympathy for his unfortunate condition, which a mask with a broad grin on it could not reasonably expect to do.

There are few pantomimic characters that afford greater scope for archæological research than the pantomime monarch. Among other hitherto unsolved mysteries that attach themselves to this potentate is the fact that he is invariably dressed in a combination of the costumes of HENRY VIII and JAMES I. Possibly this is not accidental. The monarch of pantomime has much in common with both of these sovereigns. The brutal disregard of human life, the bullying tone he adopts towards his dependants, and his unscrupulous flirtations are strongly suggestive of the former monarch, while his waywardness, caprice, and irresolution are no less characteristic of the latter.

The Pantomime Prince

It is a curious fact in that the physiology of pantomime, that, although the pantomime monarch is invariably a blustering, big-headed and bullying autocrat, his son, the heir apparent, is an undersized stripling with a lovely complexion, copious black hair (with a large comb in it), and tiniest of hands and feet, and a generally epicene appearance.

The pantomime prince is the especial *protegé* and peculiar pet of the pantomime fairy, whose principal aim in life is to get him comfortably married to a young lady of the humblest extraction. At the same time, he is the innocent object of the undying hate of the pantomime demon, whose entire existence is devoted to the keeping him a bachelor. If marriages are made in heaven, they are certainly thwarted elsewhere; at any rate, the pantomime demon always gets the best of it in the end. The well-meaning, but foolish fairy, who has been moving heaven and earth to induce the young man to contract a highly unsuitable match, no sooner finds herself pitted against a demon, than she gives up the matrimonial scheme for a bad job. If she stopped here, the prince would have every reason to thank her for not insisting upon a match which could only end unhappily to both parties; but she doesn't. The blundering spirit, apparently under the impression that she is doing his royal highness a favour, changes into a contemptible harlequin.

The Christmas public who only know the pantomime prince as a happy, chaffy, slangy, and latch-key loving royal highness, little dream that that devil-may-care-ified young fellow has, in reality, a bitter, bitter sorrow at his heart. For he knows very well that he will either grow up to be a big-headed, unjust, red-faced, and detested monarch like his disreputable father, or he will be changed into a harlequin. Although he never openly alludes to the two destinies, one of which is certainly in store for him, he must be perfectly well acquainted with their existence. Analogy would teach him the former, while the apathetic indifference, and total absence of anything like astonishment with which he watches the wearisome development of a tediously elaborate transformation scene, proves pretty clearly that he knows all about the contemptible fate in store for him in his metamorphosed condition. We don't see that we can place the situation of the unhappy victim of transformation more vivdly before the reader than by requesting him to picture to himself the consternation of HIS ROYAL HIGHNESS THE PRINCE OF WALES, if, just on eve of the approaching wedding, a blundering, but well-meaning fairy, unexpectedly transformed him and his lovely bride into a harlequin and columbine, and sent them dancing about for the rest of their lives in the London mud, jumping through windows, and converting sensible business announcements into feeble and irritating puns.

If ever there was a man who had cause to exclaim, "Save me from my friends!" that man is surely the pantomime prince, whose degrading transformation is attributable solely to the blundering officiousness of his guardian angel.

The Pantomime Giant

Educated from our earliest infancy in the firm belief that everything that was ferocious, bloodthirsty, and demoniacal centred in the person of the giant of fairy tale, we cannot easily forget our intense disappointment at the personal attributes of the only giant we ever saw who promised to realize the expectations we had formed of such a being–the giant of pantomime. True, he was big enough; true, he was much more than ugly enough; true, he expressed himself as only a confirmed and irreclaimable cannibal could be expected to express himself, but there all analogy between the real and the ideal terminated. Feeble as to his arms, contemptibly feeble in the matter of legs, as helpless with the former as he was unsteady on the latter, his appearance was far better calculated to excite ridicule than apprehension. Palpably a big, bloated bully, who threatened whole armies with annihilation, while he lacked the constitution of a canary to assist him in carrying his menaces into effect. His instrument of death was a club–huge, indeed, in size, but wicker-work in constitution, and weighing about a pound and a half.

With the estimation we had formed of the giant of fairy land, founded on the unsupported testimony of a romantic nursemaid, fell, likewise, our opinion of his conqueror. JACK, slayer of the offspring of ANAK, was no longer the lion-hearted adventurer we once supposed him; he was simply a cautious and designing impostor, who laid highly-complicated schemes to entrap, and eventually slay, a defenceless monster whom we could have tripped up with one foot–a monster whose most alarming feature was the possession of two distinct voices, one in his head and the other in his stomach, the former of which was constantly imploring the latter to keep a little steadier on its pins. With these few words, we consign to oblivion as arrant a humbug as ever threatened to do what he couldn't perform.

Gilbert started 1864 with a review of pantomimes and a two strip 'Procession of Pantomime' (16 January):

In the same issue he published 'The Physiognomist at the Play', having begun an illustrated series 'The Comic Physiognomist' in late 1863. Here he speculated on the reason people laugh at pantomines, the jokes and 'business' of which are totally familiar to them. The Physiognomist solemnly concludes they consider that to do so is to discharge a stern moral duty which everybody owes to Society. Gilbert's 'Musings in a Music Hall / By A Young Man from the Country' also inquires (28 October 1865):

> When a man sticks his hat at the back of his head,
>   Tell me, Oh, Editor, why do they roar?
> And then, when he pushes it forward instead,
>   Why do they scream twice as loud as before?

> When an elderly gentleman rumples his hair,
>> Why do they all go delirious as well?
> When he uses a handkerchief out of repair,
>> Why do they, why do they, why do they yell?

His next verses for *Fun*, 'Pantomimic Presentiments', also ask 'when will novelties begin?' for he is tired of

> Seedy sprites forever vaulting, seedy metre ever halting,
> Men of 'property' cobalting eighteen-penny devil's face;
> And the foolish culmination in a weary 'transformation,'
> Whose complete elaboration takes a twenty minutes' space!

The question of what makes people laugh is clearly a recurrent one for the coming librettist of *The Mikado*. He would live to discover the same reaction to his own lyrics in revivals of the operas he wrote with Sullivan. There, however, it was wit and rhyming dexterity, not simple repetition that induced laughter even after the first surprise was gone. (Unfortunately, however, many twentieth-century devotees tend to laugh from simple recognition of familiar lines.)

The Comic Physiognomist for 13 February 1864 found himself visited by a deputation of players who begged for his attention; so in his next the C. P., as he called himself, described the actors in a theatrical tavern (20 February). Of these the most amusing is the tragedian:

> Ha, ha! 'Tis well, but no matter. He is a great fellow is this tragedian. He feels himself so completely identified with SHAKESPEARE that he considers that he would be slighting the immortal bard if he didn't have SHAKESPEARE's head engraved on every article of jewellery upon his body. A SHAKESPEARE pin is in his cravat, an *intaglio* of SHAKESPEARE is on his little finger, and a bust of SHAKESPEARE forms a seal which dangles from his watch-chain. The tragedian can't get on in life without slow music, and as he rarely gets it when off the stage, he is seldom happy. But hush! he museth – the tragedian museth! Let there be music of the slowest possible nature, and see that the lights be down. We will away and not disturb him.

Not till 8 October and the second series did he deal with actresses.

CONCERNING SOME ACTRESSES ENCOUNTERED BY THE C. P.

"How doth the little busy bee." – *Inappropriate Quotation.*

23

This is the leading lady. This is LADY MACBETH, the Queen mother, and KATHERINE OF ARAGON. She is nearly forty, and is buxom. The stately ruins of a magnificent CONSTANCE, the splendid overgrowth of a beautiful JULIET. A good-tempered, sociable lady out of her profession, but a very devil in it. A lady who can command, but who seldom does, in her private life, but a lady who has everything her own way in her public phase. She has probably married a *jeune premier* at an early stage of their respective existences. There are youths who still love her – dissolute young libertines of sixteen who see no obstacle to the success of their suit, in the fact that she is very married indeed. They still cast bouquets to her, and if it is any satisfaction to them that she smells them publicly with a pleased smile (for her teeth are beautiful), they are perhaps repaid for their trouble. People wonder where the bouquets come from, for although an excellent actress, and probably a very good woman, she is rather past the bouquet-receiving age.

This is the singing chambermaid. It never was the C. P.'s good fortune to encounter a singing chambermaid in private or hotel life, so he is unable to apply a realistic test to this young lady's performances. Most hotel chambermaids are gaunt and forty, but then they do not sing. She is very lively, and extremely rude to everybody except her young missus and the captain (with both of whom she is on the most intimate terms). She loves JOHN, who is plain and homely in appearance, but intelligent and comic in disposition. She has red hair. Although ostensibly engaged to him, she nevertheless treats him unkindly, and although by no means prudish as a rule, invariably boxes her lover's ears when he embraces her. She has a neat leg and does not hide it under a bushel. She is greedy of comic business, and when she *is* on the stage everybody knows it.

Here is the burlesque lady. She is the PRINCE PRETTYPOP-PET, of dissipated but frank and genial disposition, with whom we are all so intimately acquainted. You are astonished to find that so girlish and epicene a young man as the prince in question is such a prodigy of valour and of strength, for his legs, though admirably formed, are not muscular, and his voice, though delightful in the abstract is a soprano. His back hair too is voluminous, and his complexion impossible. But this astonishment vanishes when the burlesque lady is known in private life. You can then understand her attempting any achievement you choose to set her and you feel sure that she will accomplish it. She has a dash and go about her which are absolutely convincing, and she is, withal, an admirable domestic manager, for she often contrives to keep her brougham (and a well-appointed one, too) out of her three pounds a week.

This is the old lady. She is not a pleasant old party, as a rule, for she often takes snuff out of a piece of paper, over the strings of a chronic widow's cap. Besides, she is authoritative and captious, and gives more trouble to authors than the rest of the company put together. She has played everything in her time, from JULIET to columbine, and is fond of recounting her provincial triumphs. Notwithstanding the widow's cap, the C. P. is not sure that the old lady ever married, but if there ever existed an excuse for that widow's cap, the excuse must have taken the shape of a big drum.

Here is the sentimental farce young lady, whose function is usually to look pretty in white muslin and blue ribbons, to be adored by a bad old – and to marry eventually a good young – man. She is often an usually – we mean, she is usually an orphan – and is superintended by a fierce and uncompromising guardian, who has but one vulnerable point. The being called "Guardy" in a wheedling and circumventing manner has a curious influence on this strange old man, and enables the farce young lady to do what she pleases with him. The farce young lady is often remarkable for having commenced her career as OPHELIA or JULIET at a large metropolitan theatre, and with great burst of advertisement. Of course the press were all for her, because the press are all for everybody, but hopeless incompetence had its way at last, and the pretty nonentity found her level.

Right and left are members of the ballet. That on the left is in a position to dance *pas seule*, and is, consequently, very ugly. It is a curious dispensation of Providence that whereas most *coryphées* are pretty, the principal *danseuse* is extremely plain. On the right is a humbler ballet girl. She is not romantic in her appearance, and is remarkable principally for the elaboration of her *coiffure* as contrasted with the seediness of her general attire. She is often a very good girl, working hard with her fingers all day, and equally hard with her toes all night. She seldom rises to any Terpsichorean dignity, but generally retires from the stage, and winds up her career in the capacity of a dresser, having married an orchestra.

Meanwhile Gilbert addressed letters to the Editor over the signature 'UNITY IS STRENGTH', the second of which asks why the opening of a pantomime and the concluding harlequinade should be utterly distinct from each other. He created a pantomime based on *Coriolanus*, in which Coriolanus, Virgilia, Tullus Aufidius, and Volumnia become harlequin, columbine, clown and female pantaloon after Coriolanus is impeached by the Roman tribunes. At this point the Fairy Thingummy appears to say, 'To stop the base ingratitude of Rome, / Come, all of you, unto my fairy home!' The play will continue as nearly as possible as the harlequinade, and Volumnia can 'combine propriety with unity' by marrying clown ('On Pantomimic Unities', 26 March 1864).

Gilbert continued the mixture of theatre and non-theatre contributions with, *inter alia*, Our Own Correspondent, who described his holiday from 13 August to 1 October 1864; illustrations to reviews written by others and occasionally by himself; a report of the Dramatic College Fête (30 July 1864), in which, among other attractions, the actor John Clarke, was supposed to have lectured on the curiosities of an antiquarian museum which included the skulls of Shakespeare at the age of fourteen and at his death; full page drawings for Christmas numbers, and so on.

In 1865 he wrote the theatre notices ('From Our Stall') from May to mid-June after which Tom Robertson took over till November 1866. Henry S. Leigh followed him, but often reviews were collaborations, Gilbert, Robertson and Leigh providing a paragraph or paragraphs each with no indication that the same hand had not written all. For example, on 15 September 1866, Robertson wrote half a column about *The Flowers of the Forest*, and Gilbert the second half, reviewing the pre-London Liverpool premiere of Tom Robertson's *Ours*. He praised the acting lavishly, adding a special word for John Hare's make-up as Prince Perovsky: 'simply marvelous'. Gilbert thought the construction of the play 'simple almost to a fault', but 'The dialogue bristles with epigram and repartee . . . .' On 6 October, after the piece opened in London, Gilbert took three-quarters of a column to castigate the *Pall Mall Gazette*'s review ('Gentlemanly Criticism'), for its criticism of the cast. This, he wrote angrily, was 'simply a contemptible piece of ill-bred impertinence . . . . grossly snobbish'. The paragraphs he quotes bear out his objections.

THE PANTOMIME THAT JACK WROTE,
AND ALL ABOUT IT.

Meanwhile, in early 1866 Gilbert had begun a series of 'Continuations of Dramatic Histories', extending the lives and fates of such popular characters as Box, Cox, Rip Van Winkle and John Mildmay[18] past the end of the plays which they inhabit. These are not particularly funny and soon disappeared. Perhaps the best is *Box and Cox* (6 January 1866):

It will be remembered that immediately on the discovery of the fact the Cox was Box's brother – in the first burst of fraternal enthusiasm – they determined to occupy MRS BOUNCER's apartments, jointly, during the remainder of their lives. But they did not get on very well together. Independently of the fact that Box was a reckless smoker, and that Cox abominated the odour of tobacco, their dispositions and temperaments were altogether uncongenial. Cox, a remarkably careful man, had saved a little money, the interest of which, added to his salary as a journeyman hatter, enabled him to live in modest comfort. He was, in short, a steady man of moderate desires, and extremely economical, not to say miserly, in his domestic arrangements. Box, on the other hand, was a "jolly dog". He was a dreadfully wild and dissipated young man, and although his occupation as a journeyman printer kept him pretty quiet during the night, yet as soon as he was released from his labours – which happened at half past six every morning – he gave full scope to his dissipated tastes, and always "kept it up" to a very late hour indeed – seldom getting to bed before two or three o'clock in the afternoon. Of course, Box used frequently to borrow money of Cox, and Cox (who had a fine disposition and loved his brother tenderly) was at first delighted to do anything to oblige him, the more particularly so as Box, on his part, was always ready to promise any amount of interest; going as far even sometimes as seven or eight hundred per cent. But, unfortunately for their domestic happiness, it turned out that Box's disposition was nothing like as fine as Cox's disposition, for when his little promissory notes fell due, he ignored them in a manner which pained his good brother exceedingly, and the little domestic differences that ensued, caused them both to regret that, in the first burst of joy, at the discovery of their relationship, they had taken a ninety-nine years' lease of MRS BOUNCER's rooms, with power to underlet, on her permission only – which she politely, but firmly, declined to give.

Then a serious question arose as to what the family name really was – whether Box or Cox? In the absence of any decisive information as to the name of their common parents, they were compelled to fall back upon the best indirect evidence they could come across. Cox vindicated his claim to that name principally on the evidence of a piece of presentation-plate, on which was engraved or printed in some description of brown ink, the family crest – two cocks crowing, with the legend, "A presente from Ramsgatte." Box, on the other hand, contended that this piece of plate was, in an archaeological sense, worthless, being (he maintained) evidently a love-token from the proprietress of bathing-machines at Margate and Ramsgate, to whom Cox was known to have been, at one time, attached – and consequently it could only have come into his possession at a recent date. Box rested his claim to the name which he had always borne, on a curious old drinking-goblet with a richly-embossed inscription, "For a Good Boy." This inscription (Box maintained) should have run thus: "For a Good *Box*", the substitution of *x* for *y* being one of those unintentional corruptions which are so frequently the result of an accidental similarity between two letters. Box backed his argument with many actual instances in this own experience as a printer, and, as he with some show of reason, observed: "You have only to take the italic capital *X* and obliterate the lower limb, and there you are!" Eventually they determined on a compromise, Box suggesting "Bocx" as the reasonable combination, and Cox suggesting "Coxb." Cox objected that Box's suggestion left his name virtually the same; and Box took the technical objection to Cox's suggestion that it looked like a misprint, and was not capable of pronunciation. Eventually, however, they decided on COXBOX as a judicious compromise.

Box (we will still call him so) ran so deeply into debt, and was so far in arrears with his share of MRS BOUNCER's rent, that he eventually found himself compelled to marry her, as the only means of squaring the difficulty. He set up as a printer, with her money, and started a religious paper and is doing well. Cox (who has started as a hatter on his own account) can get neither principal nor interest of the money lent to his unprincipled brother, and is now taking it out in serious advertisements, to Christian Young Men who want a hat, with a text thrown in.

As the verses which would become the Bab Ballads increased, Gilbert also wrote parody reviews. His other non-theatrical contributions lessened although they did not completely cease. His verse itself frequently dealt in whole or part with the stage, sometimes seriously as in Bab's 'The Pantomime "Super" to his Mask' (24 February 1866):

> Vast, empty shell!
> Impertinent, preposterous abortion:
> With vacant stare,
> And ragged hair,

And every feature out of all proportion !
Embodiment of echoing inanity !
Excellent type of simpering insanity !
Unwieldy, clumsy nightmare of humanity !
  I ring thy knell !

  To night thou diest,
Beast that destroy'st my heaven-born identity !
  Nine weeks of nights,
  Before the lights,
Swamped in thine own preposterous nonentity.
I've been ill-treated, cursed, and thrashed diurnally,
Credited for the smile you wear externally –
I feel disposed to smash thy face, infernally,
  As there thou liest!

  I've been thy brain:
I've been the brain that lit thy dull concavity!
  The human race
  Invest *my* face
With thine expression of unchecked depravity,
Invested with a ghastly reciprocity
I've been responsible for thy monstrosity,
I, for thy wanton, blundering ferocity –
  But not again !

  'Tis time to toll
Thy knell, and that of follies pantomimical:
  A nine week's run
  And thou hast done
All thou cans't do to make thyself inimical.
Adieu, embodiment of all inanity !
Excellent type of simpering insanity !
Unwieldly, clumsy nightmare of humanity !
  Freed is thy soul!

   (The mask respondeth.)

  Oh! master mine,
Look thou within thee, 'ere again ill-using me.
  Art thou aware
  Of nothing there
Which might abuse thee, as thou art abusing me ?
A brain that mourns *thine* unredeemed rascality ?
A soul that weeps at *thy* thread-bare morality ?
Both grieving that *their* individuality
  Is merged in thine ?

Another Bab, 'At a Pantomime / By a Bilious One' (28 December 1867), opens with

An actor sits in doubtful gloom,
    His stock-in-trade unfurled,
In a damp funereal dressing-room
    In the Theatre Royal, World.

He comes to town at Christmas-time,
    And braves its icy breath,
To play in that favourite pantomime,
    Harlequin Life and Death.
      . . . . . .

He cries, 'Go on – begin, begin!
    Turn on the light of lime;
I'm dressed for jolly Old Christmas in
    A favourite pantomime!'
      . . . . . .

The wand of Time is waved, and lo!
    Revealed Old Christmas stands,
And little children chuckle and crow,
    And laugh and clap their hands.
      . . . . . .

The old ones palsied, blear, and hoar,
    Their breasts in anguish beat –
They've seen him seventy times before,
    How well they know the cheat!

They've seen that ghastly pantomime,
    They've felt its blighting breath,
They know that rollicking Christmas-time
    Means cold and want and death –

Starvation – Poor Law Union fare,
    And deadly cramps and chills,
And illness – illness everywhere –
    And crime, and Christmas bills.

Those aged men so lean and wan,
    They've seen it all before;
They know they'll see the charlatan
    But twice or three times more.

And so they bear with dance and song,
    And crimson foil and green;
They wearily sit, and grimly long
    For the Transformation Scene.

Which is, of course, Death. Gilbert believed these verses were one of the best things he ever wrote.[19]

Closer to dramatic criticism are other ballads such as 'The Reverend Micah Sowls' (18 April 1868); Sowls is a ranter who condemns the theatre as 'The Presence-Chamber of the Evil One' But his wily bishop tells him to go to Drury Lane, where

> He saw a dreary person on the stage,
> Who mouthed and mugged in simulated rage,
> Who growled and spluttered in a mode absurd,
> And spoke an English SOWLS had never heard.
>
> For 'gaunt' was spoken 'garnt,'
> And 'haunt' transformed to 'harnt,'
> And 'wrath' pronounced as 'rath,'
> And 'death' was changed to 'dath'.

The actor talks for hours until Micah Sowls sleeps.

'Hongree and Mahry' (or, properly pronounced, 'Henri and Marie') was originally subtitled 'A Transpontine Romance', changed to 'A Recollection of a Surrey Melodrama', and finally to 'A Richardsonian Melodrama.'[20] This blank verse Bab (20 November 1869) is an historical melodrama in which Hongree and Jooles are rivals for Mahry's hand. Jooles would marry her; Hongree would not. He is ordered to lead a futile mission against the English, and after sixteen lines of quibbles feels it is his duty to betray the French. He does so. Jooles and the French soldiers are killed as they sleep, and Hongree marries Mahry after all.

Theatrical, but not really dramatic, criticism is Gilbert's amusing depiction of the woes undergone by a Shakespeare look-alike in 'An Unfortunate Likeness' (14 November 1868), embellished with footnotes from Shakespeare. The satire, however, is directed not only against veneration for Shakespeare, but the published commentaries which proclaimed him a member of any professional group one of his plays names. Nor are these all the Bab Ballads that refer in some way or other to the stage. Meanwhile, Gilbert was also contributing drawings of stage types and letter press about them as the Thumbnail Sketcher of *London Society*.

3 Experiments in the Genre

Superior to Gilbert's early work (the Bab Ballads aside) is his criticism in the form of burlesque drama, the parodistic playlets. These, as Edward Lauterbach says, are the only ones in *Fun* 'to make use of parody as a vehicle for genuine criticism' and are so perceptive and comic in their treatment that persons who have not read or seen the plays can appreciate them.[21] In them he began to work out an analytic form of parody, which would be heartily funny, yet would satirize the thought processes, assumptions and moral bases of melodrama in particular.

Gilbert, however, did not originate the form. For instance, an early version of it appears in the trial of Eliza Hayward's novel *The History of Miss Betsy Thoughtless*, for dullness, in Henry Fielding's *Covent Garden Journal* (22 February 1752). The trial takes place in the Court of Censorial Enquiry: the defendant is acquitted on the grounds that all Grub Street works are dull and that even Jonson and Shakespeare may be dull on occasion. In the nineteenth century, parodistic reviews began with trials of domestic melodramas in *The Man in the Moon* in the 1840s and were revived by H. J. Byron in the *Comic News* (1863) and by *Punch*,[22] which attacked Gilbert's first performed play, *Uncle Baby*. Byron continued with two burlesque notices in *Fun* (in June 1865): 'Epsom Ups and Downs; or, the Magnificent Woman and the Mysterious Minstrel' and 'The Mesopotamian Milkmaid; or, Lawks a Dairy Me!' Boucicault's *Arrah-na-Pogue* was travestied by Tom Robertson, who also wrote a self-parody of his own *Society* (*Fun*, 9 December 1865).

Furthermore, in the 1860s the *Tomahawk* used the format for a variety of subjects including dramatic criticism. The *London Figaro* continued it in the 1870s; so did *Moonshine* in the early 1880s (a very inferior imitation of Gilbert), and *Judy* as late as 1895 although only occasionally (another inferior imitation). Finally at the turn of the century St John Hankin published a series of dramatic parodies in *Punch*, second in wit and acuity only to Gilbert's and equal to many of his in dealing with Shakespeare and Maeterlinck.

In 1865 Gilbert wrote a generic parody of sensation drama and of a hypothetical new Best and Bellingham extravaganza,[23] as well as a burlesque drama based on *Geraldine* at the Adelphi, a play which the reviewer for the *Illustrated Times*, probably Robertson, described

SOCIETY.

A COMEDY IN THREE ACTS.

RE-WRITTEN FOR THE GENTEEL AND GUSHING, BY A. S. NOE.

ACT THE FIRST.

SCENE I.—*The Chambers of a Barrister in Lincoln's Inn.* MR. CHODD, MR. JOHN CHODD, *his son,* THOMAS STYLUS, *Esq., a journalist, and* SIDNEY DARYL, *Esq., a Barrister, discovered.*

CHODD.—
AM rich—so is my son—and we wish to be of service to our fellow man.

THOMAS STYLUS, Esq., and SIDNEY DARYL, Esq.—Bless you!

CHODD. — Let us start a daily newspaper — a mild and philanthropic work, that will appeal to the highest and holiest feelings of our common nature. What shall we call it?

SIDNEY DARYL, Esq. (*as if inspired*).—The Morning Milk.

MR. JOHN CHODD.— Good! Simple, natural, refreshing, and affecting. I wish to get into society.

SIDNEY DARYL, Esq.—You shall! [*Takes his hand.*

MR. JOHN CHODD.—Thanks. How blessed is union of feeling and concord of heart. Let us gaze upon the face of nature.

[*They open the windows and look upon the quad—then burst into tears.*

SCENE CLOSES.

SCENE II. — *Blank-Blank-square.* [*The inhabitants of Berkeley, Grosvenor, Belgrave, and other squares, are respectfully informed that no invidious allusion is here intended. The Beadles of the various Squares, and those of the Burlington Arcade, are earnestly requested not to feel themselves insulted.*]

Discovered LADY PTARMIGANT *and* LORD PTARMIGANT.

LADY PTARMIGANT.—Ferdinand, I fear that Sydney Daryl loves our niece, Maud Hetherington.

LORD PTARMIGANT.— Well, well, boys will be boys.

LADY PTARMIGANT (*aside*).—And girls will be girls, that's the worst of them.

LORD PTARMIGANT (*with caution*).—We were the same when we were young.

LADY PTARMIGANT (*affected to tears by the reminiscence*).—We were! We were!

They embrace. Tableau. Red Fire.

CURTAIN.

ACT THE SECOND.

SCENE I.—*Drawing-room at the Peacock's Perch. A luxurious haunt, frequented chiefly by journalists and other men of fashion. Journalists and other men of fashion discovered lounging in chairs, sofas, &c.*

MORTIMER DELAVAL, Esq.—Waiter! A demi-bouteille of Johannisberg.

ARLINGTON CHAMPNEIGH, Esq.—Waiter! Moselle, sparkling.

FALDERAL FEEBLE, Esq.—Bring me a flacon—not the Jockey Club—the Village Flowers.

MORTIMER DELAVAL, Esq.—What's the matter, Feeble?

FALDERAL FEEBLE, Esq.—Nothing, thanks, hardly of any consequence; but not an hour ago I passed a common person in the street—and he had been smoking.

OMNES (*with disgust and sympathy*).—Dear! dear! Poor Feeble!

MORTIMER DELAVAL, Esq.—Seem a physician?

FALDERAL FEEBLE, Esq.—Not yet. I shall meet Sir Saccharum to night at the Duchess's reunion.

SIGISMUND SALOP, Esq.—Waiter! Some milk and water—weak.

OLD GENTLEMAN (*who drinks spirits, and is looked down upon by the others in consequence. Aside.*)—He is going to write.

Enter SIDNEY DARYL, Esq., *and* THOMAS STYLUS, Esq.

SIDNEY DARYL, Esq.—Stylus, my valued friend, I find I have only two hundred thousand pounds about me. Could you lend me enough to make it half-a-million?

THOMAS STYLUS, Esq. (*examining a real morocco portemonnaie.*)—I haven't quite so much about me; indeed, my friend, I have but a paltry fifty thousand; but I will procure it for you. (*Crosses the stage to Arlington Champneigh, Esq.*) Champneigh, lend me three hundred thousand pounds.

ARLINGTON CHAMPNEIGH, Esq.—I have nothing but some Sardinian five per cents, to the amount of a few thous; but I will procure the rest for you. (*Crosses the stage to Mortimer Delaval, Esq.*) Delaval, lend me four hundred thou.

MORTIMER DELAVAL, Esq.—I fear I have not so much upon my person. I have, indeed, only this trifle of Brazilian scrip, but I will procure it for you. (*Crosses the stage to Falderal Feeble, Esq.*) Feeble, lend me four hundred and fifty thousand pounds.

FALDERAL FEEBLE, Esq.—I have not so much about me. I have here but a few Montevidean six per cents.; but I will procure it for you. (*Crosses the stage to the Old Gentleman.*) My very dear sir, please lend me two hundred and twenty thousand pounds four and sixpence.

OLD GENTLEMAN (*writing cheque*).—There is a cheque for the amount, payable at Coutts's.

THOMAS STYLUS, Esq. (*epigrammatically.*)—Ce n'est que le premier pas qui Coutts.

SCENE CLOSES.

SCENE II.—*A Ball-Room.*

Discovered SIDNEY DARYL, Esq., *watching a flirtation between* JOHN CHODD, Esq., *and* MISS MAUD HETHERINGTON, *the lovely and accomplished, &c.*

SERVANT (*to S. Daryl, Esq.*)—Will you take a glass of champagne, sir?

SIDNEY DARYL, Esq. (*with mild reproof*)—Not any. I am too much of a gentleman to drink—it is only common persons who do so. I trust that I am not so forgetful of my station in life.

[*Servant retires, abashed, and drinks secretly.*

SIDNEY DARYL, Esq.—I see Maud is encouraging the attentions of Mr. Chodd. If I were to go up to them—quarrel with him and up-braid her, my conduct would be spirited and dramatic; but then it would be unphilanthropic and ungenteel. Let me behave in a manner worthy of the author of a Hand-book on Etiquette. Let me remember the verses I used to sing when a child. (*Recites, mentally, "Let dogs delight, &c," with fortitude.*) Yes, that gives me strength to forgive everybody. Bless you, Mr. Chodd, bless you, Maud. I will now retire into the Square, and shed a few tears under the weeping ash."

TABLEAU. CURTAIN.

ACT THE THIRD.

SCENE.—*The Hot Wells at Spring-mead le Beau.*

Discovered, Everybody being genteel. Those who are not being genteel are being philanthropic. An election conducted on the principles of truth, and disinterestedness going on outside.

SIDNEY DARYL, Esq.—I have won the election; but shall I take advantage of that circumstance? No! Mr. Chodd, I resign. The seat for the borough is yours!

JOHN CHODD, Esq. (*protesting*).—No! no!

SIDNEY DARYL, Esq.—I entreat.

JOHN CHODD, Esq.—I cannot accept. But Miss Hetherington has accepted me.

SIDNEY DARYL, Esq. (*with a burst of feeling.*)—Bless you both!

JOHN CHODD, Esq.—But I will give her up to you! (*Gives her up. Aside, with a whited-livered wink.*) I've got the best of the bargain.

Enter LORD CLONMARVELLOUS.

LORD CLONMARVELLOUS (*after blessing everybody like a real aristocrat*).—Sidney, the Prime Minister has sent me to you—with his love—and in consideration of your abstinence from ill-temper, the use of tobacco and alcoholic liquors, has conferred upon you the post of Governor General of India.

MISS MAUD HETHERINGTON (*advancing to audience*).—And if our kind friends before us will only smile upon our efforts, no one will be more happy.

SIDNEY DARYL, Esq.—Genteel.

JOHN CHODD, Esq.—Or philanthropic.

MISS MAUD HETHERINGTON.—That—

Audience—who can bear no more—tear up the benches, wreck the theatre, and exeunt.

———————

* Possibly this manly and determined course of action was suggested by a speech made by the immortal, though amiable Mr. Packenff.

Gilbert's Fun *review of* Society

as unlikely to prove a success, being too long, insufficient in incident, and written in blank verse. No one cares now, the reviewer said (17 June 1865), for 'Crusaders, knightly vows, Welsh harpers, hereditary curses, shaven monks, or deeds of "derring-do"'. Its only good role was the heroine's and to some extent the harper's and the villainous monk's. The reviewer admitted, however, that Miss Bateman was applauded in the last act.

Gilbert, therefore, set up a new drama for Miss Bateman (*Fun*, 24 June 1865), the subtitle of which referred to Harper Twelvetrees Soap Powder, a heavily advertised product.[24] Then he labelled it '(TEMP. ED. I.)':

GEMMA DI VERGY;
OR, THE WILD HARPER OF THE TWELVE TREES

GEMMA DI VERGY .A Welsh maiden.
ALPHONZO . . . . . .A wild Irishman, beloved by GEMMA.
CINCINNATUS . . . .Lord of the Keep of Dolbardern, and
. . . . .father of GEMMA.
RODERICK DHU . .Pope of Rome.
BOCCACIO . . . . . .A Welsh harper.
RIMINI
RISTOLACCO } . . .Welsh retainers in the pay of CINCINNATUS.
SPARTIVENTO
EDWARDS . . . . . . .A Spaniard.
JULIA DOMNA . . . .A housekeeper.

ACT 1. – *The Castle of Chester*

Enter RIMINI, RISTOLACCO, *and* SPARTIVENTO.
RIMINI. –Dolts! Know ye not — *(something or other.)*
THE OTHERS. Ay, marry do we!
RIMINI. –Then out upon ye for saucy varlets!

(They out upon themselves.)

ACT 2.–*The same.*

Enter JUMBLES *and* JULIA DOMNA.
JULIA. –A murrain on thee, thou fool!
JUMBLES *(sarcastically)*. – Nay, it is thou that art the fool, and even I, JUMBLES, the poor jester, am the wise man.

Enter GEMMA DI VERGY.
GEMMA *(sternly and with purpose)*.–This jester hath amused me oft with his rare wit.

35

JUMBLES (*feeling himself called upon to say something smart*).–Then art thou forsworn, and I, the fool, am the wiser of the twain.

GEMMA.–Carses! My bitterest carses blight you both! Wow!

Enter BOCCACIO *with harp.*

BOCCACIO.–Shall I sing you something?

GEMMA.–No. Move on!

BOCCACIO.–Then carse everybody! Carse *you*, Gemma di Vergy, in particular! You'll see!

(Six years are supposed to elapse.)

ACT 3. – *The same.*

GEMMA.–I have had the measles, but now, with the exception of a slight hump-back, I am well again. How lovely is my sister Emily. Would that Alphonzo would return from the wars!

Enter ALPHONZO.

ALPHONZO.–He is here!

GEMMA.–Ah! But now that I am hump-backed —

ALPHONZO.–You are *not* hump-backed; at least nothing to speak of.

GEMMA.–Carses on you! My bitterest carses – *(recollecting herself)* I should say "blessings!" but such is the force of habit—

ALPHONZO.–Don't mention it. We will be one.   *(They coo.)*

Enter JUMBLES.

JUMBLES.–You twain one? Then that one were twice the fool he was before, and I, the poor jester, am the wisest.

ALPHONZO.–Get out!

ACT 4. – *The same.*

Enter POPE RODERICK DHU.

RODERICK.–She little thinks – but soft!

Enter GEMMA.

GEMMA.–Good father, how sweetly my sister Emily is looking!

RODERICK.–Humph!

GEMMA.–Why that "humph?" What mean you?

RODERICK. *(whispering at the top of his voice).–* She loves your husband!

GEMMA.–I'll not believe it. Carses on you for suggesting it!

RODERICK.–Well, you'll see.

Enter EMILY.

GEMMA.–My Emily! *(They embrace.)*

RODERICK.–Hah!

Enter EDWARDS.

EDWARDS.–My lord is wounded in the tournay, and is like to die!

EMILY.–Oh! poor fellow!

GEMMA.–Hah! She is sorry! Then she loves him! I will kill her!

RODERICK.–Do!

GEMMA.–Carses! May my bitterest carses, &c., &c., &c.

ACT 5.– *The same with a sofa in it.* EMILY *on it in evening dress and crinoline as worn by the early Welsh.*

Enter GEMMA.

GEMMA.–Ha! She sleeps! 'Tis well! She dies!

EMILY.–Ah, Gemma!

GEMMA.–Die!

EMILY.–No! Why?

GEMMA.–You love my husband!

EMILY.–Not particularly. I like him as a brother-in-law.

GEMMA.–Oh! Then I will die instead. Go away. *(Exit Emily.)* Now for it! *(Drinks poison.)*

Enter POPE.

POPE.–Is she dead?

GEMMA.–*(with mental reservation).–*No, but she will be soon!

POPE.–Then I will reveal myself. I am SOMEBODY ELSE!

GEMMA.–Nonsense!

POPE.–I am. Ha! ha! That strikes thee to thy soul!

GEMMA.–No, I don't care. I am about to die, but before the fluttering spirit hath fled, carses, my death-bed carses wither you up into raisins! *(Dies.)*

POPE.–Horrible! most horrible!

Enter all the characters, who curse each other all round (this effect is registered); they then curse themselves and finally the audience.

CURTAIN.

Of the above burlesques, however, that of a generic sensation drama, *Sir Rockheart the Revengeful* (*Fun*, 11 November 1865), is most ebulliently comic. It was preceded by a letter under the heading 'Vice Triumphant':

> Sir, – Sensation dramas should mirror Society as it is, not as it ought to be. But in its existing phase Virtue is invariably triumphant in the long run – I may say the very long run – and Vice is introduced simply that it may be utterly and irrevocably overwhelmed in the last act. Is this true to nature? I, for one, have spent a long and laborious life in the exercise of the strictest virtue, and I have never triumphed. Now in my old age I intend to go in for a course of hideous and blood-curdling wickedness, and, as a first step in my career of infamy, I publish a Sensation Drama in support of my views.
>
> Yours,
> AN AGED CURATE.

SIR ROCKHEART THE REVENGEFUL;
OR, A LIFE ON THE OCEAN WAVE.

SCENE.–*Drawing-room in* SIR ROCKHEART'S *castle. Enter the crew of H. M. S. Matilda Jane. They clear the room of all the furniture for a hornpipe.*

OLD BOB BACKSTAY.–My dear eyes! I am bosun's mate of the Matilda Jane. SIR ROCKHEART has invited us all to dinner in the servant's hall!

ALL.–He has. Hurrah!

OLD B. B.–Three cheers for the noble SIR ROCKHEART! May prosperity be his mainstay, and may blessings be showered—

Enter SIR ROCKHEART

SIR R.–Confound it, what are you rabble doing in my drawing-room? Bear off to the servants' hall, ye varlets, or by the Lord Harry I'll make mincemeat of every mother's son of ye!

OLD B. B.–Ay, ay, yer honour!

(They all go out disconcerted.)

SIR R. *(moodily)*.– I am SIR ROCKHEART the Revengeful, and I war against society. I have no particular reason for being revengeful, for no one has ever injured me, so I attribute it to an inherent taste for depravity of all kinds. This morning I boiled my aunt; this afternoon I chopped up my prattling babe.

Enter THE LADY CLARIBEL.

THE LADY C.–Father, I love ULRIC the Unimpeachable. Consent to our union.   *(She prays.)*

SIR R.–He is a worthy young man with an undeniable rent-roll, and perfectly unobjectionable in every respect. I know, dear CLARIBEL, that he loves you devotedly, and I am perfectly certain that bliss unutterable would characterize your wedded life. But he dies to-morrow!

LADY C.–Oh, father!

SIR R.–What?!! Dare to dictate.

(He seizes her by the feet, and is about to dash her brains out upon the wall, when who should come in but OLD BOB BACKSTAY.)

OLD B. B.–What do I see? A lubberly old three-decker bearing down upon an unarmed punt! Dash my old eyes, that ain't fair! Sheer off, yer ugly old swab, or abaft my funnel if I don't make you see more stars than were ever dreamt of in your philosophy. SHAKESPEARE, ahem!

SIR R. *(bitterly)*.– And this, *this* is a British seaman's return for my princely hospitality!

OLD B. B. *(touched)*.– No, no, SIR ROCKHEART, don't say that. I've eaten of your beer and drunk of your cheese, I know; and if so be as ever you're in want of a dinner, you may reckon on OLD BOB BACKSTAY'S sharing his last halfpenny with your honour; but the lubber who would stand by and see an innocent and conwulsively beautiful young gal slaughtered in cold blood by a weak and defenseless old man without expostulooralating is a wretch whom "twere gross flattery to term a coward!" *(Unmanned, but recollects himself and his authority.)* TOBIN, ahem!

SIR R.–You are right, worthy fellow, quite right. But I mean to kill her notwithstanding.

OLD B. B.–Then speak to the man at my wheel, if I don't summon the whole ship's crew, who will help me to secure your darned old carcase, "you burgoo-eating, pea-soup-swilling son of a sea-cook!" MARRYAT, ahem!

(He whistles. Enter six hundred and forty men of the Matilda Jane, each with a pistol in each hand, which they point at SIR ROCKHEART.)

ALL.–Surrender!

SIR R.–No!

ALL.–Then die!

(They all snap their pistols, which flash in the pan.)

ALL.–Perdition! Our twelve hundred and eighty pistols have been tampered with.

SIR R.–Ha! ha! ha! And learn, ye minions, that next time ye come to carouse in a British baronet's servants' hall, ye had best not hang up your pistols in the family umbrella stand!

ALL.–Foiled!

SIR R.–Ye may say that. *(Takes a revolver from his pocket, and shoots them all.)* Now who shall slay me?

ULRIC.–I will!

SIR R.–Not so!

ULRIC.–Yes! I love CLARIBEL devotedly, and cannot consent to stand calmly by while you are dashing her brains out.

SIR R.–This to me in my own freehold? *(Aside.)* I have a reversionary interest in all his property, and, if I kill him, twelve thousand acres of the richest pasture land, all the castles on the Rhine, the vineyards of Ay and Epernay, most of Africa, the Isle of Wight, the Summer Palace at Pekin, the Island of Ceylon, and the British Museum will all be mine! Shall I hesitate? No!

(Desperate combat, in which ULRIC is killed.)

SIR R.–So fare all in whose property SIR ROCKHEART THE REVENGEFUL has an interest in reversion or remainder! By-the-by, the property is entailed on myself and the children of my late wife. *(Sheds a tear.)* My late wife is dead *(sighs)*, and *(recovering himself)* if I kill CLARIBEL I shall be *(triumphantly)* Tenant-in-Tail-after-Possibility-of-Issue-Extinct!

> *(Kills CLARIBEL, and takes possession of all the property. His new tenantry enter and do him homage. Eventually, after a long and happy life, he dies at a good old age, surrounded by hosts of faithful and attached dependents.)*
> CURTAIN.

On 11 January 1868, Gilbert published another generic review – this one of pantomime. It consisted of reversing the expectations of the form and rendering the figures in the harlequinade completely unconscious of how to carry on their traditional violence. The scenes introduced to set and later to strike an elaborate scene being erected and dismantled behind the curtain are Gilbert's own bitter recollection of having to write covering 'front' scenes for a rainbow fountain in his 1867 pantomime *Harlequin Cock Robin and Jenny Wren*.

OUR OWN PANTOMIME.

Pantomimes are said, by envious cavillers, to derive their principal attractions from magnificent dresses and romantic scenery. There is no good reason why Pantomime writers should suffer under such imputations. A tale of love need not be the less stirring because its surroundings are of nineteenth century date, as the subjoined précis of Our Own Pantomime will testify.

HARLEQUIN WILKINSON;
OR, THE FAIRY PEWOPENER, AND
THE VICAR OF PENDLETON-CUM-TURNIPTOP

SCENE 1. – *Vaults beneath Pendleton Church.*
The Black Beadle of Pendleton discovered surrounded by his familiars. He informs them that it is high time that their Vicar was married, and suggests that Matilda, the only daughter of old Watkins, the village attorney, would made him a fitting helpmate. Familiars express approbation, and pledge themselves to assist Black Beadle in carrying out his designs.

SCENE 2. – *The Fairy Pewopener's Second Floor.*

The Fairy Pewopener appears, and summons her Attendant Throngs. She explains that Matilda Watkins loves Wilkinson, a local printer – a person every way undesirable, being poor, uneducated, and depraved. She also announces the plot that Black Beadle has concocted, to unite her to the Vicar of Pendleton – a gentleman of the highest respectability, and in every way worthy of her. The Attendant Throngs express indignation at Black Beadle's unromantic designs, and pledge themselves to defeat his schemes, if possible. This determination is celebrated by a grand

BALLET OF OLDEST INHABITANTS!!!

SCENE 3. – *Attorney Watkins's Office.*

Comic clerks discovered, taking out writs of *ne exeat regno* against everybody. The cheers of an excited populace without stimulate them to increased exertions. Enter Mr. Watkins. He signifies that as on next Tuesday three weeks he will be within a month of sixty-one, all his clerks may take a holiday. They throw their arms up in token of their joy, and go off.

Enter the Vicar of Pendleton. He expresses a wish to be united to Matilda. Watkins immediately consents. Duet and comic dance, suggestive of Mutual Satisfaction.

SCENE 4. – *Back-yard of Printing Office of the "Pendleton-cum-Turniptop Denouncer".*

ONE-O'CLOCK DANCE OF PRINTER'S DEVILS.

Enter Printer Wilkinson. He expresses in pantomime his love for Matilda – his expectation of finding her here – and his disappointment at her absence. He consoles himself with an old file of the "Denouncer". Airy music. Enter Matilda, dancing. The lovers embrace. Chord. Matilda tells William of her father's design of uniting her to the Vicar of Pendleton. Wilkinson's despair. Slow music. Appearance of the Fairy Pewopener. Astonishment of Lovers. Chord. She tells them not to despair (twiddling music through all this), as she is determined to thwart the Old Attorney's laudable design. The Lovers embrace more than ever. Enter Mr. Watkins, led by Black Beadle. Mr. Watkins mildly reproves Matilda. But Matilda don't care. Eventually, with assistance of Black Beadle, he carries her off. Printer vows that he will dismember

Mr. Watkins at an early opportunity. Tableau. Wilkinson pretending to dismember Watkins.

SCENES 5, 6, 7, 8, 9, 10, 11, 12, 13, 14, 15, 16, 17, 18, 19, 20 and 21.

These scenes are introduced to allow time to set a Magic Drinking Fountain, or an Æthereal Washhand Basin, or a Chromatic Pump, or a Lime-Lit Tub, or any other elaborate "property" which the Management may think fit to introduce into the story at the last moment.

SCENES 22, 23, 24, 25, 26, 27, 28, 29 and 30.

Have no reference to the plot, but allow time to "strike" elaborate property aforesaid.

SCENE 31. – *Doors of Pendleton Church. (Gates.)*

Enter Fairy Pewopener, meeting Black Beadle. Black Beadle intimates that he will never give in; and Fairy Pewopener mentions her intention of transferring everybody to her Blissful Home. Black Beadle much enraged at this, and gives vent to this emotion in a

SONG ON TOPICS OF THE DAY.

In which the words "No Lamps" will frequently occur; "Not for Joe" will form the refrain of every verse.

SCENE 32. – *The Peaceful Pewopener's Ritual Realms.*

(In this scene the novel effect of Five Hundred Peaceful Pewopeners opening Five Hundred Real Pews to an Organ Voluntary will be introduced.)

The Fairy Pewopener expresses her intention of (somehow) putting an end to all strife by changing
  Wilkinson into Harlequin,
  Matilda into Columbine,
  Watkins into Pantaloon, and
  The Vicar of Pendleton into Clown.

Rally.

SCENE 33. – *Doctors' Commons. Harlequin and Columbine attempt a "trip," but not being used to it fail, and go off abashed.*

Enter Clown and Pantaloon. They seem very much ashamed of their new condition. Enter a Costermonger with carrots – Clown does not steal any. Enter an Invalid on crutches – nobody throws him down. A small boy intimates to Clown that he wants to be shaved. Clown refers him to a barber. Enter a man with advertising placard, "No Lamps – A Meeting To-night." He stands in the centre of stage – nobody slaps his board, so he goes off. Enter a Policeman with practicable head to come off. Clown looks on ruefully. Exit Policeman with practicable head to come off. Enter an Old Lady who asks Clown the way to Hicks's Hall. Clown politely informs her. He does not steal her reticule. A small boy enters and tells Clown that the police are coming. Clown remarks that it concerns him in no way. Enter the Police. Exeunt the Police. Enter the Archbishop of Canterbury with Sir John Phillimore and the Dean of Arches. Clown, overcome with confusion, rushes into shop and purchases overcoats and umbrellas for himself and Pantaloon, with which they disguise themselves.

Prompter, at wing, "Now then – Cascade – Come!" Clown, "We do not know how to do a Cascade! Spare us!"

Merciful Prompter "rings down".
                                    The End.

For two of the years during which Gilbert wrote his burlesque reviews for *Fun*, he also wrote straightforward criticism, frequently of the same plays, for the *Illustrated Times* (1868-1870). Occasionally he also wrote for the *Observer*, but his contributions there are untraceable. His viewpoint was essentially the same, but he altered the proportions, as, for example, in his criticism of Edmund Yates's *Tame Cats*, which he reviewed for the *Illustrated Times* on 19 December and for *Fun* on 26 December 1868. His first notice contained elements of reportage, which he considered were necessary in a review. *Tame Cats* was an unsuccessful comedy, which, as the *Athenaeum* pointed out, failed to please or interest the audience and was hissed. Gilbert began his *Illustrated Times* review with the problems faced by a novelist who turns to writing a play:

> There is very little sympathy between Mr. Mudie's library
> and the stage.* Novels rarely dramatise effectively, and profes-
> sional novelists seldom succeed as dramatic authors. In point of

---

*Mudie's Library, founded by Charles Edward Mudie (1818-90), opened in Oxford Street in 1852. Criticised in some quarters (G. A. Moore) for exercising a form of censorship through its selection of stock.

fact, two of the essential requisites of a good novel – forcible word-painting and constant change of scene – are terrible barriers in the way of a genuine dramatic success. The novelist who attempts to write for the stage generally overcharges his dialogue with long soliloquies and tedious descriptions – elements which would tell effectively in a story (where they would probably take the form of editorial remarks), but which in a comedy would simply have the effect of hampering the dialogue and arresting the action of the piece. So with change of scene. A novelist usually seeks for opportunities of diversifying his venue, as much as is reasonably possible; whereas a comedy-writer of the higher class modern school ventures into treacherous waters whenever he changes his scene in the course of an act.

Mr. Yates, in his comedy, "Tame Cats," which was produced, with equivocal success at the PRINCE OF WALES'S THEATRE, last Saturday, has wisely avoided the errors into which novelists are most prone to fall when they write for the stage. His dialogue is usually to the point; and his three acts tell the story, such as it is, without intermediate change of scene. So far, he has done wisely; but Mr. Yates hardly seems to have acquired the art of placing his story dramatically before the audience. This is something like the scheme of the piece:– Two personages of the play enter, and they converse while a third person listens. They go off; the third person comes to the front and soliloquises. To him enters a fourth; these two converse, as the previous pair did, and a fifth enters unperceived. When the stage is clear for him, the listener comes down, and, after a soliloquy, he enters into conversation with a sixth, while a seventh, concealed in the conservatory, overhears all that takes place; and so on throughout the whole list of characters. I really believe I am not exaggerating when I say that whenever a dialogue of any importance took place in the course of the comedy, somebody, lying in ambush, overheard it all.

The leading idea on which the comedy is based is sufficiently suggestive. A good-natured gentleman is surrounded by a set of social blood-suckers, who make his house their own, and who treat his wife with contemptuous indifference. She sees easily enough through the hollowness of their pretensions, and, with the unsought assistance of a mysterious personage, whose real character is not revealed until the end of the piece, contrives to let her husband see them in their true light. The mysterious personage who busies himself throughout the piece with thwarting the schemes of the "Tame Cats" turns out at last to be an eminent thiefcatcher of a superior order – one Captain Collars, the chief (if I understood rightly) of some Australian mounted police corps, and the uncle of the good-natured gentleman on whom the "Tame Cats" have been preying. So far, good. The idea is not exactly a new one, but it was, at all events, open to novelty of treatment. But the unfortunate and unnecessary complexity of the story, and the inartistic manner in which it is treated by Mr. Yates, together, no doubt, with the unsatisfactory manner in which a certain female character in the piece was played, excited the ire of the exceptionally critical audience that assembled to sit in judgment on it last Saturday. It remains, however, to be seen whether the average paying public (who are not half so difficult to please as those who go into a theatre for nothing) will indorse the unfavourable verdict that was passed upon the piece by the first-night audience. A good deal of judicious compression (especially in the parts of Mr. Tweedie and Mrs. Soppet) and a reduction of the unconscionable "waits" between the acts, may do something to bring about a reaction in favour of the play. There is much in the dialogue that is good – particularly in the scene between Ezra Strad (a begging-letter imposter, most artistically "made up" by Mr. Hare) and Mr. Waverham; and also in that between Mrs. Waverham and Mrs. Langley (a flirting "grass widow"), capitally played by Miss Addison and Miss Wilton. There is little novelty in the little bit of "character" with which Mrs. Langley is endowed by the author. He makes her a young lady of a poetic and generally gushing temperament, who is constantly at a loss for the very words in which she intends to convey the point of her speeches, but the exquisite delicacy with which this temporary oblivion is suggested by Miss Wilton invests this rather hackneyed character with singular freshness. Miss Carlotta Addison, who, with the face and form of a girl of seventeen, has all the aplomb and self-possession of a middle-aged actress, effectively filled up a rather sketchy outline of the neglected wife. A singular earnestness about Miss Carlotta Addison's acting seems to enchain the attention of the audience whenever she is on the stage. She is remarkably lady-like in her demeanour, and, while she gives the fullest effect to every line she has to speak, never falls into the mistake of over-acting her part. At the Prince of Wales's she is likely to meet with a range of parts calculated to display her special talents. Mr. Montague plays Mr. Waverham capitally, although it is quite out of his usual range of character. Mr. Hare, as the begging-letter imposter, who holds a secret which, if revealed, would, as he believes, strike a deadly blow to the fortune of the good-natured Mr. Waverham, avails himself of a capital opportunity for an artistic make-up. As a picture of utter servility combined with almost womanish spite, Mr. Hare's performance was simply perfect. I am not usually led into raptures by an ordinarily good piece of acting; but every part that this finished artist has undertaken stands forth in such favourable contrast to the conventionalities of nineteen out of twenty so-called "character actors" that it is difficult to overrate his importance, both as a means of chastening public taste and as an example to other and older actors who profess his special line of business. Mr. Clayton, of the new Queen's Theatre, is almost the only "eccentric-actor" who approaches Mr. Hare in the matter of careful "make-up". Mr. Bancroft plays the part of an (ostensibly) soft-headed poet, who is really a very acute sharper; but the part seemed scarcely fitted to this gentleman's unmistakable talents. The part is not a good one in itself, and in saying that it is unsuited to Mr. Bancroft I have no doubt I am simply echoing his own opinion. A Mr. Collette made his first appearance in a subordinate part, and played it nicely; but he was so hampered by the preposterous enthusiasm of foolish friends (who appeared to occupy at least two thirds of the stalls and half the private boxes) that his success was greatly imperilled more than once. Mr. Montgomery played a gentleman's valet, and being neither in gorgeous livery nor in a chophouse waiter's pumps, looked like the real thing. The scenery is capital.

In his parody review Gilbert concentrated on the pattern of overhearing and soliloquising and incorporated the noisy behaviour of Collette's enthusiastic admirers into the subtitle:

TAME CATS; OR, THE TRIUMPH OF COLLETTE

ACT 1. SCENE–*Interior of* MR. WAVERHAM'S *house, Twickenham.*

Enter BIDDLES, *a valet (and* NOT *in pumps, thank goodness!)*
BIDDLES.–This house is Mr. Waverham's – a gentleman who

inherited a large fortune from his aunt. It is over-run by toadies whom we call Tame Cats. There are three of them now in the house, and their speciality is that while two of them engage in conversation, the third is always listening unperceived.

YOUNG MEN IN STALLS.–But Collette. Where is Collette? Why don't he come?

Enter MR.COLLETTE.
(The part he plays is that of CHARLES HAMPTON, *a War Office Clerk, but his part is of no importance.)*

MR C.–Ha!

Y. M. IN STALLS.–Hurray!

MR. C.–This must be the house.

Y. M. IN STALLS.–Never saw anything like it in all my life. Beautiful!

MR C.–Now for the signal!   [*Claps three times.*
A signal which is enthusiastically taken up by his injudicious friends.

Enter ANNIE TEMPLE.
ANNIE.–My Collette!   [*They embrace.*
MR C.–What will the War Office say to my being here?

(It is impossible to describe the ecstasy of the Young Men in the Stalls at this remark, which appeared to be susceptible of some special construction with which we were, unfortunately, not familiar. But we believe the War Office is still going on.)
                    [*Exeunt* ANNIE *and* MR. COLLETTE.

Enter MRS. LANGLEY.
Young Men in Stalls subside into apathy.

MRS L.–I am a "grass-widow", and my husband is in India. I am carrying on a flirtation with a person named Wedgwood, a poet, who is one of the Tame Cats in this establishment.

(Somebody, we forget who, is listening, unperceived, to all this.)

Enter MR. WEDGWOOD.
WEDGWOOD *(But really there is no reason why we should trouble our readers with dialogues between subordinate characters*

played by such insignificant artists as MISS MARIE WILTON *and* MR. BANCROFT. COLLETTE *is our only joy.)*

[Exit MRS. LANGLEY.

Enter MR. WAVERHAM *(a bad part very well played by* MR. MONTAGUE, *and quite out of his ordinary line).*

WAVERHAM.–Wedgwood, I want to consult you on money matters – I have some thousands to invest. What would you advise me to do with them?

[Somebody listening – oh, yes, it's MR. TWEEDIE.

WEDGWOOD.–Really, my dear Waverham, I am a mere child in money matters – I know nothing about them.

WAVERHAM.–That is precisely why I always consult you when I make heavy investments. It is my business-like way.

WEDGWOOD.–Well, I know nothing about it; but I believe there are some things called Cotopaxis.

WAVERHAM.–You recommend them? Good. I will invest everything I possess in them. Here is a note to my stockbroker to that effect.

Gives note to servant to post, it is taken from servant by old TWEEDIE *unperceived.*

Really we feel we are trifling with the reader's patience. There is no more of MR. COLLETTE *in this Act. It is only necessary to say that* MR. WAVERHAM *neglects his wife, who is insulted by his guests; that* MRS. LANGLEY *is carrying on a flirtation with* WEDGWOOD, *who also has designs on* ANNIE TEMPLE'S *fortune, and that a very tiresome old lady is constantly overhearing everything, except when she is being overheard herself. Also, that a begging-letter imposter (admirably made up and played by* MR. HARE*) has a secret which concerns the stability of* WAVERHAM'S *fortune. But let us get on to* MR. COLLETTE.

ACT II. *Interior of* MR. WAVERHAM'S *House.*

Enter MR. COLLETTE. *The Young Men in the Stalls stretch themselves, and indicate in pantomime to Young Men in Private Boxes that here is something worth living for at last.*

MR C.–This *must* be the house.

Y. M. IN STALLS.– This reminds us all of Betterton in his best days.

MR C.–Now for the signal.

[*He claps three times. The Young Men take up the applause as before.*

Enter ANNIE.

ANNIE.–My own! Is not this rather imprudent?

MR C.–No.   [*Great laughter.*

ANNIE.–But you are forbidden the house.

MR C.–Yes, I know.   [*Loud cheers.*

ANNIE.–And here you are in the drawing-room.

MR C.–I am, I am.   [*Sensation.*

Enter MRS. WAVERHAM *(who has been listening to all this).*

MRS. W.–Mr. Collette, don't you think you had better hide in the conservatory?   [*A* MRS. SOPPET *is listening now.*

MR C.–Why?   [*Loud laughter.*

MRS. W.–Because if my husband were to return he would kick you out.

MR C.–Oh! Then I'll go.

    [*Tremendous cheering. Exit* MR. COLLETTE.

Well, really, as the rest of it lies entirely between such uninteresting persons as MISS WILTON, MISS CARLOTTA ADDISON, MR. HARE *and* MR. MONTAGUE *(two of them conversing, and a third overhearing all that is said), we will content ourselves by saying that* MRS. WAVERHAM (MISS ADDISON), *noticing the flirtation between* MR. WEDGWOOD (MR.BANCROFT) *and* MRS. LANGLEY (MISS WILTON), *cautions* MRS. LANGLEY, *who pretends to accept the caution, but who eventually turns the tables on* MRS. WAVERHAM, *by accusing her of carrying on an intrigue with* MR. COLLETTE, *and charges her with having concealed him in the conservatory. Her husband (a moral cad) believes this until it is shown that the conservatory is empty.* MR. TWEEDIE *has let* MR. COLLETTE *out. All this has nothing to do with the plot, and is interesting only because* MR. COLLETTE'S *name is connected with the charge.*

ACT III. *Library in* WAVERHAM'S *House. Enter* MR. WAVERHAM.

WAVERHAM.– All is lost! The Cotopaxis have gone down, and I am ruined! Assist me in this embarrassment. (*Somebody listening, we forget who. Enter* WEDGWOOD.) My dear friend Wedgwood, I am ruined!

WEDGWOOD.– Oh, but this house is yours.

WAVERHAM.– Yes, but it is mortgaged for £4,000. Of course, I do not know who the mortgagee is – a mortgager seldom does!

WEDGWOOD (*coming out in his true light, the serpent*).– I am the mortgagee, and I will foreclose tomorrow.

WAVERHAM.– You? Monster! is it thus you repay my hospitality?

WEDGWOOD.– It is!

Enter EZRA STRAD, *the begging letter imposter (who has been listening to all this).*

EZRA S.–Stop! The house was not yours to mortgage. The uncle you thought was dead still lives, and all this property is his! *That* is my secret, *that* is my secret!   *[Chuckles.*

WEDGWOOD.–Sold!

WAVERHAM.–Undone!

Enter MR. TWEEDIE (*who, it is hardly necessary to observe, has overheard all this*).

TWEEDIE.–Not so. *I* am that uncle, and all I have is yours!

WAVERHAM.–Oh. This is satisfactory as far as it goes, of course; but how about the Cotopaxis that I invested in?

TWEEDIE.–I knew it was a bubble company, and so I intercepted the letter. Behold it here.

Enter MR. COLLETTE. *Great excitement in Stalls.*

MR. C.–I am so glad!   *[Extraordinary demonstrations of delight.*

WAVERHAM.– Take Annie and be happy.

MR. C. (to ANNIE).– My own!   *[Loud cheers.*

MRS. L. (*Well it don't much matter;* MR. COLLETTE *has nothing more to say, and it is only a tag finishing up with the words* "TAME CATS".)

CURTAIN.

EVERYBODY.– Collette! Collette! Collette!

But MR. COLLETTE *being, to all appearance, a gentleman, and being, no doubt, disgusted with the preposterous folly of his friends in the stalls, did not reply to the call.*

OURSELVES.– It is impossible to speak with high favour of the plot of this piece. It is very disjointed, and conveys the idea rather of a smart novel with the descriptive passages omitted, than of a comedy of modern life. At the same time, much of the dialogue is good and to the point. If the story had been a little more probable, and a little more intelligible, the dialogue might have carried it through. It is admirably acted by MISS MARIE WILTON, MISS CARLOTTA ADDISON (who, if the piece had been a success, would have made an enormous advance in her profession by her performance of MRS. WAVERHAM), MR HARE, who is excellent in every way, and MR. MONTAGUE. MR BANCROFT'S part does not appear to suit him; this very clever actor's peculiar talents seem to have been quite ignored by the author. MR. BLAKELEY and MRS. BUCKINGHAM WHITE are simply in the way throughout the piece. This is not MR. BLAKELEY'S fault, who makes the best of a very bad part. MR. COLLETTE played the insignificant character assigned to him in a quiet and gentlemanly manner. He did not attempt to make too much of the part – but his friends did.

The absurdity of those friends becomes even more ridiculous when one considers that, as Ourselves said, the cast included Marie Wilton and her husband, Squire Bancroft (albeit miscast), who were phenomenally successful in Tom Robertson's plays; Carlotta Addison, who had made her debut in Gilbert's first burlesque (*Dulcamara! or, The Little Duck and the Great Quack*, 1866) and was rapidly becoming a significant actress on the prose stage; John Hare, a youthful member of the Bancrofts' company, who specialised in old men's and character roles, a perfectionist in making up, and John Clayton, who would create an important role in Gilbert's *An Old Score* (1869). Even so, and in spite of the ill-judged clamour for Charles Collette, *Tame Cats* ran for only eleven performances.

4 Compression and Extension

The first of Gilbert's travesty reviews to deal immediately with a specific work seems to be 'Draco Beach' under the title 'What We Have to Put Up With' (29 July 1865).[25] Its real title was *Solon Shingle*, and its author, the American John E. Owens, played Solon. A clever actor, his piece was 'utterly destitute of merit', according to the *Illustrated Times* (8 July 1865). It includes a pair of clerks, one virtuous, one wicked, who plants a stolen watch and a confession on the good clerk; a starving mother; a law court, and an American farmer, who constantly spits and searches for his barrel of apple sass. It ends with the audience exclaiming, 'What an insult to place such a piece before a London audience. But we have brought it upon ourselves by our confounded good nature, and there's no help for it.' At least it furnished Gilbert with an amusing play on words.

On 4 November 1865 Gilbert's much better-developed criticism of Reade's *It's Never Too Late to Mend* appeared with its title translated to 'IL N'EST TROP TARD POUR RACCOMMODER!' This is the play that moved F. G. Tomlins to rise and rebel, and Henry Morley to describe its prison scene as 'a repulsive excrescence', which 'does not advance the story by a syllable'.[26] Reade, who was serious, not merely sensational, about prison reform, had adapted the play from his own popular novel of the same name, and in the hands of skilful actors it was no doubt compelling.

Gilbert's technique in dealing with *It's Never Too Late to Mend* was basically that of extension and compression. While Reade specified some accompanying music, including 'Home, Sweet Home', Gilbert introduced two dozen other songs, whose titles are presumably appropriate to the dramatic moment at which they are supposedly played. Thus Joseph, the potato thief, expires to 'Death of Nelson' and Hawes, the demonic prison governor, cuts off the gas in a cell to the air 'The light of other days has faded.' When Reade's Hawes orders fourteen days of bread and water, Gilbert's orders seven years. When Reade's church bells ring in the distance but are silenced in the space of three speeches, Gilbert's bells, *which are several miles off, in an adjoining county, are stopped immediately*. In Reade's play Isaac Levi, turned out of his home by the villain, takes the house next door, bores a hole through the party wall, observes a criminal action, and brings about the downfall of villain and accomplice. Gilbert's Levi announces: 'He turned me from my home, so for seven years I have lived bricked up in one of the walls with no other companion than a solitary but effective lime-light; and there I have patiently awaited an opportunity for detecting him in his crimes.'

On the other hand, Gilbert cut the plot to the barest of bones, deleting Reade's connective dialogue, but sometimes using Reade's own sentences or reducing a long speech to a précis. Thus Gilbert's Faithful Black receives a box of lucifer matches for finding a lump of gold weighing several tons, a reward which Reade gives his savage Jacky only after carefully building up Jacky's awe and delight in the matches. Thus, too, both Gilbert and Reade use the title of the play as a tag line, but Gilbert makes it a complete *non sequitur*.

For his early parodies, Gilbert did not speak avowedly *in propria persona*, but by late 1866 he began occasionally to attach a paragraph labelled 'Ourselves'. At first such paragraphs were minimal; Boucicault's *The Long Strike* elicited only three lines: 'After all, it is by no means a bad piece, and it's capitally acted – especially by Mr. Emery, Mr. Cowper, and Mr. and Mrs. Boucicault; but we're such a fellow – we must have our joke!' (*Fun*, 29 September 1866). 'Ourselves' did not reappear regularly until 19 January 1867 in the review of *A Lesson for Life*: 'Well, it's a pretty piece, but faulty in construction; a great deal too goody-goody in sentiment, and n-not [*sic*] particularly well played.' Thereafter 'Ourselves' generally increased his paragraph length, although sometimes a mere sentence or two of exasperation sufficed: 'Well, of all the trash! But no matter!' (*Rouge et Noir*, [*Fun*, 26 January 1867]) or 'Oh, Mr. Halliday! Mr. Halliday! Have we deserved this?' (addressed to the author of *The Great City*, [*Fun*, 11 May 1867]). Occasionally, but infrequently Gilbert illustrated these reviews, as he did Palgrave Simpson's *The Siren* (Lyceum, 11 November 1869).

Gilbert's satiric techniques were by no means limited to those we have already seen, which, in any case were not his alone – although he was superior in maintaining the original plot line while rendering it absurd. Sometimes compression and the omission of connectives put what remained out of context, often reducing it to triviality. For instance, Watts Phillips's spectacular play, *Theodora: Actress and Empress*, which opened at the Surrey

THE SIREN.

ACT 1.—SCENE, *Old Villa on the Bay of Naples.* SARTORIUS, *an old fiddler, discovered, with* FIDES, *his daughter.*

SARTORIUS.—Yes, Fides, your poor old father is by chalks the greatest composer of this or any other day. But he is very old and he dawdles and dobbers about in a manner which I am sure must irritate 'em.

FIDES.—Caspar Albano's opera is produced to-night.

SARTORIUS.—And he never sent me a box, though he is my pupil! Ungrateful scoundrel! (*Drivels.*) But I must be firm! (*Proudly.*) I am a great composer. (*Composes himself.*)

Enter CASPAR.

CASPAR (*with appropriate action*).—Here is a box for my opera. Caspar, particularly—(*Exit* FIDES.) Caspar, above all things, lead a respectable life! (*Caspar quails.*) Now I'll go and dress.

Enter FIDES (*dressed*).

FIDES.—Here I am—and how do I look?

CASPAR (*leaving his legs akimbo*).—Exquisite! I love you.

FIDES.—Caspar—this is sudden—

CASPAR (*wagging his head*).—It is.

FIDES.—But my father will not let me marry a fiddler.

CASPAR (*slapping his heart*).—I will ask him—If he consents?

FIDES.—I am yours. [*Exit* FIDES.

Enter COUNT CARNIOLI, CASPAR's *patron.*

CASPAR (*winking his eye*).—Count, I am going to be married.

COUNT (*in sad dog*).—Never! It is ruin to a young man. (*Aside.*) I will introduce him to the lovely Princess Leonora Falconieri—she shall swamp his faculties. [*Exeunt to the Opera.*

ACT II.—SCENE 1. *Saloon of Opera Box. Wild Neapolitans discovered in opposite box.* PRINCESS FALCONIERI *discovered with a fat man of easy manners. Also a Countess in pink net.*

PRINCESS.—The first two acts of the opera are charming. (*Fat man waves his hand, with an action that speaks volumes.*)

PRINCESS.—Ah, here is Count Carnioli—he will tell us about the composer. (*Fat man changes his leg with an air of quiet resolve.*)

Enter COUNT CARNIOLI (*Fat man hooks his fingers into his waistcoat pocket and sniffs.*)

COUNT.—The composer is a young fellow who was formerly a goatherd. I took him from his goats, educated him, and this is the result.

PRINCESS.—Charming! Ah, the third act is commencing.

COUNT.—This is the most exquisite air in the piece. The Moorish chief, El-Strange, is supposed to be bidding adieu to the Alhambra.

(*The Moorish Chief bids adieu in an air which suggests a feeble amateur practising the bass part of a very long and slow choral grace. The sham audience applauds—the real audience don't.*)

PRINCESS.—They are calling the composer. (*Throws bouquet.*) There! I have thrown my handkerchief too! How very awkward!

SCENE 2.—*House of* PRINCESS FALCONIERI, *lately the property of* JOHN MILDMAY, ESQ., *and before that, the residence of the Pumpydoor.*

Enter the PRINCESS *from the opera.*

PRINCESS.—I wonder if the young man, Caspar, will call to-night? Oh, he will not dare—he must know that the handkerchief was thrown

Enter Servant.

SERVANT.—A young man, madam; this is his card.

PRINCESS.—'Tis ha! Show him up.

Enter CASPAR, *he trembles.*

PRINCESS.—Are you not well?

CASPAR (*throwing out his chest*).—Oh, passing well—passing well! (*thumping his ribs*). Down, little flatterer.

PRINCESS.—May I ask to what I owe this visit? It is 12 p.m.

CASPAR (*winding his watch*).—It is—I—a—

PRINCESS.—You seem confused. Have you been drinking?

CASPAR (*clearing his throat*).—Drinking? No, I—I—I want to play you a little thing of my own.

PRINCESS.—Do, (*aside.*) I will slip out unobserved, and so shall not hear him! (*Does so.*)

(CASPAR *sits down to an organ and plays a long amateur fugue, recognised at once by the audience as the work of the master who composed the Choral Grace. After five and twenty minutes of this*)

PRINCESS (*re-entering, in desperation*).—Look here. If I allow you to sit with your arm round my waist, will you leave that fearful instrument?

CASPAR (*working all over*).—I will. (*He does.*) [*Tableau.*

ACT III.—SCENE 1. *Boudoir at Villa Falconieri.* CASPAR *and* PRINCESS *discovered.*

CASPAR (*crying like a child*).—It is now six months since the commencement of our relations (to which I will not more particularly allude) and you have changed much. You do not love me, Leonora!

LEONORA.—Ridiculous. I love you considerably.

CASPAR (*flinging himself on a sofa*).—No. You love that young operatic tenor. It is all over between us.

LEONORA.—Nonsense. Do, (*aside.*) (CASPAR *weeps, like a travelling donkey as he is.*) I hate men who cry! (*And so do we.*)

CASPAR (*looking at his "Bradshaw"*).—Farewell! I leave you!

LEONORA.—Stay—I did but jest! (*Looking earnestly into his eyes.*) I do love you!

CASPAR (*working his right arm*).—You do? Ecstacy! I remain! [*They embrace, thus exit* LEONORA.]

Enter a Servant with note, which she gives to CASPAR. *He reads:—*
"Farewell! I do not choose to let my lovers leave me—I prefer to leave them. Leonora."

CASPAR (*trembling like a jelly*). She has eloped with the tenor. I will after them! (*He afters them.*)

SCENE 2.—*Some Ruins by a Lake. Enter a person of grotesque appearance whose name is not in the cast. He nods awkwardly to the audience, who for some unaccountable reason hiss him. (Exit grotesque personage.) Then enter* CASPAR *and* COUNT CARNIOLI.

CASPAR.—They left in a carriage and pair and are sure to drive through this very intricate ruin.

Enter a carriage and pair, with small portmanteau on roof.

CASPAR (*presenting a pistol, not at postilion, who may fairly be supposed to have the immediate control of the horses, but at the portmanteau on the roof*).—Stop!

The carriage door opens and old SARTORIUS, *apparently standing in drink, descends.*

CASPAR (*feeling for his eye-glass*).—My old tutor!

SARTORIUS.—Gentlemen, my daughter Fides is dead—I am taking her home to bury her—I have packed her in that portmanteau, and she passes as luggage.

CASPAR (*tearing out his hair by the roots*).—Pass on, old man!

The PRINCESS *and the tenor cross the lake in a gondola.*

CASPAR (*writhing with internal convulsions*).—It is she!

(*Dies in great agony.*)—CURTAIN.

OURSELVES.—The piece, (a very unwholesome one), is cleverly adapted by Mr. PALGRAVE SIMPSON. On the whole, it is detestably acted. Exceptions, however, may be made in the cases of Miss KATE SAVILLE and Mr. COGHLAN.

Part of Gilbert's Fun *Review of* The Siren

Theatre on 9 April 1866, is simultaneously reduced in *Fun* (28 April 1866) to half a column and yet made more repetitive, repetition being one of Gilbert's most frequently used devices.

THEODORA

ACT I.– *Constantinople. Enter an* EFFEMINATE OFFICER.

E. O.–Bai Jove!   *[Exit* EFFEMINATE OFFICER.

Enter CREON.

CREON.–I am the adorer of Theodora – Good, that!

Enter THEODORA *and* RABBLE.

THEO.–Save me!

CREON.–I will.   *(Saves her.)*

ACT II.–*Encampment of Roman Army at Carthage.*

Enter CREON *and his son* PHILIP.

CREON.–Nineteen years have elapsed since the last act.

PHILIP.–Since the last act?

CREON.–Yes. You were not born then.

PHILIP.–Not born then?

CREON.–No.

PHILIP.–No?

CREON.–No. You are the son of Theodora and of me.

PHILIP.–Of Theodora and of me?

CREON.–Go to her. She is Empress now.

PHILIP.–Empress now?

CREON.–Go and demand my recall from banishment.

PHILIP.–Recall from banishment? Yes.

                     [Exit to Constantinople.

Enter MIRIAM.

MIRIAM.–Ha! ha! ha! But no matter!   *[Exit* MIRIAM.

ACT III.– *Interior of Byzantine Palace.*

Enter THEODORA.

Grand Ballet of women in blue masks and dominoes

Enter PHILIP.

PHILIP.–You are my mother.

THEODORA.–Nay. *(To Guards.)* Pretend to behead him in yon

56

jam cupboard. *(They pretend to behead him. But he don't care.)*

ACT IV.– The same.

THEODORA.– Ha! A tumult.

Enter a TUMULT.

TUMULT.–Abdicate, or we revolt.
THEODORA.–Never!   *[They revolt.*

ACT V.– The caverns. Philip dying.

Enter THEODORA.

THEODORA.–Ha! Can it really be my son?

Enter MIRIAM.

MIRIAM.–It can!

TABLEAU. CURTAIN.

In fact, Gilbert's review is almost perfunctory in its brevity, and the play was not a success, spectacle over-riding drama. There was not enough publicity, and Avonia Jones was miscast as Theodora. Charles Fechter, Dion Boucicault, and others thought it was an adaptation, although Phillips insisted it was original.

Perhaps Gilbert's most 'cutting' review, however, is a full-page parody of Edmund Falconer's *Oonagh; or, The Lovers of Lisnamona* (6 December 1866), which opened Her Majesty's Theatre on 19 November. Here he regularly inserted brackets of deletion. He also repeated and re-repeated the miser's 'cairshes' and 'I am like a dog with his tongue out.' Falconer himself played Fardourougha.

OONAGH;
OR, THE LOVERS OF LISNAMONA.
IN FIVE FITS

FIT I (SCENE 1.)– *The* O'DONOVAN'S *Farm House. Enter* CONNOR O'DONOVAN *meeting* BARTLE FLANAGAN.

BARTLE F.*(seizing* CONNOR *by the throat)*.– Your father is a miscreant. He has ventured to ask me to pay him what I owe him – none but a double-dyed villain would do such a thing to a bhoy of the Oirish pisintry. He is a blaygaird; but I want him to take me into his employ.

CONNOR O'D *(mildly)*.– Nay; he is my father, and to put it gently, your remarks are in bad taste – especially as you come to ask a favour.

BARTLE F.–It would perhaps assist to give an Irish tone to our conversation if I here remarked, "Musha alanna avick!"

CONNOR O'D. *(firmly, but kindly)*.– It would, Bartle.

BARTLE F.–Then consider it done.

CONNOR O'D.–I will! I will!

> *[They rush into each other's arms.*

BARTLE F.–Connor, Oonagh O'Brien loves you!

CONNOR O'D.–Ah, get along wid ye blarney! *[Simpers R.*

SCENE 2.– *A Hayfield. Enter* LADS *and* LASSES *dancing.*

A LAD.–Faix, bhoys—

[A conversation, twenty minutes long, between A LAD *and* A LASS, *cut out for want of space. Apologies to* MR. FALCONER. *–Ed.*]

A LASS.–Thrue for yez!

ALL.–Musha! *[They musha.*

Enter CONNOR O'DONOVAN, *meeting* OONAGH.

CONNOR O'D.–Oonagh, I am but an Oirish bhoy, while you are a respectably dressed young person, suggestive of a music mistress – but I love ye.

OONAGH.–Ah, avick alanna machree! Also acushla!

> *[Comes down and blushes.*

CONNOR O'D.–We will marry!

OONAGH.–But not without the consent of pa. He is an extensive landed proprietor, and you are only a farm labourer, or something (pardon me) equally common, and he might – I say he *might* object. It's unlikely, but he *might*.

CONNOR O'D.–My father, Fardourougha, the miser.

OONAGH.–Whom everybody loathes!

CONNOR O'D.–The same – shall go and ask his consent.

OONAGH.–My own Connor! *[They entwine.*

SCENE 3.– *Interior of* O'BRIEN'S *Farm House*

[Episode of some length about Lent, cut out for want of space. Apologies to MR. FALCONER.– *Ed.]*

Enter O'BRIEN *and* FARDOUROUGHA.

FARD.–Mishther O'Broien, my son loves your daughter.

O'BRIEN.–Well, as I haven't the plishere of knowing him, and as he is far below me in the social status – I should say shtathus – and as, moreover, he is the son of the biggest ould blackguard —

FARD (*sternly*).– You mean blaygaird.

O'BRIEN.–I beg your pardon – blaygaird for miles around, why I must take time to consider.

FARD.–Ha! My bittheresht cairshes on yez for not jumping at an alloince wid the house of O'Donovan. I am like a dog with his tongue out. Cairsh ye! cairsh ye! cairsh ye!

[Goes into Fit the First.

Enter BARTLE FLANAGAN.

BARTLE F.–I will entice O'Connor to the quarry where the Ribbon men* hold their secret meetings. He shall become one of us,–and then I will betray him. For no particular reason.

Dance by all the characters.

FIT II.– *The Quarry.* RIBBONMEN *discovered.*
[A lecture on Ribbonism, an hour and a quarter long, cut out for want of space. Apologies to MR. FALCONER. *–Ed.]*

Enter CONNOR O'DONOVAN *and* BARTLE FLANAGAN.

BARTLE F. (*introducing him*).– A comrade, bhoys!

CONNOR O'D.–Niver! I came because I expected to meet my young woman here. We always meet here by moonlight. It is not correct, perhaps; but never mind that.

ALL.–We don't! We don't! *[They don't.*

SOMEBODY.–Here is a person called Peery Clancy. We will bury him and cut off his ears!

ALL.–We will! *[They bury him, all but his head, and cut off his ears.*

BARTLE F.–We will leave him here, and Phil Curtis shall watch over him.

---

*Ribbon men belonged to the Irish nationalist Ribbon Society and wore green ribbons in opposition to the Protestant Orange Ribbon Society.

ALL.–He shall.   *[He does.*

    Exeunt all but PHIL CURTIS *and* PEERY CLANCY'S *head.*

PHIL C.–Clancy, I will murder you!
AUDIENCE.–Cut it short!
PHIL C.–Never! I will smash your head with a stone.

               Enter CONNOR O'DONOVAN.
CONNOR O'D.–Not so!   *[Points at him.*
PHIL C.–Foiled! Humph. Another time!   *[Tableau.*
FARD.–Ah, musha, then!   *[Goes into Fit the Second.*

FIT III. *(considerably curtailed).– Exterior of a Savings Bank.*

               Enter FARDOUROUGHA.
CROWN.–The bank has stopped!
FARD.–And I am ruined! Cairshes on ye! I am but a dog with
his tongue out!   *[Goes into Fit the Third.*

FIT IV.– *A Court of Justice.* CONNOR O'DONOVAN *being tried*
    for something which doesn't appear.

COUNSEL FOR THE CROWN.– I am going to call five hundred
witnesses for the prosecution.
COUNSEL FOR DEFENCE.– And I two thousand for the defence.
  [Evidence of ninety-two witnesses cut out for want of space.
     Apologies to MR. FALCONER.– *Ed.]*
JUDGE.–I am obliged to clutch at my desk or I shall tumble
over it into the court. But (*recklessly*) no matter!
COUNSEL FOR DEFENCE.– I will now call my seventy-second
witness—
JUDGE.–No, hang it all – I know it's in your part, but – dash
it. You know – I can't stand it. Even *they* (*indicating audience*),
who can stand a good deal, can't stand it!
AUDIENCE.–We can't. Hear! hear!
JUDGE.–What say you, gentlemen of the jury, is he guilty?
JURY.–He is! he is!
  [Great joy of audience, who hope that CONNOR O'D. *will be*
taken out and shot. But he isn't.

FARD.–Musha avick! I am like a dog with his tongue out. Cairshes on the judge – cairshes on the – cairshes on —

[Goes into Fit the Fourth.

FIT V.–*The Condemned Cell.* CONNOR O'DONOVAN *discovered.*

CONNOR O'D.–I suppose no one ever saw a condemned cell with a groined and mullioned cathedral window before. But Danson is as Danson does!*

[Weeps resignedly.

Enter FARDOUROUGHA.

FARD.–I am like a dog with his tongue out. Cairshes on society at large! [Faints.

Enter BARTLE FLANAGAN *in custody.*

BARTLE F.–I am in custody, and I must die; but what of that? The Oirish bhoy laughs a hideous laugh of scorn at death.

[Laughs a hideous laugh of scorn at death. All shriek.

Enter the SHERIFF OF CORK.

FARD.–Sheriff of Cork, what if I cairshed yez?

SHERIFF.–Oh that were too fearful! Spare me!

[Goes on his knees.

FARD.–I will. I am like a dog with his tongue out! But stay – I will reveal all!

[Is about to reveal all – by which he probably means that he will explain the allusion to a dog with his tongue out; everyone listens eagerly to hear this awful mystery explained, when a ground cloth to be used in the next scene makes a premature appearance from the back of the stage, and cuts all the performers off their legs.]

FARD. (recovering his balance).– I will reveal ALL!

[Same business – all pick themselves up, and go on as if the phenomenon was a familiar characteristic of all condemned cells.]

FARD.–I will reveal ALL!

*A scene designer, several times referred to by Gilbert.

[Same business. They all hurry off, and reveal ALL *in the Green Room.*

SCENE 2.– *Behind the Scenes.* FARDOUROUGHA *and* STAGE CARPENTERS *discovered. But no – this scene is too awful.*

SCENE LAST.– *A Hayfield.* LADS *and* LASSES. *Enter* OONAGH.

OONAGH *(supported).*– My lover is to be hanged today. How annoying!

Enter O'BRIEN.

O'BRIEN.–Nay; he is reprieved. Bartle has confessed!
OONAGH.–Oh, I am pleased to hear that. Ah, he is here!

Enter CONNOR O'DONOVAN – OONAGH *and* CONNOR *fondle.*
[Three-quarters of a hour's dialogue between the lovers, cut out for want of space. Apologies to MR. FALCONER. *–Ed.]*
FARD.–Then all is joy again. I am no longer like a dog with his tongue out; and I revoke all the cairshes which I have had occasion to make during the piece. *(The* SHERIFF OF CORK, *the* JUDGE, JURY, O'BRIEN, BARTLE FLANAGAN, *and all others cursed in the previous scenes, enter in high spirits.)* I will faint no more; and if *(addressing a person at the back of the pit),* you, sir, who alone have sat out the performance, will signify your approbation, you shall have the dying blessing of Fardourougha, the Lover of Lisnamona, which is a place and not a lady.

[Goes into Fit the Fifth, all over the Stage. Tableau.

CURTAIN.

The mishap with the ground cloth did, in fact, take place. *Oonagh* lasted until 2:30 a.m. (12:40 according to another review), Gilbert staying to the end, although most of the audience had long since melted away. When the carpenters pulled the cloth so that seven or eight characters standing in a line near the footlights unexpectedly fell flat on their backs, the audience 'broke into a yell of laughter'.[27]

The same dramatist's *Innisfallen; or, The Men in the Gap*

(Lyceum, 17 September 1870) was, as 'Ourselves' objected, 'inordinately – preposterously – long' even though it contained two good situations. Most of Gilbert's paragraph, however, took the audience to task for disgracefully guying two actresses in a tedious scene, which was the author's fault, not theirs. He admitted that Falconer gave the audience great provocation, for, as the *Athenaeum* remarked in its review (24 September 1870), 'Among long-winded playwrights, Mr. Falconer is simply the most long-winded.' After a large audience had laughed at and derided *Innisfallen* for two hours, he thanked them and said that 'emboldened by the success of his new piece' he would continue with similar works. A martyr to a religion of self-worship, said the *Athenaeum*.

Falconer's *Oonagh* very likely prompted Gilbert's verses 'How to Write an Irish Drama', which appeared in *Fun* (1 December 1866) less than a month after the play opened and closed at Her Majesty's. Dion Boucicault's Irish plays of the 1860s also must have hovered around Gilbert's pen.

> If you'd write an Irish drama,
>   Be awhile attentive, pray,
> While I show a panorama
>   Of ingredients in the play.
>
> Take, oh take some lads and lasses,
>   Take a dreary moonlight glen,
> Take a comic spy who passes
>   Through a lodge of Ribbon men.
>
> Take a burly Irish squire,
>   Take a wretch to work the harm,
> Let him set a barn on fire,
>   Take a mortgage on a farm.
>
> Take a chain of circumstances
>   Implicating innocence,
> Take a chambermaid who dances,
>   Take unworthy evidence.
>
> Take a secret still, and work it,
>   Take a rattling Irish jig;
> Take a judge who sits on circuit,
>   In his flowing full dress wig.
>
> Take a lawyer in a fury—
>   Evidence that's most unfair,

Take an idiotic jury
With moustache and flowing hair.

Take a colleen, flirty, jilty,
Take a crowd in court to yell,
Take a verdict, too, of guilty,
Take a priest and take a cell.

Take a noble sheriff, bringing
Pardon, which the convict claims,
Take the village bells a-ringing,–
Take and pitch 'em in the Thames.

A last instance of repetition is the irrelevant, but prevalent catch-word or catch-sentence spoken by low comedy characters. Gilbert frequently objected to this, since it violated his general principle that 'all humour, properly so-called, is based upon a grave and quasi-respectful treatment of the ridiculous and absurd'.[28] As he said in a prose review of *Guy Fawkes*, a Strand burlesque, when it flagged, which it often did, 'Mr. James has only to exclaim, "Make no blooming error!" and a "certain portion"... shriek with unrestrained delight.'[29] In the parodies he repeated catch-sentences from the plays at inappropriate times. 'Oh my delicate sensibilities! Somebody please kick me,' reiterates the comic servant in *Nellie's Trials* (20 January 1866). Someone kicks him, and he says again, 'Oh my delicate sensibilities.' Blinker *(Lost in London)* constantly refers to Tiddy's biceps (30 March 1867), which he does only occasionally in the original play, and Toole punctuates *The Fast Family* (26 May 1866) *'for some reason best known to himself'* with 'Ha! I have missed another post!'

Numerical extension, related to but not identical with repetition, produced visual comic effects. For instance, in the second act of *Rouge et Noir* (*Fun*, 26 January 1867) five characters faint simultaneously; in the parody of *School* (*Fun*, 30 January 1869), Bella tells Lord Beaufoy that eighty-seven of the schoolgirls have recently eloped; and in Boucicault's and Byron's drama *Lost at Sea* (Adelphi, 2 October 1869) twelve Adelphi widows and orphans conduct business with twelve Adelphi stockbrokers in the open street (*Fun*, 16 October, 1869).

LOST AT SEA

ACT I. SCENE 1.–*Franklin's Villa at Acton.*

Enter LORD ALFRED COLEBROOK *and* LAURA FRANKLIN.
LORD ALFRED.–My love!
LAURA.–My own. *[They do.*

Enter the PR*NCE *and* PR*NC*SS OF WALES *to Royal Box.*
Enter at the same moment MR. C. H. STEPHENSON *as*
FRANKLIN, *to Stage. Enthusiastic reception of* PR*NCE
and PR*NC*SS OF W*LES *by audience, and graceful*
acknowledgement thereof by MR. STEPHENSON.

MR FRANKLIN (*still rather surprised by his reception*).–
Away, I would be alone! (*They away.*) I would indeed be alone,
or rather, a loan that I might borrow myself, and place the
bank once more on a satisfactory footing. *Enter his wicked*
cashier RAWLINGS.

RAWLINGS.–The Bombay Castle in which Walter Coram,
your principal creditor, was returning to England from India,
has gone to the bottom and all hands are lost!

MR. FRANKLIN (*devoutly*).–Heaven be praised! *[They pray.*
At this moment, great excitement of snobs and snobbesses at
O. P. end of dress circle. They have just discovered that
with a little manoeuvering the R*y*l *back hair can be*
distinctly seen over partition of box. Special excitement of
one dowdy snobbess in third row, three from the end.

Enter LORD ALFRED *and* LAURA.

LORD ALFRED.–Laura, I can never marry you. Can I say
more?

LAURA.–You cannot, my ever frank and noble Alfred!
[They fall into each other's arms.

SCENE 2.– *Exterior of Jessop's Herbarium, Love Lane, Lambeth.*

Enter JESSOP.

JESSOP.–I had three months for practising without a
diploma, but somehow a month of my time has been remitted.

Enter RAWLINGS.

RAWLINGS.–It has, and through my agency. The Home Secretary is a customer of ours, and I told him that if he didn't release you, I wouldn't let him overdraw.

JESSOP.–My best of friends. But your object?

RAWLINGS.–I want you to personate a dead man, one Coram, who was our principal creditor. He is drowned, but we can easily account for his escape, and you shall have half the swag, £30,000.

JESSOP.–Agreed!

SCENE 3.– *Interior of Jessop's Laboratory.*

Enter KATEY JESSOP *and* WALTER CORAM *(who for some reasons best known to himself is passing as* MR. WALTERS.)*

CORAM.–Katey, you saved my life, when I was desperately ill, and as a return, I will tell you its story. 'Tis now some thirteen thousand years since—

KATEY *(interrupting him).*– No; pray don't.

CORAM.–At all events you will listen to my escape from shipwreck?

KATEY *(resignedly).*– Well, go on.

CORAM.–I was to have returned from India by the Bombay Castle, round the Cape, having taken the unusual precaution of sending my shirts and socks by overland mail. However, I *didn't* sail by the Bombay Castle, which was lucky, as all hands went down with her.

KATEY.–And your shirts and socks?

CORAM.–Came overland as usual. It is an expensive mode of transit for heavy goods, but I love my shirts and socks and would not put them to the inconvenience of coming round the Cape with me if it could be avoided. Besides, I am an old opium-eater, and do many eccentric things under its influence. I have £50,000 a year, but I take lodgings in Love Lane. Again, I love you–yes, you, Katey!

KATEY.–Oh, forbear, kind sir–I love Rawlings.

Enter RAWLINGS, *with several boxes.*

RAWLINGS.–Yes, sir, she loves me. I am sorry.

CORAM.–Oh, don't mention it, I'm sure.

RAWLINGS.–You're very good.

CORAM.–Not at all–it's of no consequence. *[Exeunt.*

CORAM.–Ha! those boxes! They are mine, and they contain my shirts and socks! How came they here?

Enter RAWLINGS.

RAWLINGS.–Looking at those boxes, sir? Ah, there's a curious tale connected with them. They belong to one Walter Coram, who commissioned me to bring them here.

CORMAN *(sagaciously, aside).*–There is some imposture here, but I will dissemble. *(Aloud, with hidden meaning).*– Oh, indeed!

RAWLINGS.–Yes; I'll tell you all about it—

Tableau. Act drop falls.

ACT II. SCENE 1.–*The Gardens at Acton Villa.*

Enter MR. FRANKLIN, RAWLINGS, *and* JESSOP, *disguised as* CORAM.

MR. FRANKLIN.–I am so glad, Mr. Coram, that you did not meet a watery grave! *(Aside)* Wretch! why were you not drowned. *[Exit.*

RAWLINGS.–Jessop, all prospers, so far. You are supposed to be Coram, and you have Franklin completely in your power. Now, I love his daughter, Laura, and you must insist on his giving her to me. You agree.

Enter FRANKLIN.

JESSOP.–Franklin, let Rawlings marry your daughter.

FRANKLIN.–Never! She is engaged to Lord Alfred. *[Exit.*

Enter KATEY *to find her father.*

KATEY *(sees* JESSOP*).*–My father in that strange wig? Why, oh, why is this? *(Faints.)*

Enter LORD ALFRED COLEBROOKE.

LORD ALFRED.–A fainting girl! I will see her safely home.

Enter LAURA.

LAURA.–Lord Alfred with his arm round a young woman!

SCENES 2 AND 3.–No matter.

SCENE 4.–*Hungerford Bridge by night.*

A poorly painted tricky scene. A scene painter with no sense of shame (and scarcely any of perspective) rushes on and bows. We thought we had put an end to this impertinence.

Enter KATEY.

KATEY.–I will commit suicide!

Enter WALTER CORAM.

CORAM.–Not so!   *[Takes her away.*
(And it was for this that we were compelled to sit out two long and meaningless front scenes! Well, well, this is a vale of tears.)

ACT III. SCENE 1.–*Lombard Street.*
(Twelve Adelphi widows and orphans are discovered on the pavement, selling shares of all kinds to twelve Adelphi stock brokers who buy and pay in the open street.

Enter somebody from a bank. He sticks a placard outside "Payment stopped," as in pantomimes. The Adelphi widows howl, and the Adelphi stockbrokers assume the attitudes of triumphant fiends. Rally.

SCENE 2. No matter.

SCENE 3.–*The Bank and Bank parlour. Clerks and cashiers discovered. Adelphi customers transacting business.*

RAWLINGS.–There is a run on Franklin's. When will Jessop arrive with the forged cheque for £20,000, which I have arranged shall be dishonoured, so that he may have Franklin in his power?

Enter JESSOP. *He presents a cheque for £20,000.*
CORAM *(from somewhere).*–Here is the money! *(Pays it*

across the counter and pockets the cheque, forged with his own name. It seems weak of him to do this, but he is an opium-eater and has reasons of his own.

SCENE 4.–JESSOP'S *Room in Charing-cross Hotel.*

Enter JESSOP *and* RAWLINGS.

JESSOP.–The cheque was honoured by no other than Walter Coram himself! What shall we do? He will be down upon us directly.

RAWLINGS.–We must murder him!

SCENE 5.–*The lost man's room.* CORAM *discovered.*

CORAM.–[Of all the eccentricities of this wealthy opium-eater, his shutting himself up in one unfurnished back attick, with barred windows, in Love Lane, Lambeth, is the most remarkable.] *(They bring him coffee–he takes it.)* Ha, this coffee is drugged with opium! No matter–I am an old opium-eater, and I like it.

[*Drinks it without further inquiry.*
(In the mean time flames have burst through the floor of his room, the boarding of which is quite consumed. Eventually it attracts his attention.)

CORAM.–Ha! Fire? No matter. I am an old Parsee, and I have a great respect for fire. And yet, perhaps, I had better give the alarm *(Goes to window.)* Ha! It is barred! Strange that I should never have noticed that before. Well, well, no matter.

SCENE 2.–No matter.*

SCENE 3.–*The attic floor and roof of Love Lane. (The house is shown in flames. With a view to the satisfaction of visitors to the Adelphi, they are requested to forget that the ground plan of the theatre resembles the longitudinal section of a squirt, the pointed end of the instrument representing the exit into the Strand.)*

---

*Scenes 2 and 3 seem to be repetition, but the content of scene 3 is different from that of scene 3 above. This burlesque play originally was very badly set in type.

Enter SMYLEY and KATEY, *scrambling over the roofs, especially Katey. They plunge into the flames with the insane view of rescuing the unfortunate* CORAM. *Tableau.*

ACT IV.–*The Villa at Acton. All enter.*

CORAM.–I am Coram.

ALL (*except* RAWLINGS *and* JESSOP).–Astonishment!

RAWLINGS *and* JESSOP.–Confusion!

CORAM (*to* RAWLINGS *and* JESSOP).–Give me my shirts and socks, go to Australia, and I will forgive you.

RAWLINGS *and* JESSOP.–We will.

LORD ALFRED.–Laura, will you marry me?

LAURA.–I will.

CORAM.–Katey, will *you* marry *me*?

KATEY.–I will!

CURTAIN.

OURSELVES.–The piece opens very well. The first Act is ingeniously conceived, and smartly written–indeed, the play throughout is, in a literary sense, not unworthy of its authors. But its construction, told, as the story is, in thirteen scenes, is childish, and the plot is wildly improbable. It is fairly well acted by MR. BELMORE and MR. ATKINS. MISS ELIZA JOHNSTONE plays a street-boy very cleverly. MR. BEVERIDGE is an acquisition to a theatre where satisfactory actors of gentlemen are not too numerous. The scenery, as usual, is ridiculous.

5 Adelphi Supers and Halliday Inferiors

Gilbert repeatedly satirized the ineffectual, badly costumed Adelphi supers and their ilk at other theatres (although no other ilk was quite as bad). In Benjamin Webster's *Ethel; or, Only a Life* (*Fun*, 27 October 1866), they were guests:

> the gentlemen in frock coats, white waistcoats, pumps, and wigs; the ladies in pink silk or black velvet bodies, made high, and trimmed with silver, fancy skirts, and black shoes.

Sir Ralph, on-stage in Watts Phillips's *Maud's Peril* (*Fun*, 7 December 1867), addresses them off-stage:

> Good bye, gentlemen. I won't ask you into the drawing-room after dinner–you'll excuse me, I'm sure–Adelphi guests, you know–hardly presentable. Terrible people to have to dinner; but I must ask them, as they possess astounding county influence. I met them first at Hilton's drawing-room, where Ethel; or Only a Life, died on the piano; and then they turned up at Ferns Villa where Nellie Armroyd, lost in London, was discovered by her husband. On both of these occasions they behaved themselves so abominably that nothing but their extraordinary county influence could induce me to invite them here.

A crowd of female Olympic Theatre supers assist in Little Nell's apotheosis in Andrew Halliday's adaptation of *The Old Curiosity Shop*, which Gilbert re-titled 'Nell in a Nutshell' (*Fun*, 3 December 1870):

> The roof comes off the church. The congregation dressed in pink ball dresses and black lace mantillas (bad taste for going to church) bearing NELL, ascend to Heaven on the machinery that took UNDINE down to–Well some weeks ago. Music, 'Oh where and oh where is my bonny NELLY gone?'–which we were sorry to hear as it seemed to imply a doubt as to her ultimate destination.

'Ourselves' called this play an outrage: 'Everyone concerned in it is to be pitied for his or her connection with such a caricature of the lamented author's work.'

The *Athenaeum*'s review (26 November 1870) had already made the same point, although in less downright language: Halliday's overcrowded canvas left many threads unfastened; there was a want of apparent connection between scenes; Quilp's death by conflagration was merely an excuse for one of the absurd fire scenes so prevalent in recent drama; someone who did not know the novel 'might complain with justice of want of intelligibility'. The *Athenaeum* reported that at the first performance there were some hisses because of the play's length, but it had now been shortened.

Gilbert's review of *Nell* was perhaps the last straw for Andrew Halliday, who began a correspondence which the *Theatrical Journal* (11 January 1871) promised would shortly appear in print. Halliday believed that Gilbert was sometimes vindictive in his parodies, and Gilbert was ready for controversy, but evidently their cross-comments were never published. It is true that Gilbert did not admire most of Halliday's work, the early part of which was collaborative, and half the latter, adaptation. His first parody review of Halliday (11 May 1867) burlesqued *The Great City*, which opened at Drury Lane on 22 April:

THE GREAT CITY

ACT I. SCENE 1.–*Exterior of Charing-cross Hotel.*

Enter ARTHUR CARRINGTON.

ARTHUR C.–I am here to meet Edith, who is coming by train from Canterbury. I will not go and meet her on the platform, but I will wander about in front of the Charing-cross Hotel. What more natural than that I should avail myself of this opportunity to remark, with much melodramatic action, that I am disinherited by my uncle in favour of Jacob Blount, M. P., because I get drunk?

[Wanders about the Strand.

Enter EDITH *with large trunk and bandbox.*

EDITH.–I have just arrived, but where is my Arthur? I suppose the fond youth is drunk as usual. I will sit on my trunk in the middle of the Strand and await him.   *[Does so.*

Enter from the Hotel, JACOB BLOUNT, M. P., MENDEZ, *and*
MAJOR O'GAB.

BLOUNT.–A lovely gal? I will deceive her!

MENDEZ.–I will help you s'help me! My grey hairs and false nose will inspire confidence.

BLOUNT.–Away! (*To* EDITH.) Young thing, let me protect you–I see you are alone in the Great City.

EDITH.–I will! I will!

BLOUNT.–Come and sup with me at an hotel under the shadow of St. Paul's.

EDITH.–Under the shadow of St. Paul's? Then it *must* be all right!   *[Exeunt, cooing.*

Enter MOGG, *a returned convict.*

MOGG.–Ha! The Strand still here, I see; and Trafalgar-square, too. But where, oh, where is my Hungerford-market?
                                                          [Weeps.

SCENE 2. *Street near St. Paul's. Enter* BLOUNT.

BLOUNT.–I have taken the timid young thing to the hotel under the shadow of St. Paul's, and I have stood her a supper of broiled fowl and Moselle, and I have selected this spot–the site of the Holborn Improvements–as a conveniently secluded place in which to lay my plans for the future. Let me meditate before I return to Edith at the hotel.   *[Meditates.*

Enter MOGG.

MOGG.–All the evening have I been wandering about in search of Hungerford-market. Can it have strayed into Holborn-valley?

BLOUNT.–Mogg!

MOGG.–Blount!

BLOUNT.–Thief!

MOGG.–Forger!   *[They garotte each other.*

MOGG.–Keep my counsel.

BLOUNT.–I will.   *[Keeps his counsel, and Exit.*

SCENE 3.– *Waterloo-bridge.*

Enter EDITH *and* BLOUNT, *apparently from the Inland*

73

Revenue Office.

BLOUNT.–Notwithstanding the Moselle, she still believes I am actuated by the purest motives. Simple are the children of Canterbury. We are now going to Kennington–I have walked with her to this spot to bring it within a shilling cab fare.

EDITH.–Away, then, to Kennington!

BLOUNT.–Away!

They get into a cab, which has just arrived by a penny steamer.

Enter ARTHUR, *drunk.*

ARTHUR.–Edith! *[Falls senseless.*

ACT III. SCENE 1.–*Drawing-room in Edith's House in Belgravia. Acres of rooms with domed and fretted ceilings, suggestive of Belgravian Luxury. Tall ices handed round as usual. Grand saturnalia of witless Honourables in Berlin gloves and chin tufts. Card tables, chess tables, &c., as usually found in Belgravian Ball-rooms. Four Noblemen discovered, dancing with four Peeresses in their own Right.*

EDITH.–Last night I was a wanderer in London–to-day I am wealthy, and go into the best society. Somebody has died in Australia, and left me millions. This is a room in my mansion in Belgrave-square. It has a domed roof, like the interior of a Mosque, which adds to its effect, but interferes with the arrangements of the apartment over it, the floor of which is difficult to walk upon. Witless Honourables crowd about me, and seek my hand in regular marriage, notwithstanding the awkward fact that I, a girl of eighteen or so, am living alone in this mansion, and giving parties without any chaperone.

Enter MENDEZ *and* BLOUNT.

MENDEZ.–Oh, s'help me, my tear!

BLOUNT.–Readily, my friend. *[S'helps him R.*

Enter a COMIC FLUNKEY.

COMIC F.–Mr. Blount, M. P., this appears to me to be a fitting opportunity to tell you the history of my life and my dawning prospects.

BLOUNT.–Certainly. Go on.

[C. F. *tells him all this, and exit, like a pigeon.*

BLOUNT.–Edith, I love you.

EDITH.–Fiend, be off! Last night you attempted to lead me from the paths of virtue, when I was but a poor wanderer. To-day I am rich, and have a house in Belgrave-square, and an extensive circle of witless Honourables in my train, and you would marry me. Go! [He goes.

Enter a DIRTY CONVICT.

DIRTY C.–Pip!–I should say Edith! I am your papa, Magwitch–I should say, Mogg! It is 4 a. m., and a more fitting opportunity for making this announcement may never occur. 'Twas I who furnished you with £5,000 a-year last night.

EDITH.–Ha! I see it all. "Great Expectations" all over again!

MOGG.–Here is my address, a thieves' kitchen in Saffron-hill. Happy to see you when you like to call.

[Exit, *molto agitato.*

Enter BLOUNT.

BLOUNT.–I have hidden under a sofa, and I heard all. I will denounce him. [Exit.

EDITH.–Ha! I may yet warn him of his danger. *(To servant.)* Quick, an opera cloak, I will walk as I am to Saffron-hill.

Puts opera cloak over ball dress and walks to Saffron-hill.

ACT III. SCENE 1.–*The Jolly Beggars' Club.*

Enter MOGG, *drunk, followed by about a hundred jolly beggars, and* MENDEZ, *in Turkish costume.*

MENDEZ.–Ha! ha! Kitchen in Saffron-hill–Belgrave-square, just now. Such is life, my tear.

Enter EDITH, *in ball dress, with her hair down to express Mogg's danger.*

EDITH.–Papa Mogg, the crushers are upon you!

MOGG.–Ha! I will conceal myself down a trap. [Does so.

Enter CRUSHERS, *of course with moustachios, and headed by* BLOUNT.

EDITH.–Saved! Saved! [Faints.

SCENE 2.–*A Board-room.*

Enter BLOUNT, MENDEZ, and some WITLESS HONOURABLES.
BLOUNT.–Gentlemen, we will get up a company.
ALL.–We will!
[They get up a company. Then exeunt all but MENDEZ.

To him enters his THIN SISTER.
THIN SISTER.–Stout brother, your daughter has been deceived by Blount, M. P.
MENDEZ.–Ha! Revenge! Revenge! I will denounce him!
[Comic dance and off.

SCENE 3. *Housetop, with view of London by night.*

Enter MOGG.
MOGG.–I am pursued. How to escape? Ha! These telegraph wires!
(Pulls down four telegraph wires, calculated to bear a strain of about five tons each, twists them into a rope, and descends over parapet.*)

Enter BLOUNT *and* BEARDED CRUSHERS.
BLOUNT.–He will escape me yet! I have it. My trusty pocket-knife will cut through the four telegraph wires in rather less than a twinkling!
[Cuts wires with pocket knife. Groans from smashed MOGG.

ACT IV. SCENE 1.–*Room in Edith's House.*
Smashed MOGG *on couch, conveniently placed between folding doors.* EDITH *and* ARTHUR CARRINGTON *nursing him.*

MOGG.–I die in great agony. See me plunge.   *[Plunges.*
EDITH.–But look here; before you die couldn't you contrive to bless us. Arthur has taken the pledge, and won't get drunk three times a day any more.
MOGG (screams).–Ya-How!   *[Dies in convulsions.*

SCENE 2.–*Railway Station. "Profile" train ready to start. Crowds of Passengers on platform. They object to get into a profile train.** Officials explain that all the "made-out" trains have struck.*

---

*A clothes line in the play itself
**As its name suggests, this was a low flat cut in the shape of a train.

Enter BLOUNT *and a* YOUNG WOMAN.
BLOUNT.–Away! Away!   *[They away into a carriage.*
Enter MENDEZ.
MENDEZ.–Stop him! Stop him!
(Officers arrest Blount. Realization of MR. FRITH'S *Railway Station. Great joy of everybody who has not seen the picture.)*

CURTAIN.

OURSELVES.–Oh MR. HALLIDAY! MR. HALLIDAY! Have we deserved this?

(At least Halliday himself supplied the phrase 'witless Honourables' which Gilbert made so much of.)

The 'trial' in the *Tomahawk* (1 June 1867) also showed Mogg's character as a version of Magwitch's and found that although some of the dialogue was good, it was Beverley's scenery rather than Halliday's 'fertile imagination' (as Halliday is forced to call it) which was responsible for any success *The Great City* might have had. Other words the *Tomahawk* put into Halliday's mouth included 'I am much patronised by the members of the [insane] Asylums.' Mendez's obviously false nose was commented on.

Fortunately, Gilbert eventually found Halliday's *Notre Dame; or, The Gypsy Girl of Paris,* which he reviewed on 29 April 1871, less culpable. In fact, having opened at the Adelphi on 10 April, it ran for nearly two hundred performances. Gilbert delicately entitled his burlesque

NOTRE———

ACT I.–SCENE 1. *Public Garden in Paris. Ball going on.*

Enter CLAUDE FROLLO, *a Goblin Monk, followed by* QUASIMODO.
FROLLO.–Quasimodo, do you love me?
QUAS.–Love you? Have you not, &c.? *Did* you not, &c.? *Will* you not &c.? And you ask me if I love you! Ha! ha! ha! *(He is much tickled by the idea.)*

FROLLO.–Then aid me with all your love. *(Pointing off.)* You see yon gipsy girl. *(Loud applause at wing from invisible crowd.)*

QUAS.–I do.

FROLLO.–I hate her–she has enchanted me–the cunning gipsy girl! *(Crowd applaud as before.)*

QUAS.–Ha! She dies!

FROLLO.–No she don't. I want you to follow her and ascertain whether she commits herself in any way, and if she does, I will have her burnt as a witch.

QUAS. *(doubtfully).*–As a which?

FROLLO.–Yes. Ha! here comes the gipsy girl. *(Crowd as before. "Gipsy Girl" is evidently a standing cue for crowd to applaud.)*

QUAS.–Claude Frollo, I will do your bidding!

FROLLO *(aside).*–He little thinks that I love her–but soft–

QUASI. *(aside).*–He little thinks that I love her–but–soft–

Enter ESMERALDA. *She dances and sings a song.*

ESMERALDA.–Ha! that monk! He follows me everywhere! Claude *Follow*, I call him.   *[Twirls and exit.*

FROLLO.–How I love her!

Enter SOMEBODY.

SOMEBODY.–Now for the great Festival of Fools which has been prepared at enormous expense for the amusement of Society at Large. Ha! Nobody here? No MATTER! *(Fact.)*

Grand Festival of Fools.

SCENE II.–*The Cell of the Goblin Monk.*

Enter CLAUDE FROLLO.

FROLLO.–I love her, and she *must* be mine!

Enter QUASIMODO.

QUAS.–Master, I have done your bidding!

FROLLO.–Have you detected her in her sorceries?

QUAS.–No; but she meets Captain Phoebus in the Coor dy Mir*rak* to-night, at nine.

FROLLO.–In the Cure dy Me*rack*? I will be there!

QUAS.–And so will I!

SCENE 3.—*The Gipsies' Revel in the Cour des Miracles. (Somewhere near the "Corps Legislatif", if one may judge by the view from the window.) Many clean Gipsies enjoy themselves. They all wear perfectly new and clean clothes, unnecessarily patched with cloth of a violently discordant colour. Enter* PIERRE GRINGOIRE, *a poet, in custody.*

GIPSY.—This person has intruded into our sanctuary.

ALL.—Then he dies! *(They prepare to hang him.)*

GRINGOIRE.—Don't

KING OF THE GIPSIES.—His life may be spared if he can induce one of our band to marry him.

Enter ESMERALDA.

ESMERALDA.—I will! *(Marries him.)*

KING.—Now to leave the newly-married couple alone together.   *[Gipsies politely retire.*

ESMERALDA.—I married you to save your life. Now, jump out of the window into the Seine, and escape. *(He does so.)* Now to receive Phoebus, whom I arranged to meet here. I hope none of the gang will see him, or he will be hanged. Perhaps, on the whole, I could not have selected, in all Paris, a less appropriate spot for my trysting than this Care dy Mee-rarch.

Enter PHOEBUS.

PHOEBUS.—My love!

Enter CLAUDE FROLLO *and* QUASIMODO.

FROLLO.—He dies! *(Stabs him. Enter everybody.)*

ALL.—Who stabbed him?

QUAS.—*She* did! *(indicating Esmeralda.)*

ALL *(who were about to hang Pierre Gringoire a minute or two ago).*—Burn her! She is a witch! *(They drag her off.)*

ACT II.—SCENE 1. *The Prison.* ESMERALDA *discovered.*

ESMERALDA.—I am about to die!

Enter GUDULE, *a Wild Woman*

GUDULE.—Ha! ha! I am glad you are to die!

ESMERALDA.—Why?

GUDULE.–Because you are a gipsy, and gipsies stole my child seventeen years ago. She would be just your age. This is her shoe. *(Produces a shoe.)*

ESMERALDA.–Ha! And here is its fellow! *(Produces a shoe.)*

GUDULE.–Can it be? Then you are–ha! ha!–my child!

ESMERALDA.–My mother! *(They embrace.)*

Enter FROLLO.

FROLLO.–Love me, and you shall be free!

ESMERALDA.–Never!

FROLLO.–Then ho! guards! To execution! *(Guards seize her, and hurry her off.)*

SCENE 2.–*Notre Dame. Procession of soldiers leading* ESMERALDA *to execution. Enter a number of little chorister-boys, who oughtn't to see such a sight.* QUASIMODO *enters from church, and coolly rescues* ESMERALDA *from guards, and walks off with her into Notre Dame. General consternation.*

ACT 3.–SCENE 1. *The Cloisters of the Cathedral.*

Enter ESMERALDA *and* QUASIMODO.

QUAS.–I have saved you. They will not search for you here.

ESMERALDA.–Why not?

QUAS.–I don't know. I am going up to the tower to look at my bells. Good night.   *[Exit.*

ESMERALDA.–I will follow him *(Does so.)*

Enter FROLLO.

FROLLO.–Esmeralda! and alive! I had thought that by this time she must be dead. I will follow her. *(Does so.)*

SCENE 2.–*Paris by night from the roof of Notre Dame.*

Enter QUASIMODO.

QUAS.–Now to bid good night to my bells. *[Exit into tower.*

Enter ESMERALDA

ESMERALDA.–Now to seek Quasimodo.   *[Exit into tower.*

Enter FROLLO.

FROLLO.–Now to see Esmeralda.   *[Exit into tower.*

ESMERALDA *(in tower).*–Ha! Frollo!
FROLLO.–Yes, pretty one–be mine!
ESMERALDA.–Never!
FROLLO.–Ha! Then this good right arm shall–
QUAS.–Never! *(They struggle.* FROLLO *is pitched off tower.)*

Enter GUARDS.

A GUARD.–She is pardoned!
ALL.–Why?
A GUARD.–I don't know!

CURTAIN.

OURSELVES.–A capital piece of its class. If accepted as an Adelphi melodrama, it leaves little to be desired. It has a connected and intelligible story, and gives opportunities for plenty of scenic effect and "powerful" acting. MISS FURTADO and MR. FERNANDEZ did ample justice to their parts. MR. KING, as Quasimodo, was too tragic, and failed altogether to import the necessary element of quaintness into the part. The acting in other respects, was fairly good. The scenery is above the Adelphi average. On the whole *Notre Dame* is an excellent melodrama and immeasurably superior to the same author's *Nell.*

6 Criticism of Construction and Plot

Much of Gilbert's criticism as 'Ourselves' was directed against construction or plot, plot being the story and construction the way in which the scenes were put together. He objected in one instance to thirteen scenes, in another to fifteen. One plot he called childish; others, too conventional, loose, or sloppy. Sometime he objected to both plot and construction, Boucicault's *Jezebel; or, The Dead Reckoning* at the Holborn Theatre (5 December 1870) being one of the prime offenders. Gilbert reviewed it in *Fun*, on 24 December, but Boucicault could hardly call Ourselves' comments a Christmas present.

JEZEBEL

ACT 1.–*Room in* GEORGE D'ARTIGUES' *House at Bordeaux.*

Enter MADAME D'ARTIGUES. *Her long skirt and her tightly-done hair show what a bad character she is.*
MADAME D'ARTIGUES.–I am a female fiend, but I have reasons of my own for not wishing this to be generally known.

Enter GEORGE, *her husband.*
GEORGE.–My wife, here is Alfred Ravel, a navy surgeon, and an old friend of mine.
MADAME D'ART. *(aside).*–I will poison him! *(Aloud.)* I welcome you, sir, *(Starts.)* Ha! That *face!*
RAVEL.–Ha! *that* face!
GEORGE.–Let us hie to the gaming-table and play fiercely.
RAVEL.–We will!   *[Exeunt* GEORGE *and* RAVEL.
MADAME D'ART.–He recognised me! I will poison him–or better still, will marry him first and poison him afterwards! *(Wildly.)* I will marry everybody first, and poison them all afterwards! It is my mission. *(Gnaws her lips.)* It–is–my–mission! *(Smacks her forehead.)*

Enter GEORGE.
MADAME D'ART.–Your eye is wild.

GEORGE.–It is. I have detected (*somebody whose name escaped us–say* DON QUIXOTE)–I have detected Don Quixote cheating at cards, and I have challenged him!

MADAME D'ART. *(aside).*–This must not be! Don Quixote is my lover–I want to marry him first and poison him afterwards! How to prevent this duel? Stay, a thought. Where is my cyanide of prussic strychnine? It is here! Now to poison my husband's draught! (*Poisons his light claret. He sees her do it but pretends ignorance.*)

GEORGE (*sadly*).–She cannot love me or she would not attempt to poison me, (*Swallows another glass of claret, as she isn't looking. She thinks he has swallowed the poisoned wine.*)

MADAME D'ART. *(bitterly).*–How are you, now?

GEORGE (*with deep meaning*).–Far from well–far from well.

MADAME D'ART. *(aside).*–The poison works bravely!

GEORGE.–Woman! you have poisoned me! Fie! (*Dies.*)

MADAME D'ART.–Dead!

Enter RAVEL.

RAVEL.–You have killed your husband. It was an error and must be expiated!

MADAME D'ART.–But how?

RAVEL.–You must come with me to a seaport in South America.

MADAME D'ART. *(aside).*–In South America people commit bigamy three times a week, and poisons grow on every hedge! (*Aloud.*) Done, along with you!

RAVEL.–Along with me it *shall* be done! (*Three stamps and off, with their right arms in the air.*)

ACT II. *Inn at Sea Port in South America.*

(*This is rather a vague address. But dramatists always seem to regard South America as a compact little colony. Who would think of describing a scene as taking place in a "Tavern in Africa", or a "Restaurant in Asia"?*)

Enter CHRISTAL, *a comic person of serious aspect.*

CHRISTAL (*darkly*).–I am a bigamist. I was sentenced to death for the crime, and should have been hanged if it had not been that there was a difficulty in finding someone who wasn't a bigamist to hang me.

Enter CAPTAIN BREITMANN

BREITMANN.–My niece, Gretchen, was to have married a party. Where is that party now?

SOMEBODY *(either* RAVEL, *or* CHRISTAL, *or* MR. DANVERS*, *out of his element).*–Where, indeed?

BREITMANN.–Ha! Does anyone dare to breathe the breath of slander against the fair fame of my niece Gretchen, who married D'Artigues?

RAVEL or CHRISTAL or MR. DANVERS.–He does!

BREITMANN.–Ah!

THE OTHER.–Oh!

BREITMANN.–Very well then.

THE OTHER.–No doubt.

Enter MADAME D'ARTIGUES. *She marries them all round.*

ALL.–Happiness!

(They fill high. She poisons their draughts. They drink.)

ALL.–Agony!   *[Tableau.*

ACT III.–*Rosenfels on the Rhine.*

Enter GRETCHEN *(who has been married in the interval to* GEORGE*).*

GRETCHEN *(simply).*–I am so happy!

GEORGE *(remorsefully).*–Suppose I turned out to be a big–a big–a big–

GRETCHEN *(simply).*–A big what, dear?

GEORGE *(thinking better of it).*–A bigot! *(Aside.)* Artfully evaded!

GRETCHEN. *(simply).*–I should not care, dear, so that you still loved me. Besides I know that you are a man of strong convictions.

GEORGE *(bitterly).*–I shall be some day! Down! down! down! *(To his fluttering heart.)*   *[Exit* GEORGE.

Enter MADAME D'ARTIGUES.

GRETCHEN *(simply).*–Who are you, and what do you want?

MADAME D'ART. *(sarcastically).*–Who am I? Ha! ha! ha!

GRETCHEN *(simply).*–Are you a tramp?

---

*An actor, Edward Danvers.

MADAME D'ART.–Am I a tramp? Do I look like a tramp?

GRETCHEN (simply).–Yes.

MADAME D'ART. (aside).–I will marry you first and poison you afterwards! (Aloud.) I want my husband. Give him to me!

GRETCHEN (simply).–This is a large order! I have not your husband!

MADAME D'ART.–You have! George is my husband!

GRETCHEN. (simply, but still with firmness).–George is my husband.

MADAME D'ART.–I beg your pardon! (GRETCHEN pardons her.) Here is my certificate. (Gives paper to GRETCHEN.)

GRETCHEN (simply).–Then my husband is a bigamist?

MADAME D'ART.–He is–and he married me first. I poisoned him, and he pretended to die in the first act. I thought he was dead, but I find he lives, and has married you.

GRETCHEN (simply).–But, dear me, ma'am, you have been on the stage a considerable time, and your experience ought to have told you that MR. HENRY NEVILLE never dies in the first act of a three act drama*

MADAME D'ART.–That experience would have told me that MISS LYDIA FOOTE always appears before the last act of a three act drama, but in this case it would have told me wrong.

GRETCHEN (simply).–I stand corrected. (Weeps.)

Enter GEORGE.

GEORGE.–Ha! my first wife?

MADAME D'ART.–Yes!

GEORGE.–Undone!

GRETCHEN (simply).–Never mind, dear George. I love you in spite of this and we will be happy together notwithstanding. (Fact!)

MADAME D'ART.–I claim my husband!

Enter CHRISTAL.

CHRISTAL (sees MADAME D'ARTIGUES).–My wife, whom I married and ran away from, and then married somebody else!

---

*Henry Neville made noted successes at the Olympic Theatre as leading man in Taylor's *Ticket-of-Leave Man* (1863) and *Henry Dunbar* (1865), and in his own adaptation of *Les Miserables* (as *The Yellow Passport*, 1868). At the Adelphi in 1867 he played Job Armroyd to perhaps his greatest critical approbation. In 1873 Neville became manager of the Olympic, where he produced Gilbert's *Ne'er-Do-Weel* (1878) and his *Gretchen* (1879); neither succeeded. Lydia Foote began her London career as a child actress in 1852 and played leading adult roles from the mid-1860s onward, including Clara in *The Frozen Deep* and Esther in *Caste*. The *Athenaeum* praised the delicacy of her acting.

MADAME D'ART.–Sold!
(And MADAME D'ARTIGUES *has no further claim upon* GEORGE–*who has learnt this valuable moral lesson–that bigamy is no moral crime if your first wife is a bigamist too.)*

OURSELVES.–A very confused and wholly impossible story, with a wholly unnecessary second act. When nothing else can be said in favour of a piece it is customary to praise its construction. But with due deference to the generally expressed approbation on this score, we submit that a piece in which the three principal persons commit either bigamy or trigamy–and in which the scene is shifted for no necessary reason from Bordeaux to South America and from South America to the Rhine–and in which the only personage in whom one is expected to take any sympathetic interest does not appear until the last act–and in which all the characters turn up together in different quarters of the globe without any sufficiently ostensible reason for doing so–and in which the second act lands the audience nowhere–is not entitled to praise on the score of skilful construction. The piece is very well acted by MISS RODGERS, MISS FOOTE, and MR. NEVILLE, but the characters are too broadly marked to admit of very delicate handling. The scenery is good.

Just as sensational but far more rigorous in structure was *A Life Chase* by John Oxenford and Horace Wigan, produced at the Gaiety Theatre on 11 October 1869. Gilbert approved of its single plot, but nevertheless did not like it. His review (*Fun*, 23 October) subtitled it 'Who Killed Cock Robin', although it had elements which, in earlier days, might have been used for a tragedy.

A LIFE CHASE

ACT I.–*Office of the Juge d'Instruction. Juge d'Instruction discovered.*

Enter MADAME BONVAL.
MADAME BONVAL.–Detect me the murderer of my husband.
JUGE.–I will! We have a suspected man in custody.
MADAME BONVAL.–I will hide behind this curtain while he is being examined.

JUGE.–It is very irregular, but be it so!   *[She hides.*

Enter ALMIVAR.

ALMIVAR.–Of what am I accused, Monsieur le Juge?

JUGE.–Of the murder of Maurice Bonval. You were seen in his company late on the night of the murder. His money was found upon you, and you owed him a grudge.

ALMIVAR.–But I didn't do it

JUGE *(impressively)*.–Are you sure of that?

ALMIVAR.–Quite sure.

JUGE.–In that case I will release you.   *[Does so!!!*

MADAME BONVAL *(entering from behind curtain)*.–That man is the murderer.

JUGE.–But, Madame, you forget–he denies it *in toto.*

MADAME BONVAL.–He may have interested motives for doing so.

JUGE.–Hardly. A gentleman would scarcely deny a crime if he had really committed it. Still, perhaps I was in error when I allowed him to go free. I will away and consult a higher authority on the subject. It is rather late to do this, but no matter. *(Exit to learn his duty).*

VAUBERT, *a police spy, comes forward.*

VAUBERT.–That man is the murderer.

MADAME BONVAL.–How know you that?

VAUBERT.–Professional instinct. Follow my instructions and I undertake to bring the crime home to him.

MADAME BONVAL.–My hand on it!

BOTH.–He is the murderer!!!

ACT II.–*Salon in the House of* MADAME ST. ANGE. *Spasmodic footman discovered.*

SPASMODIC FOOTMAN *(with appropriate action)*.–Madame St. Ange.

Enter MADAME ST. ANGE.

MADAME ST. ANGE.–The guests have not arrived, Pierre?

SPASMODIC FOOTMAN *(with appropriate action)*.–No, Madarm.

MADAME ST. ANGE.–You can go.

SPASMODIC FOOTMAN *(with appropriate action).*–Yes, Madarm.   *[Exit, with illustrative gesture.*

Enter guests. Like all Frenchmen, they wear crop wigs coming to a point over the forehead. They interchange repartees, and are much amused with each other. The audience are much amused with them.

Enter poor MISS FARREN, *as a French marquis in a crimson tie. Lets off an intellectual fire-work, as first guest. Then exit poor* MISS FARREN.*

Enter MADAME BONVAL *and* VAUBERT

VAUBERT.–Madame St. Ange, let me introduce a lady who is anxious to know you.

MADAME ST. ANGE.–Welcome, lady.

VAUBERT *(aside to* MADAME BONVAL*).*–Almivar will be here anon. You must fascinate him.

MADAME BONVAL *(with full reliance in her powers of fascination).*–I will!

Enter ALMIVAR.

ALL.–Welcome, Almivar.

ALMIVAR.–Thanks, friends. I have been charged with the murder of my notary, and honourably acquitted. Amusing mistake, wasn't it?

ALL.–Ha! Ha!

MADAME BONVAL AND VAUBERT *(aside to each other).*–Ho! ho!

SOMEBODY.–Come–a turn at Baccarat.

ALL.–We will!

(MADAME BONVAL *gazes steadily at* ALMIVAR *under the mistaken impression that she is fascinating him.)*

ALMIVAR *(aside).*–That woman is extremely annoying!

They play at Baccarat. MADAME BONVAL *stares* ALMIVAR *out of countenance all the time. He loses.*

ALMIVAR.–Confound the woman's impertinence! *(He changes his seat, but she follows him. He loses more than ever.)*

ALMIVAR.–Oh hang it, I can't stand this!

VAUBERT *(aside to* MADAME BONVAL, *and jumping at a conclusion).*–He is the murderer!

---

*Nellie Farren usually played cheeky boys in Gaiety burlesque, and seems miscast here.

89

ACT III.–MADAME BONVAL'S *apartment.*

Enter MADAME BONVAL *and* VAUBERT.

VAUBERT.–The scheme works bravely.

MADAME BONVAL.–Almivar will be here directly.

VAUBERT.–You must continue to make love to him.

MADAME BONVAL.–I will!

VAUBERT.–We are all to sup at the Café Anglais to-morrow. Give me the dagger with which your late husband was slain.

MADAME BONVAL.–Behold it here!–Oh horror! *(Tumbles over a sofa, after giving him a curious weapon, which we know to be a dagger because it is expressly stated. It is elaborately chased, apparently the work of* BENVENUTO CELLINI *in early infancy.)*

Enter ALMIVAR.

ALMIVAR.–Madame Bonval!

MADAME BONVAL.–Monsieur Almivar.

ACT IV.–*Cafe Anglais. Enter* ALMIVAR, VAUBERT, *and* MADAME BONVAL *to wholesome light supper of champagne and apples. They sit down.*

VAUBERT *(by way of making himself agreeable at a supper party).*–Behold this dagger–it is the weapon that stabbed Maurice Bonval.

ALMIVAR.–Ha! *(Shrinks.)*

VAUBERT *(aside to* MADAME BONVAL*).*–He is the murderer!

MADAME BONVAL *(aside to* VAUBERT*).*–Evidently.

VAUBERT *(aloud).*–The weapon is elaborately carved.

ALMIVAR (coolly).–So was its victim, ha! ha!

VAUBERT *(aside to* MADAME BONVAL*).*–He is the murderer!

MADAME BONVAL *(aside to* VAUBERT*).*–Evidently.

VAUBERT *(aloud).*–It struck him to the heart!

ALMIVAR *(who don't like this sort of thing at supper).*– Don't, there's a good fellow.

VAUBERT *(aside to* MADAME BONVAL*).*–He is the murderer!

MADAME BONVAL *(aside to* VAUBERT*).*–Evidently.

ALMIVAR *(who is getting rollicking).*–Come, one more apple, before we part!

VAUBERT *(aside to* MADAME BONVAL*).*–He is not the murderer!

MADAME BONVAL *(aside to* VAUBERT*)*.–Evidently! And what is more, I love him! *Tableau.*

ACT V.–*Apartment on the Quays.*

Enter VAUBERT *and* MADAME BONVAL *(as usual).*

VAUBERT.–I have changed my mind since I gave the cue for the end of the fourth Act. He is the murderer!

MADAME BONVAL *(who is beginning to have a poor opinion of* VAUBERT'*s qualifications as a detective).*–Oh, you get out. *(Sends him on to the balcony.)*

Enter ALMIVAR.

ALMIVAR.–Madame BONVAL, I love you! May I hope?

MADAME BONVAL.–You may! *(He hopes.)*

VAUBERT *(from balcony).*–He is NOT the murderer!

MADAME BONVAL.–I must tell you who I am–I am the widow of Maurice Bonval, whom you were suspected of having murdered!

ALMIVAR.–You! *(Aside.)* Oh, agony.

Enter VAUBERT *from balcony.*

VAUBERT.–Stop! Behold this dag– Oh! *(as in pain.)*

ALMIVAR AND MADAME BONVAL.–Are you unwell?

VAUBERT.–No; it is nothing. *(Fumbles at his tail pocket, and eventually produces pantomime dagger from it)*–Behold this dagger!

ALMIVAR.–Ha! ha! I will confess all! I *did* kill Maurice Bonval!

ALL.–Ha!

ALMIVAR.–And thus–thus he is avenged! *(Stabs himself, and dies in great agony.)*

VAUBERT *(with inspiration).*–He is the murderer!!!

CURTAIN.

OURSELVES.–An ingeniously conceived, but very unpleasant story. The second act is very poor–the first and fifth are good. That the piece is successful is attributable to the fact that it is strongly sensational, and that the story, unencumbered with underplot, is kept well in view throughout. MR. WIGAN played a very unpleasant part in a masterly manner. MR. CLAYTON, careful and conscientious, did full justice to a part which is quite out of his line. MISS NEILSON was artificial and extravagant to the last degree.

(Poor Miss Neilson. Her Juliet had been praised the year before, but even then she sometimes was a little artificial; reviewers agreed she showed great promise but had much to learn. Unfortunately, she had little time to learn it—she died at the age of thirty-four.)

Artificial exposition was regularly parodied as in the bald opening statements of *How She Loves Him!* (*Fun*, 4 January 1868), a travesty of Boucicault's play, which had opened at the Prince of Wales's on 21 December 1867. Here Mr. Nettletop is discovered '*much bandaged, looking through telescope at ladies bathing*'. He says:

> I am divorced from my wife—it doesn't clearly appear how, for although I allowed her to think I went astray, I was guilty neither of cruelty nor desertion, as the act requires. I find I still love her, and in order to induce her to return to my arms, I affect to be an utterly helpless invalid, and in that enticing character I expect to prove irresistible.

Likewise, Patty's first speech in Watts Phillips's *Nobody's Child* (*Fun*, 28 September 1867) is made to run:

> My uncle, Peter Grice, is Postmaster of St. Arven. Joe, the village idiot, is our servant. Lewcy Tregarvon, my foster-sister, is the daughter of Sir Robert Tregarvon, a long-haired, horsemanship-looking bart. Captain Dudley Lazonby was formerly engaged to Miss Lewcy, but is now thrown over for George Penrhyn. Now you know all about us.

Other plot elements which Gilbert invited his readers to laugh at included inappropriate reactions, leapings to conclusions, and astonishing coincidences, as in his review of the 1866 version of *The Frozen Deep* (17 November 1866). Wilkie Collins and Charles Dickens had originally written it for amateurs in 1857, and it then had three public performances in Manchester. Nine years later, Collins revised it and in doing so lost the original elements of its success, nor could a professional actor emulate the startlingly intense acting of Dickens himself in the leading role.[30] Gilbert seized on its long narrative passages and made the snow an obvious stage trick, ending with a ridiculous interrupted tag line and inappropriate joy:

THE FROZEN DEEP

ACT I. SCENE 1.–*A Country House in Devonshire.*

Enter LUCY CRAYFORD *and* MRS. STEVENTON.

LUCY.–
MRS. S.– } 'Tis now some seventeen years since—

LUCY.–Oh, I beg your pardon.

MRS. S.–Not at all, go on.

LUCY.–'Tis now some seventeen years since Clara Vernon first met Lieutenant Crayford. It's a long story–I will tell you all about it.

MRS. S.–No–don't–some other time. *I*, also, have a long story to tell. It takes twenty minutes; but, nevertheless, I will give it to you.

LUCY.–Spare me!

MRS. S.–Never!   [*Tells her a long story that lasts twenty minutes. Any jumble about the Arctic regions, polar bears, and second sight will do.*

LUCY (*awaking*).–You astound me! Now let *me* tell you the story of the loves of somebody in the Arctic regions–say Lieutenant Frank Aldersly?

MRS. S–Well, it's certainly your turn. (*Sighing*) Do get on with it!

LUCY.–But soft–Clara is coming; we will dissemble.

[*A door opens of its own accord, and in comes* CLARA, *frantic.*

CLARA (*hysterically*).–Ha! ha! I have seen him in a dream! I have seen Lieutenant Frank Aldersly, and he is dying at the hands of Lieutenant Crayford!

LUCY (*meditatively*).–In our family we always call Lieutenants by their naval rank, however intimate we may be with them. But (*rousing herself*) no matter!

CLARA (*to* LUCY).–
MRS. S.–   } I will tell you the story of—

CLARA (*to* MRS. S.).–Oh, I beg your pardon.

MRS. S.–Pray don't mention it–go on.

CLARA.–I will tell you the story of my engagement to Lieutenant Frank Aldersly and Lieutenant Crayford. Lieutenant Frank has long loved me–he told me so–and we were engaged. Then came a person called Lieutenant Crayford

93

whom I knew but slightly. After telling me that he was going off to fight the Paynim foe in Central Africa he informed me that he should consider himself engaged to me, and before I could expostulate he kissed me, and exitted to Central Africa.

LUCY *(decisively)*.–That was rude.

CLARA.–It was. He returned from killing the Paynim foe, and then he claimed me. I told him that I was engaged. He said, "Ha! ha!" (You know how he stamps when he is excited.) "I will kill him!" And in furtherance of his determination, he exitted to the Arctic regions

LUCY.–Humph!

CLARA.–You are right. Well–Lieutenant Crayford and Lieutenant Frank are on board the same ship! Ha! I see them now through my back hair!

Enter a London fog. Then the party-wall at the back opens, and discovers a room in the next house. A gentleman is lying on the floor asleep, and another, on the top of a gigantic twelfth cake, is about to shoot him; Fireworks at the back.*

CLARA.–Ha! ha! The Frozen Deep. The Frozen Deep.

ACT II.–*Hut in the Arctic Regions.*

Enter LIEUTENANT CRAYFORD *and* LIEUTENANT STEVENTON.

LIEUT. S.–
LIEUT. C.– } Let me tell you all that has happened since—

LIEUT. C.–Oh, I beg your pardon.

LIEUT. S.–Not at all–go on.

LIEUT. C.–I was going to recapitulate to you all that has happened since we left England.

LIEUT. S.–So was I.

LIEUT. C. *(disappointed)*.–Oh. Then I suppose I needn't go on.

LIEUT. S.*(dismally)*.–Oh, do.

LIEUT. C.*(cheerfully)*.–Well, I will.

[*Tells him everything that has happened since they left England.*

Enter FRANK ALDERSLY *with the scurvy.*

FRANK A.–I have got the scurvy. I have had it for months.

---

*Now called a Twelfth Night cake, lavishly iced with white sugar and surmounted by miniature sugar figures and scenes. One is still cut at Sadler's Wells during the annual party of the Vic-Wells Association.

Enter RICHARD WARDOUR.

RICH. W.–Yah! I do not yet know that Frank Aldersly is my hated rival. But I shall learn it 'ere long.

LIEUT. C. *(aside to* STEVENTON*)*.–He is rough, but he means nothing. He is the best-hearted fellow in the world. I will tell you a story about him. 'Tis now some twenty-seven years since—

Enter, providentially, CAPTAIN HELDING. *Somebody shovels some snow over him at the door.*

CAPT. H.–I should be glad to know why you station a party, in a white cap, at the door to shovel snow over your superior officer whenever he comes in or goes out?

LIEUT. C. *(to* FRANK–*aside)*.–Richard Wardour's story another time!

CAPT. H.–We will cast lots to see who shall go away from this, and who shall stay.

Enter the SHIP'S COMPANY. *A party in a white cap heaps a shovelfull of snow on each as he enters. They expostulate.*
LIEUT. C.–Now for the dice!
[*They cast lots.* WARDOUR *is to stay, but* ALDERSLY *is to go with the exploring party. Then exeunt all but* WARDOUR. *Party in white cap shovels more snow on to each man as he goes out. This is, perhaps, a preventative against scurvy.*

RICH. W.–I am incensed–I know not why–and to relieve my feelings I will break up the hut. Let me begin with Frank Aldersly's berth. Yaah! Wow! *(Chops up* FRANK'S *berth, which has been roughly put together with tin tacks. On one of the planks he sees the letters* E. B.*)* That must stand for Clara Vernon! At least she's called Vernon in the bills, though her real name is Burnham. Clara Burnham! *(Muses.)* Burnham wood! This is young Aldersly's berth–then he *must* love Clara; or why did he cut E. B. in the plank? He must die!

Enter LIEUTENANT CRAYFORD.
LIEUT. C.–What's all this?
RICH. W.–Listen. I will tell you a story. 'Tis now some ninety-two years since—

LIEUT. C.–No, no. What is the upshot of it?

RICH. W.–The upshot is that Aldersly must die!

LIEUT. C. *(wheedlingly).*–Oh, don't kill him!

RICH. W.–I must. He has carved E. B. on his berth. That means Clara Vernon.

LIEUT. C. *(weakly).*–Well, I wouldn't kill him for all that.

Tableau.

ACT III.–*A Cavern on the coast of Newfoundland.*

Enter CLARA *and* LUCY.

CLARA.–Well, here we are in a cavern in Newfoundland. Why did we come here?

LUCY.–Oh, I don't know! And yet I do. I will tell you. You must know that two hundred and three years ago there lived—

CLARA.–Oh, bother. Suppose we should come across the explorers from the North Pole! Wouldn't that be a coincidence?

LUCY.–It would, indeed. Ha! Here they are!

Enter LIEUTENANTS CRAYFORD, STEVENTON, *and* OTHER EXPLORERS.

LIEUT. C.–Lucy! You here? Who *would* have thought of seeing you. How dedo?

LUCY.–I will tell you how I am. 'Tis now some—

CLARA.–But my Lieutenant Frank–where is he?

LIEUT. C.–Ha-a-a-h! Who shall say?   *[Weeps.*

CLARA.–Lieutenant Steventon, where is my Lieutenant Frank?

LIEUT. S.–Ah, me!   *[Weeps.*

CLARA. *(to a* SAILOR*).*–Sailor, where is my Lieutenant Frank?

SAILOR.–Belay!   *[Weeps.*

CLARA.–My gift of second sight, taken in conjunction with your tears, convinces me that there is something wrong. I will go home and faint.

Enter RICHARD WARDOUR, *ragged and hungry.*

RICH W.–Ah, give me to eat!

LIEUT. C. *(recognising him).*–Richard Wardour! What have you done with Lieutenant Frank? I know–You have eaten him!

RICH. W.–Ha! Lieutenant Frank? Wait a bit.

Exit–then re-enters with the ghost of LIEUTENANT FRANK.

CLARA.–My Lieutenant Frank's ghost! Oh, joy! *[Hugs him.*

RICH. W.– ⎫
LIEUT. F.– ⎬ Let me explain.

RICH. W.–Oh, I beg your pardon.

LIEUT. F.–Don't apologise–proceed.

RICH. W. *(politely).*–After you.

LIEUT. F.–Oh, I couldn't think of it!

RICH. W.–Well, then, I didn't kill him; but, on the contrary, I saved him. I wandered to Newfoundland with him, where, by a curious coincidence, we have all met at the same moment. I was starving–starving–starving!

LIEUT. C.–But–you are English officers–why didn't you apply to the British Consul?

RICH. W.–Well, do you know, it's very extraordinary, but that never occurred to me. To resume. I was starving, and seeing that you were eating, I came to you, and lo! you turned out to be–start not!–Lieutenant Crayford!

LIEUT. C. *(musing).*–Strange!

RICH. W.–But true. And now let the revels commence; and there won't be a merrier party in any cavern in Newfoundland! And if our friends in front will—But, ha! This is death! *[Dies in excruciating agony.*

GENERAL JOY. CURTAIN.

The absurdity of the initials on the bunk was caused by Clara Vernon's name having been Burnham in the original version. Her vision of Frank dying at Crayford's hands is a mistake, whether Gilbert's or *Fun's* compositors'. Moreover, in 1866 as in 1857, it is Wardour, not Crayford, who goes to Africa. The allusion to Wardour's having eaten Frank is a reminiscence of Dickens's interest in Sir John Franklin's last, fatal Arctic expedition of 1845, which suggested the idea of *The Frozen Deep*. In 1854 it was reported that Franklin and his men had finally been driven to cannibalism, which Dickens ardently refused to believe.

Before he settled on 'Ourselves', and sometimes after, Gilbert used tag lines, which in mid-Victorian drama summed up the final situation and generally asked for applause. As J. B. Buckstone explained to the Italian actress, Miss Binda, the conclusion of Fanny Kemble's play *Mademoiselle de Belle Isle* unfortunately divided one sentence between the two leading characters:

> This ending for us would be too abrupt–our people like to see the principal actor or actress, advance, and speak a sort of epilogue–I have ventured to finish thus ... has it not brought me that which has long been a stranger to my heart–Happiness?–My truth proved–my honour unsullied–my father–my brother free–and he that I have fondly loved through years of sorrow–mine!–can there be greater happiness in store for Gabrielle de Belle Isle?–Yes–one thing more–*advancing to the audience*–your kind approval.[31]

Gilbert's tag lines were, of course, comic. His version of Tom Taylor's *Henry Dunbar* (*Fun,* 23 December 1865) ended with

> DUNBAR.–I am about to die, and if our friends in front will only look kindly on my efforts, there will not be a happier old dog in England than Henry Dunbar!   [*Dies in great agony.*

while Miss Miggs's tag ending the burlesque of *Barnaby Rudge* (24 November 1866) might almost be an 'Ourselves' paragraph:

> ...And if our friends in front can make head or tail out of what we've been doing, or can derive the slightest gratification from the preposterous farrago of coarse nonsense we have set before 'em, there won't be a happier party in all England than Harlequin Barnaby Rudge; or, the Fairy Varden and the Yankee Gal from Down East.[32]

7 Melodrama and an Intrusive Scene-Painter

Although Gilbert's reviews of Tom Robertson's plays were, for the most part, mild and often enthusiastic, he could not keep himself from guying the eminently guyable Adelphi melodrama *The Nightingale* (29 January 1870). 'Ourselves' had said of *Caste* (*Fun*, 4 May 1867): 'Well, it's a capital piece; extremely well written, though perhaps a little prosy in the third act. Beautifully placed upon the stage, and excellently acted by the best company in London. But we must have our joke, for all that.' (And his joke is infinitely superior to the irrelevant but brutal blows which the *Tomahawk* dealt Robertson in its own 25 May trial.) But Gilbert obviously felt that *The Nightingale* could or should not succeed; the public evidently agreed with him, for the play was cut, altered, and polished after the first night (15 January 1870) without securing a long run. Its plot forecast, in certain respects, the plot of Conway and Carr's *Called Back* as synopsized in the *San Francisco Argonaut* (quoted in the Chicago *Tribune*, 9 November 1884): 'Act 1–My God! He is blind! Act 2–My God! She is mad! Act 3–My God! She is sane! Act 4–My God! He is dead!'

THE NIGHTINGALE; OR, THE TERRIBLE TURK AND THE GREAT TIDAL WAVE!

ACT I.–Mary's *House. Enter* HAROLD.

HAROLD.–As I am now forty, it is high time I began to think of choosing a profession. I shall go to Cambridge, and take orders.

Enter CHEPSTOW, *in high spirits.*
CHEPSTOW.–Harold! Congratulate me! I have just been gazetted to an ensigncy in the Twenty-second!
HAROLD.–I do! We were at Rugby together. My early education having been neglected, it occurred to me, at the age of

thirty, that it would be well if I went to school. And that is how I came to know you. *(Aside.)* Heavens, I love Mary.

Enter ISMAEL, *a Terrible Turk, and* WILLIAM WAGE.
WILLIAM.–Ismael, you are my tutor.
ISMAEL.–I am.

Enter MARY.

MARY.–William!
ISMAEL *(Aside).*–Take her hand. *(He does so.)* Bless you both!
HAROLD *(Aside).*–All is lost!

ACT II.–*The Italian Inn.* MARY *(now married to* WILLIAM*) discovered, with a roguey-poguey in a cradle. Also, an impertinent but faithful female servant,* KEZIAH.

MARY.–My dear husband is dying in the next room. I am convinced that Ismael is poisoning him; but I will not interrupt them.

Enter ISMAEL.

ISMAEL.–There is no hope. He can't live through the night. When he is dead will you marry me?
MARY.–Villain! Know that the pure English wife seldom (if ever) listens to overtures of marriage until her husband is quite, quite dead. *(*ISMAEL *quails.)*   *[Exit* MARY.

Enter WILLIAM, *very poorly.*

WILLIAM.–Villain! You have poisoned me. You have insured my life heavily, and you have committed forgeries in my name!
ISMAEL.–Pardon me, you err. *(But he has, the bold, bad man!)*
WILLIAM.–You–ha! I die!   *(wriggles and dies.)*

Enter Adelphi Johndarmes.

JOHNDARME.–I arrest William Wage for forgery.
ISMAEL.–It is too late. He is dead.

ACT III.–*A Portsmouth attic. Fine Sea View. Enter* MARY,
KEZIAH, *and* ROGUEY-POGUEY.

MARY *(explains).*–After the death of my husband, I took to the operatic stage, and came a dreadful cropper. Failing abjectly as a prima donna, and having nothing in my pocket, I put my pride in it, and accepted an engagement in the Portsmouth chorus at two pounds a week. Hence I am known to the world as the Nightingale.

KEZIAH *(aside to* ROGUEY-POGUEY *in a whisper).*–Hush, then, it mustn't make faces at the audience and spoil its mother's best scenes. It must be a good boy, den, and concentrate its little attention on the business of the stage.

MARY.–The sea view is charming, but as the sea comes right up to the attic window sill in calm weather, it is not pleasant to think of the consequences of anything like a gale of wind. Thank heaven we are not on the ground floor!

[Exeunt, leaving ROGUEY-POGUEY.
(A boat is rowed up to the window, and ISMAEL *enters through that aperture. Flight of steps conveniently placed for that purpose.*

ISMAEL.–Now to steal the child and insure its life. But first to give it an anticipatory dose of poison. *(To child.)* Oh, nicey, nicey, nicey! *(Gives the child a table-spoonful of arsenic and exit into the sea.)*

Enter MARY *and* KEZIAH.

MARY.–Where is the child?

KEZIAH.–I don't know. *(*MARY *rolls her eyes.)* Ha! Missus is mad! I will run away and leave her all alone. *(Does so, like a faithful creature as she is.)*

*(*MARY *steps out of window into a boat. Enter the Great Tidal Wave. The house is swamped and disappears.* MARY *alone on the wild waste of waters in boat. The sea rises very much indeed. Happily the presence of a lime light suggests that human aid is not far off. The sea runs mountains high, but the boat behaves well. Tableau!)*

ACT IV.–*A London Square–real gas lamps and actual pillar post. Showy house, with fashionable ball going on. Adelphi guests arrive on foot, and all at once. This is accounted for by the fact that they had been spending the*

earlier part of the evening with "Ethel; or, Only a Life";
but were summarily dismissed from that lady's house in
consequence of her sudden death on the piano.

Enter MARY, *very poorly clad, but quite sane again.*

MARY.–If it had not been for the lime-light man I had perished. I have lost my situation in the Portsmouth chorus, and, consequently, I am no longer known as the Nightingale. Ha!, I faint. *(Does so.)*

Enter ISMAEL, *in gorgeous turban and gilt-trousers.*

ISMAEL.–This is the house at which I am going to conjure. Such is life! Ismael, whom no one recognises as the cruel Bahadur Khan, the inciter of that famous Indian mutiny which was suppressed two years ago by Mr. Eburne and Mr. Robert Romer* in *"A Sister's Penance,"* has come down to earning half-guineas by conjuring at fashionable entertainments! It is Allah's will.   *[Exit into house.*

MARY *(on ground)*.–Gurgle! gurgle! gurgle!
(At this point all the Adelphi guests–who can stand a good deal but not a conjurer–leave the house in a body and walk home through the snow).

(Enter from house) HAROLD *and* CHEPSTOW.

HAROLD.–Yes, Chepstow, I changed my mind about going into the Church, and I bought a commission in your regiment instead. We fought together in India, and here we are.

CHEPSTOW *(seeing* MARY, *lying on the snow)*.–Hullo, here's a lark. Here's a dying woman! *(Chaffs her, like an officer and a gentleman.)*

Enter from house ISMAEL.

ISMAEL *(sees* MARY*)*.–It is Mary Wage.

HAROLD.–And you–you are Bahadur Khan! Vengeance!
                    [Exit ISMAEL *very quickly. Tableau.*

ACT V.–*The Village Church. Enter* MARY *and* ISMAEL.

---

*William Eburne and Robert Romer were actors of middle-aged character parts. In *A Sister's Penance* (1866) Romer played Colonel Leslie in Act 2, during which the Indian Mutiny takes place, incited by Ammedoolah, an educated Hindu turned villain. In *The Nightingale*, the inciter of the Mutiny is Bahadur Khan, now disguised as Ismael.

MARY.–No, Ismael, I can never love you. You murdered my husband, and you kidnapped my child. It would only be Christian to forgive you, and I do so with all my heart, but I do not think I could ever be truly happy with you. Where is my child?

ISMAEL.–Alas, he is dead! Here is his grave.

MARY.–Dead! *(Goes mad again.)*

Enter KEZIAH *with* ROGUEY-POGUEY.

KEZIAH.–Not so! The arsenic turned out to be nothing but Epsom Salts. He forged the child's burial certificate, having first insured his life.

MARY.–My boy! *(Becomes as sane as an Adelphi heroine can be.)*

ISMAEL.–Ha! Foiled! But I will be avenged! *(Seizes child and presents pistol at its head.)*

Enter HAROLD *and* CHEPSTOW, *with a company of ridiculous soldiers, armed to the teeth with penny canes.*

HAROLD.–There is your prisoner, the cruel Bahadur Khan!

(They seize him. Tableau!)–CURTAIN.

OURSELVES.–This piece is not worthy of MR. ROBERTSON. As the leading dramatist of the day he has a valuable reputation to sustain, and he should be careful how he risks it by producing pieces that his own good sense and great experience must tell him could never succeed. The story is at once ordinary and impossible. It offers little opportunity to the actors engaged in it. The scenery is contemptible.

Robertson was indeed not a writer whose style suited the Adelphi; *The Nightingale* was a failure in spite of the presence of Mrs. Mellon and Miss Furtado in the cast. Webster was too old for his role, and the *Graphic* (5 February 1870) said that, while he could not act badly, 'as Ismael he does his worst.' Gilbert illustrated this review with a large, very dark picture of Miss Furtado in her boat and several little figures:

It was not the melodrama *per se* to which he objected but the melodrama *per Adelphi*. His parody contained yet another allusion to *Ethel; or, Only a Life* (13 October 1866), which entered his store of references after his full-scale review on 27 October. He evidently considered it an archetypal Adelphi 'society' drama, intensified by the supers whose description I have already quoted.

ETHEL; OR, ONLY A LIFE

ACT I.–*Room in Cambric House.*

Enter THOS. WORDLEY, *and* HILTON WORDLEY, *his son.*

WORD.–I am a retired linendraper.

HILTON.–And I am your only son!

WORD.–I am also a cad.

HILTON.–You are. And I am a cub.

WORD.–You are–you are! *[They embrace.*

Enter ISABEL WORDLEY.

ISABEL.–I am your daughter, and am receiving music lessons from Ethel; or, Only a Life.

WORD.–True. Here is Mr. Langdale, our family doctor, who has come to see how you are.

Enter LANGDALE.

LANGDALE.–Isabel–*how* are we this morning?

ISABEL *(looking deep into his eyes).*–Better *(with empressment)*, better now! *(Squeezes his hand.)* Oh, Mr. Langdale! *(Sighs at him.)* Ah, Mr. Langdale! *(Fondles him.) (Aside.)* How shall I let him know that I love him? The maiden heart is shy, and shrinks from discovering its preferences.

HILTON.–Once I seduced a young lady whose name is inaudible at the back of the dress circle. She committed suicide.

Enter MRS. MONTGOMERY.

MRS. MONT.–Not so. She is here! I did *not* die!

HILTON.–You did!

MRS. MONT.–I didn't. I am a wealthy widow–far and away the richest person in the world–and I have come to buy your house.

WORD.–This way, and I will show it to you.

Exeunt all but HILTON *and* ETHEL; *or Only a Life.*

HILTON.–Ethel, I have orange hair and no forehead to speak of, but I adore you.

ETHEL.–I am a most superior young person, yet, cub as you are, I worship you!

Enter WORDLEY.

WORD.–Ha! my son proposing to a music mistress! Miss Chatteris, here is ninepence for the last three lessons. Now be off! *[Exit* ETHEL; *or, Only a Life.*

HILTON.–Dear papa, do not be angry–I am only going to deceive her! I am going, dear papa, to run off with her to Paris under pretence of marrying her, and when I am tired of her I will desert her, and leave her to perish, dear papa. That's all!

WORD.–Ho! ho! Sly dog! Sly dog!

[They dig each other in the ribs.

ACT II.–*The Terrace, Richmond. Enter* ETHEL; *or Only a Life.*

ETHEL.–The scenery is by Danson. They call him the Danson swell.

Enter MR. LANGDALE.

LANGDALE.–How dedo? Oh, by-the-by, I love you! Will you marry me?

ETHEL.–Oh, do you? Well, I'm awfully sorry, but I'm engaged or I would with pleasure.

LANGDALE.–Oh, it's of no consequence. I am going to India, and I thought I'd mention it. Good bye.

[Goes to India.

Enter HILTON.

HILTON.–We fly to Paris to-morrow!

ETHEL.–We do!

SCENE 2.–ETHEL'S *Lodging in High-street. Spring, 1866.*

ETHEL.–These are my lodgings. They are painted by Danson. They call him the—Ah! Who is there?

Enter WORDLEY.

WORD.–Ethel, my son is deceving you!

ETHEL.–Impossible!

WORD.–Read.   *[Gives letter.*

ETHEL.–Too true!

WORD.–I fly!   *[Flies.*

Enter HILTON.

HILTON.–Dearest Ethel.

ETHEL.–Monster in human shape! Fiend unapproachable! Skeleton of the wilderness! Avaunt!

HILTON.–Never! *(Aside)*–Baffled!

Enter MRS. MONTGOMERY.

MRS. MONT.–What is this? Ah, I see it all. He refuses to avaunt to oblige a lady! Ah, well! The world is, after all, but a big spinach-garden, in which the aloe and pandemonium struggle unsuccessfully for mastery, my dear! I'll soon cure him. *(To* HILTON.*)*–Avaunt, directly.

HILTON.–Ha! foiled! But a time will come!

[Avaunts R. U. E.

MRS. MONT.–It's always so, my dear. Life has its palladiums, but still it often happens that poppies grow up among the bear-gardens of our choicest intimacies, whether we will or no!

ACT III.–*Chelsea, London, S.W.* ETHEL'S *Rooms in Park-walk.*

Enter ETHEL.

ETHEL.–This is Chelsea, London, S. W. How poor are my rooms! Danson has painted them on the back of the last scene. They call him—but no matter.

Enter ABIGAIL HAWCROFT.

ABIGAIL.–I am Mr. Wordley's niece, and I have been staying in Yorkshire.

ETHEL.–My own old friend!

ABIGAIL.–Give me some refreshment.

ETHEL.–I have not a farthing in the world.

ABIGAIL.–I thought not. I will go and buy you some hams.

[*Exit.*

Enter MRS. MONTGOMERY.

MRS. MONT.–Ah, Ethel! I am going to marry that cad Hilton.

ETHEL.–Oh! Mrs. Montgomery, how can you?

MRS. MONT.–Ah, my dear, when you have seen as much of the world as I have, you will learn that though we may *desire* to travel by Life's Limited Mail, yet Atropos often steps in and, flaring the bright dazzling torch of inconstancy before our eyes, compels us to declare on the side of intemperance and virtue. You will learn that when the mob pulls down the Hyde-park railings next summer.

Enter a YOUNG PERSON.

YOUNG P.–Miss Chatteris, a man called Starkie loves you!

ETHEL.–Never!

YOUNG P. *(wheedlingly).*–Have Starkie!

MRS. MONT.–Better have him, my dear. High spirits may do much to alleviate the agony of a soothed soul; but depend upon it, my dear, Limited Liability is the best mainstay that the mottled soap of affection can afford us, after all.

Enter MR. ROBERT ROMER.

MR. ROBERT R.–I have come for some rent, madam. I am a very poor man, and if you could oblige—

ETHEL.–Never! Audacious!

Enter ABIGAIL, *with some raw hams.*

ABIGAIL.–There's nothing like a raw ham when you are really hungry, and want your dinner in a hurry.

MR. ROBERT R.–I want my rent!

ABIGAIL.–What! Dare to want your rent! Take that!

[*Knocks* MR. ROBERT ROMER *down with a raw ham.*

MRS. MONT.–Ah, my dear, decrepitude is all very well, in theory, but when you are my age you will know that one cannot pay too much attention to the benisons which an ungrateful world hurls at the head of impoverished tutordom! I am seventeen, and I ought to know.

ACT IV.–HILTON'S *Drawing-room in Cromwell-road, S. W.*

Enter HILTON *and* WORDLEY.

WORD.–Now I am a pauper, but you are married to MRS. MONTGOMERY, and this mansion is yours!

HILTON.–True. It never occurred to me before!

Enter MRS. WORDLEY MONTGOMERY.

MRS. WORD.–Oh, the guests have not arrived. I may mention then, that infancy and old age are twin butterflies, whose only care is to increase their store and to accept sharing-engagements wherever the goddess Bradshaw may waft them.

Enter LANGDALE *and* ISABEL.

LANGDALE.–Isabel, we are married!

ISABEL.–Bless your honest, truthful nature--it scorns deception! We are!

Enter GUESTS–*the gentlemen in frock coats, white waistcoats, pumps, and wigs; the ladies in pink silk or black velvet bodies, made high, and trimmed with silver, fancy skirts, and black shoes. They admire the beauty of the rooms, and direct each other's attention to the elegance of the cornices, and especially to a portion of the South Kensington improvements which, in the shape of a deadwall covered with crimson drapery, projects far into the room; also to a wide expanse of champagne country in the distance.*

Enter ETHEL.

ETHEL.–I have come to play the piano at this evening party. What a beautiful room! It is painted, I hear, by my old friend Danson, who "did up" my rooms at Richmond and at Chelsea. They call him the Danson swell, and well they may. This is quite the Danson cheese.

LANGDALE.–Ethel!

ETHEL.–Mr. Langdale. Oh, I am so glad to see you. I want to tell you that as I can't get any one else, except Starkie, I will marry you–so come along!

LANGDALE.–But–it's very awkward–I am married already.

ETHEL.–Oh! *(Hysterically.)* Ha! ha! ha! Only a Life! Only
a Life! *Falls over the grand piano and dies.*
CURTAIN.

The *Illustrated London News* (20 October 1866) was kinder to this
play than Gilbert evidently was, for it praised the ambitious effect
produced by the author, the younger Ben Webster. It did find the
dialogue prolix, however, and some scenes unreasonably prolonged.
The allusion to the Hyde Park riots was added in rehearsal, but
'excited great disapprobation', perhaps because it linked intemperance and virtue. A new Reform Bill was being slowly gestated, and
when a pro-Reform mass meeting was forbidden in Hyde Park, riots
began on 23 July and continued for two days. Rioters broke down the
railings near Marble Arch.

Perhaps it was the assumption that a melodramatic play
portrayed 'real' life which Gilbert decried. He evidently had no objection to what he called a 'fine old crusted absurdity', *Mazeppa*,* when
Adah Isaacs Menken played it yet again in her last London season.
Other reviewers might object, but Gilbert in his review for *Fun* (2
November 1867) found it 'always worth seeing'. Nevertheless, this
did not hinder him from exploiting its impossibilites to the utmost.

MAZEPPA

ACT I. SCENE I.–*Exterior of* OLINSKA'S *Apartments. Night.
Sentry on Battlements.*

Enter MAZEPPA.

MAZEPPA.–Olinska, the dewy night is, &c.–the soft beams
of early zephyrs will soon, &c., and under these circumstances
I call on thee to come forth!

OLINSKA. *(coming from chamber into balcony).*–My
Cassimir!

SENTRY.–Ha, a conversation! It must be the wind. I will
report the phenomenon to my employers.   *[Exit to do so.*

---

*Loosely based on a long poem by Lord Byron, *Mazeppa* frequently strained its audiences'
credulity, especially in the title character's long ride. Originally conceived for a male actor, the role
became a tantalizing female lead, especially when played by Menken, its leading proponent.
Wearing only a flesh-coloured body-stocking and a strategic wisp of costume, she appeared to be
naked as the 'wild' horse bore her about the stage.

OLINSKA.–I am to be married to the Palatine!

MAZEPPA.–Never! *I* will prevent it.   *[Exit to do so.*

Flourish. Enter the CASTELLAN *and Suite.*

CASTELLAN.–My daughter, you are this day to be marryed to the Palatine.

OLINSKA.–This is indeed sudden.

CASTELLAN.–It is. It is now 4 a. m., and I expect him here at 5. At 5:30 a. m. the nuptials will take place.

Enter a MESSENGER.

MESSENGER.–My Lord, heven now a princely cavalcade can be distinguished by the naked hi in the far distance.

[Points off Left.

CASTELLAN.–It *must* be the Palatine. They have walked over from Warsaw before breakfast.

Enter immediately the PALATINE'S *Procession from Right. The Palatine himself in a Tent Bedstead.* MESSENGER *suddenly points off Right. It is observed that the Nobility of Poland wear their frocks fastened behind, and do not wash behind their ears.*

OLINSKA.–Ah me!

THE PALATINE (*suddenly appearing from behind curtains of Tent Bed*). Boh! 'Tis hi!   *[Awkward pause.*

OLINSKA (*aside to Castellan*).–Go on, it's you.

CAST.–Eh? I think not.

Ghostly Whisper.–My Lord, I THANK you for this honour!

CAST.–My Lord, I thank you for this honour.

PALATINE.–The orty Olinska will soon be my-ine!

CAST. (*aside*).–This is going flat. (*Aloud.*)–We'd better get on with the toornymong.

Grand Toornymong. Knights in crumpled armour prod their horses with their swords, and engage. General triumph of everybody in turn, and all at the same time. Everybody crowned–no blanks.

SCENE 2.–*The* PALATINE'S *private apartment.*

PALATINE.–It were a right royal spectacle! But if the orty

Castellan had spent less money on his toornymong, and more on furnishing his guests' chamber, it would have been better.

Enter MAZEPPA, *cloaked and masked.*

MAZEPPA.–I have come to kill thee.

PALATINE.–Does it not occur to you that this is an uncalled-for liberty?

MAZEPPA.–It does. But no matter. There is a sword. Fight.

PALATINE *takes sword, fights, and is killed.*

Enter EVERYBODY.

EVERYBODY.–'Tis Cassimir who killed him.

CAST.–Then tie him to the wild horse of Tartary!

MAZEPPA.–This is too awful. True, the horse is a compatriot, but to be lashed to his back! Ah, 'tis a dreadful doom! *Tableau.*

SCENE 3.–*Eligible Building Plot in Poland.* ATTENDANTS *bringing in the Wild Horse.* MAZEPPA *is tied on to his back, all scream, and the horse trots off. Tableau.*

ACT II. SCENE 1.–*Tartary. Enter* TARTAR SOLDIERS *and* THAMAR.

THAMAR.–The crown will one day be mine. Then I will buy a jacket that is big enough for me.

Enter PEASANTS *screaming.*

PEASANTS.–The wild horse of the Volpas! He is coming!

(The wild horse of the Volpas trots across the stage with MAZEPPA *on his back.)*

SCENE 2.–*Another part of Tartary. Enter* THAMAR.

THAMAR.–The crown *must* some day be mine. Then, ha! ha! a new helmet.

Enter PEASANTS.

PEASANT.–The wild horse of the Volpas!

COMIC PEASANT *(to give a local colouring).*–The wild 'orse of the Wollopers!

111

*Enter the wild horse of the Volpas as before. Shrub falls on
him. Wild horse (a nervous animal) faints.*
Enter the KHAN.

KHAN.–Ha! This is evidently my long-lost son, Mazeppa.
Twenty years ago, when only three weeks old, he ran away to
Poland, and I have never seen him since. Bear him to my
chamber!

THAMAR.–Then the crown will not be mine! But I will be
avenged! The jacket and the helmet shall yet be mine.

KHAN.–Bring out the cheap Mazeppa banner that we've
always kept in readiness for an event of this description!

*The Mazeppa banner ready emblazoned is brought forth with
pomp. Tableau.*

SCENE 3.–*Interior of* KHAN'S *tent.* MAZEPPA *borne in senselss
on litter.*

KHAN.–My long lost son! I will take a nap.
[Goes to sleep on the floor. MAZEPPA *wakes up.*

MAZEPPA.–Ha! Where am I? *(Looks out of tent.)* The name on
the street-corner says Tartary. Have I then ridden from Poland,
right through Russia into Tartary? It must be so! It must have
taken me about eighteen months to accomplish the journey, and
yet, although I have been tied hand and foot to a wild horse for
that considerable time, and have had nothing to eat or drink,
here I am beautifully clean and as fat as ever. A little more, and
it would have been almost miraculous. I will celebrate my deliv-
erance by some appropriate gesticulation.

*Defies the lightning; overhears a conspiracy; ties his sandal;
kills Abel; triumphs over Satan; impeaches Warren
Hastings; salutes Caesar, the emperor; bids farewell to
all his greatness; carries off the Sabine Women; leaps
into the Gulf in the Forum; orders off that bauble; rises
from the sea; murders Rizzio, and exit to see what sort
of night it is.*

Enter THAMAR *and* CONSPIRATORS.

THAMAR.–Now to strike the bul-low that will make me

master of Tartaria and a new suit! Die, thou aged Can!

The KHAN *starts up, defends himself, and is almost overpowered when* MAZEPPA *comes to his rescue. The* KHAN *takes new courage and he and* MAZEPPA *finally triumph over the whole body of conspirators.*

Tableau (MAZEPPA, KHAN). *"The meeting of Wellington and Blucher after Waterloo."*

MAZEPPA.–And now to conquer Poland!

KHAN *(not unnaturally).*–But why Poland?

MAZEPPA.–Because my Olinska, whom I love, is there.

KHAN *(politely).*–Quite so!   *[Exeunt to conquer Poland.*

ACT III.–*Poland. Preparations for marriage of the* PALATINE.

Enter a COMIC AND INDELICATE SERVANT.

COMIC S.–Nearly everything I have to say has a double entendre, and I stagger about the stage as if intoxicated. My performance throughout this part is considered the best imitation of drunkenness ever seen in a British theatre. But where are the wandering Tartar acrobats who are to perform before the mighty Palatine?

Enter the KHAN, MAZEPPA, *and others, disguised.*

MAZEPPA.–We are here! *(Aside.)* To-day she is to be married to the Palatine. We are, as usual, just in time.

Enter OLINSKA, *in high spirits, being about to be married to someone she hates.*

MAZEPPA *(aside).*–Olinska–do not start–'tis I! We walked over from Tartary this morning. We were three hours crossing Russia.

OLINSKA.–My Cassimir!

THE CASTELLAN.–Let the a-sporruts commence.

Enter thousands of sham acrobats, who take Poland by force of arms. Combats of two everywhere. Violent death of all of OLINSKA'S *relations, and ecstasy of* OLINSKA *herself, who, we hope, will enjoy the change from civilized Poland to barbaric Tartary. Fires of all sorts, and triumph of Tartaria. Banners emblematic of the victory (always kept*

ready) produced at the moment of Poland's downfall.
Flourish. Curtain.

OURSELVES.–Fine old crusted absurdity; very well mounted, and always worth seeing. MAZEPPA'S dresses in first and third acts worth (probably) millions; in second act, about fourpence-halfpenny.

Another drama featuring a horse was Edith Sandford's *Firefly*, at the Surrey Theatre beginning 17 May 1869. Although Gilbert's review (*Fun*, 5 June) says nothing about its antecedents, *Firefly* was heavily indebted to Ouida's novel *Under Two Flags*, published with tremendous success in 1867. The hero's noble self-sacrifice to save his brother's reputation, his batman Rake (Rock in the play), his enlisting in the Foreign Legion in Algiers, his childhood friend now a Princess (Duchess in the play), his striking a superior officer, and the devotion of the piquant vivandière Cigarette (Firefly, played by Miss Sandford herself)–all are represented, although the play ends very differently from the novel.

FIREFLY

ACT I.–*Somewhere in Baden Baden. Enter* LEONARD GRANTLEY.

LEONARD.–My brother Harry has forged a bill, and I am suspected of having done it! *(Enter* MORDECAI, *a Hebrew, and* LORD CASTLEFORD.
MORDECAI.–This bill is forged by you!
LEONARD.–It is not!
MORDECAI.–What proofs have you?
LEONARD.–Proofs? What need of proofs when one's conscience is all right?
LORD C.–He speaks truly. I am sure he is innocent.
MORDECAI.–Not so *(To Officers of Justice.)* Arrest him!
(The Officers attempt to arrest him. He knocks them all down, especially MORDECAI, *and springs over a wall and so escapes.)*

ACT II. SCENE 1.–*Algiers. The French Army discovered bivouacking.*

A SOLDIER.–Hurrah for the bold Chassoores!
ALL.–Hurrah!

Enter LEONARD GRANTLEY, *in the uniform of a private Chassoore, together with* ROCK, *lately his servant, but now also a Chassoore.*

ROCK.–My noble master!

LEONARD.–Nay, Rock, we are no longer master and servant, we are equals in rank, and fight side by side.

ROCK.–The Colonel dislikes you.

LEONARD.–He does. I don't know why, for I am the finest soldier in the French army.

ROCK.–May it not be because you *will* wear your whiskers, although, by the rules of the French army, you are bound to shave them?

LEONARD.–It may be that. Very likely it is. At all events, we will hope so. *(To the Army.)* Soldiers of France, we will hope so!

THE ARMY.–We will!

Enter COLONEL *and the* DUCHESS DI RHONA.

COLONEL.–Private Grantley.

LEONARD.–Here!

COLONEL.–Dog!

LEONARD *(aside).*–Ha! But no matter.

COLONEL.–The Duchess would see specimens of your ivory carving.

LEONARD.–Behold them!   [*Shows some specimens.*

DUCHESS.–How much?

LEONARD.–They are yours for a glance of those soft eyes!

DUCHESS *(aside).*–A gentleman, evidently! *(Aloud.)* Nay, I must pay for them.

LEONARD.–I will not take money for them. A glance is all I want.

COLONEL.–Don't trouble yourself, Duchess, *I* will give him the glance!

LEONARD.–Nay, it must come from her Grace.

COLONEL.–Insolent hound!

LEONARD.–Ha! But no matter!

COLONEL.–Away! I will settle with you anon!

DUCHESS *(confidentially to audience)*.–I love that ivory carver! *[Exit, blushing.*

Enter FIREFLY, *a Vivandière, on a pale horse with weak eyes.*

FIREFLY.–I have achieved another victory! The Arabs have fled, and Algiers is ours!

LEONARD *(mildly)*.–*Are* ours. Algiers *are* ours.

FIREFLY.–Always right, my noble boy!

THE ARMY.–Three cheers for Firefly!

ALL.–Hurrah for the bold Chassoores!

SCENE 3.*–COLONEL DURAND'S *Quarters.*

Enter Colonel DURAND *and* CAPTAIN DE VIGNY.

CAPTAIN.–Colonel, the French army has collared a little Arab child. She made a desperate resistance, but the armies of France were too many for her. After a protracted struggle she capitulated.

COLONEL.–May France ever triumph over her haughty foes! They cannot now say that we have not taken a single prisoner. Load the captive with chains and bring her in.

[They bring the captive in, securely guarded.

COLONEL.–Ha! A right truculent countenance! Away with her to the unprotected cottage on the Algerian frontier.

CAPTAIN.–But–excuse me–her Arab father has only to walk over and take her back.

COLONEL.–Silence, dog! *(Enter* LEONARD GRANTLEY.*)* Here, you–I'll send you on a message of certain death. Take a flag of truce and this letter to her Arab father. "If you don't capitulate your daughter shall be smashed."

LEONARD.–I go! *[Goes.*

SCENE 4.–*The Arab Encampment.*
ALDARIM, *Chief of the Khalifas, discovered, surrounded by his tribe.*

ALDARIM.–Changed are the days since Aldarim was the

---

*Gilbert evidently misnumbered scenes; he indicated no scene 2 cockney Jew Mordecai in the first act!

ALL.–They are.

Enter LEONARD *(with Flag of Truce), and also* FIREFLY, *on the Horse of the Crimson Eyelids.*

LEONARD.–I bear a message from the Franks.

ALDARIM.–They are dogs!

LEONARD.–Most of them. Listen. "If you don't capitulate your daughter shall be smashed."

ALDARIM.–Ha! Bear him to his death!

FIREFLY.–Not so.

ALDARIM.–Why not?

FIREFLY.–Because I, the Vivandière of the Franks, decline to sanction such a proceeding.

ALDARIM.–Oh. That alters the case, of course. *(To* LEONARD.*)* If Firefly remains with us as a hostage you can return to your Army. Otherwise, you die. Which will you do?

LEONARD.–I will return and leave her here. It is better that she should die than I, for I am the finest soldier in the French army. Farewell, Firefly!

FIREFLY.–But–I say–

LEONARD.–No, thanks–I am only too happy to give you another opportunity of showing these Arab dogs how well a Frenchwoman can behave under circumstances of immediate danger.   *[Exit very quickly.*

ACT III.–*The* DUCHESS DE RHONA's *Apartments.*

Enter LEONARD, *meeting the* DUCHESS.

DUCHESS.–I want to pay you for those ivory carvings.

LEONARD.–Nay. All I require is a glance of those soft eyes.

DUCHESS *(aside).*–He *is* a gentleman! Are you not Leonard Grantley?

LEONARD.–I am.

DUCHESS.–Then I am your early playmate.

LEONARD.–Ha! My own Di Rhona.   *[They embrace.*

Enter COLONEL DURAND.

COLONEL.–What do I see? Private Grantley embracing my Duchess!   *[Exit* DUCHESS, *very red.*

LEONARD.–She is my early playmate, Colonel.

COLONEL.–Oh, yes, I dare say. She is engaged to me, and you must permit me to object to your fondling her at your pleasure.

LEONARD.–There are some insults that even a soldier of France can't stand, and this is one of them. Have at thee, monster! *[Gives him one for himself.*

COLONEL.–Ha! A blow! Seize him! *[Soldiers seize him.*

LEONARD.–Why, what have I done?

COLONEL.–Away with him, and shoot him!

LEONARD.–Oh, Duchess di Rhona! My early, early playmate!
[They hurry him off.

ACT IV.–*The Desert. Enter* ARABS *and* FIREFLY.

ALDARIM.–The Frankish dog has not returned with my child, so the woman he bravely left as hostage shall die.

ALL.–It is just! *[They are about to stab her.*

ALDARIM.–Stay! A death by stabbing were far too easy and merciful. Tie her to yon tree with a handkerchief, while we retire and ponder on our vengeance.

[They tie her to a tree with a cotton handkerchief, and exeunt.

FIREFLY.–How to break the irresistible bond that holds me prisoner. Ha! My trained Etna, with his wonderful Horse Effects!

Enter ETNA, *the pink-eyed horse. He unties the slip-knot and* FIREFLY *is free.*

FIREFLY.–Free! Free! Away to other climes! But first, my Etna, ring the belfry bell, that the Arabs may know that I am going. *[Etna rings bell.*

Enter ARABS, FIREFLY *mounts Etna, shoots all the Arabs and escapes.*

LAST SCENE.–*The Falls of Arena.* (JOHNSON.)

PEOPLE BEHIND.–Hold him back. Don't let him rush on!

Enter SOLDIERS *and* LEONARD, *a prisoner.*

LEONARD.–And I am to be shot for thrashing my commanding officer. I have said a good deal of clap-trap in the course of the piece about the admirable treatment French soldiers recieve at the hands of their superiors, and I have often compared their happy condition to the miserable existance passed by our British troops, but I begin to think I was mistaken.

COLONEL.–Shoot him!

ALL.–We will!

COLONEL.–At a yard and a half. Ready! Present–

Enter FIREFLY, *just in time.*

FIREFLY.–Hold!

COLONEl.–Why?

FIREFLY.–I don't know!

COLONEL.–Ha! The forest is on fire!   *[So it is.*

FIREFLY.–Indeed! Ha! the child in the hut!

Rides up rake to hut at back of stage. A child is obligingly handed out to her at the end of a pole by some devoted creature within. FIREFLY *returns, and presents the child to the Soldiers of France.*

ALL.–Hurrah!

The Curtain falls, and LEONARD GRANTLEY *(we hope) is shot forthwith.*

OURSELVES.–The piece is terrible trash; but it is expensively mounted, and is illustrated by some excellent scenery. The last scene (by MR. JOHNSON) is especially good. MISS SANDFORD is an accomplished equestrian, and her horse is remarkably well trained. A word of praise for MR. EDGAR, who played Colonel Durand very effectively. He seems to know how a uniform should be worn.

Earlier that year Johnson had been presented as a fictional character in Watts Phillips's drama *Not Guilty* at the Queen's Theatre, 13 February 1869. The stage directions for 'CURTAIN' in Gilbert's *Fun* review (6 March) are enhanced by his *Illustrated Times* review of the same play (20 February 1869). He found it 'impossible to give a clear outline of the plot', but acknowledged the elaborate sets. 'Mr Johnson, the scenic artist,' he wrote, 'took the liberty of rushing on the stage four or five times' during the performance whenever his sets were applauded. Gilbert suggested he should wait to take his bow with the actors at the end of the piece. In another *Illustrated Times* review (of Halliday's *Little Em'ly*, 16 October), Gilbert described the sets as 'cleverly contrived', but disapproved of Johnson's coming on stage in answer to moderate applause. The better class of scenic artists had lately abandoned this impertinence, 'But Mr. Johnson has shown himself to be simply irrepressible in this particular.'

The *Athenaeum* considered the view of the ship in *Not Guilty* 'a new and remarkable effect' (20 February), but dismissed the piece as merely 'a fairly interesting play of a bad class'.

NOT GUILTY;
OR, "A PARTY BY THE NAME OF JOHNSON"

ACT I. SCENE 1.—*The Bar-Gate, Southampton (1847).* SERGEANT *discovered with Recruits, and* ROBERT ARNOLD, *a locksmith, and* TRIGGS, *a lawyer's clerk. Enter* JOHNSON, *a scene-painter.*

ROBERT.—That mysterious man again. Why does he dog my path?

JOHNSON *(to himself).*—On second thoughts, no!

[Exit JOHNSON, *bowing apologetically.*

SERGEANT.—Come Robert, I have enlisted everybody in Southampton except you.

ROBERT.—I will. *[Enlists.*

Enter POLLY, *a barmaid.*

POLLY.—As to-morrow is Good Friday, and I shan't be wanted till Easter Tuesday, I'll just pop on a bonnet and shawl and run over to India. *[Exit.*

Enter SILAS JARRETT, *a beggar.*

SILAS.—A nice line of life this for a man who has played at Homburg.

Enter MRS. ARMITAGE, *in great woe.*

MRS. A. *(to* SILAS, *as an eligible person to confide in).*–My child is dying for want of necessaries. Give me some money.

SILAS.–No. Get out. *[Exit.*

Enter ROBERT.

ROBERT.–Mrs. Armitage? In tears? Take this fiver!
[Gives note.

MRS. A.–Bless you! Bless you! *[Faints.*

ROBERT.–She has fainted!
[Carries her off, leaving basket of tools behind him.

Enter SILAS.

SILAS.–A basket of tools *(Examines them.)* A bunch of skeleton keys? I will commit a burglary, then away to India.
[Commits a burglary (only it isn't a burglary, for it's daylight) on MR. TRUMBLE'S *house, and exit with many thousand pounds.*

Enter MR. TRUMBLE.

MR. T.–Hurrah! I have been appointed trustee for all the inhabitants of Southampton during their temporary absence in India! *(Sees indications of burglary.)* Robbed! Ha! ha! ha! ha!
[Exit senseless. Tableau.

SCENE 2.–MRS.ARMITAGE'S *garret.* MRS. ARMITAGE *discovered tending sick child. Enter* JOHNSON.

MRS. A.–That inscrutable creature again! What–what can he want with me? Avaunt!

JOHNSON *(to himself).*–Ah, another time!
[Exit, bowing apologies.

MRS. A.–The child is dying of fever, so I will take it out for a walk. *[Does so.*

Enter SILAS JARRETT.

SILAS *(pursued).*–If I can only continue to escape over the tiles all may yet be well.
[Leaves basket of tools on table, and escapes over tiles.

Enter Soldiers and Police, meeting ROBERT ARNOLD.

SOLDIERS.–Where is the burglar? Ha!   *[They seize him.*
ROBERT.–What would you?
SOLDIERS.–You are our prisoner. For burglary.
ROBERT.–I am Not Guilty!   *[Tableau.*

SCENE 3.–*The Madras ship off the Cape on her way to India
in a dusty sea. The stern of the vessel is towards the audience. The ship behaves well. Eventually the stern of the
vessel disappears, and discovers the saloon, with* SILAS
JARRETT *counting his ill-gotten gains, and a* MR. ST.
CLAIR *asleep on settee.*

JOHNSON *appears furtively on deck.*

STEERSMAN *(a well-spoken man was he).*–That dreadful
man again! What have I done that this spectral shape should
ever haunt my path?
JOHNSON *(to himself).*–No–later!
                    [Bows apologetically to Steersman, and exit.
SILAS *(in cabin).*–It is convenient to be able to remove the
stern of the vessel when the cabin becomes stuffy. It looks
more dangerous than it is, for there is still a gauze curtain
between the cabin and the raging dust without.
MR. ST. C.–Ha! Counting money? I'll help you! *(Picks up a
note from the floor.)* Hullo, this note is mine!–I handed it over
to Mr. Trumble before I left. Villain!   *[Collars him.*

Enter all the Crew, who have been listening at the keyhole.
SILAS *breaks from them.*

SILAS.–You think you are sure of me, but you do not know
the resources of a really ingenious man. I will fling myself into
the gale and swim to Plymouth!
                    *[Does so as an agreeable alternative to a possible
                    conviction for breaking into a dwelling house.*

ACT III.–*The Quarries at Dartmoor.* CONVICTS *discovered at
work.*

Enter JOHNSON.
CONVICTS *(gloomily).*–Our punishment is severe enough
without *his* constant presence.

122

JOHNSON *(to himself)*.–My scheme works bravely–but no matter! Anon! anon! *[Exit, bowing apologetically to Convicts.*

JACK SNIPE *(a comic Convict)*.–Gather round me and I will sing you a comic song.

[Convicts do so while he sings a rollicking song.

[NOTE.–The tendency of this scene is to show what a particularly jolly, happy-go-lucky time of it Convicts have, and that penal servitude in its severest form is little more than a healthy and agreeable exercise. But as there is no ballet in this scene, there is nothing in it to arrest the attention of the Lord Chamberlain.]

Enter SILAS JARRETT *(now a Warder).*

SILAS.–No matter how I became a Warder. Perhaps I have a face which is its own recommendation; perhaps I got the place through the interest of Johnson. Anyhow, here I am.

JACK SNIPE *(to* ROBERT ARNOLD, *who is working out a sentence of penal servitude for the robbery in the first act)*.–This fearful man is even more terrible than Johnson. He actually seeks to stop my comic songs.

SILAS *(mildly)*.–I do. It is against regulations.

(The Convicts chaff their warders for a quarter of an hour. The Warders bear it as gentlemen of easy manners should.)

SILAS *(to* SECOND WARDER)*.–I rather think the convicts wish to plan their escape. It would perhaps be ungentlemanly to listen.

SECOND W.–Quite out of the question. Let us retire. Poor fellows! *[Exeunt Warders, weeping.*

CONVICTS.–Let us rise and murder every one! There are sixteen of us against five warders. Come!

(They rise, and try to kill their Warders. The Warders with a fine faith in the virtue of an emblem, show them their staves. The Convicts do not quail. The most diabolically disposed of the Warders feels that a time for decisive action has arrived, and fires his rifle in the air. The Convicts are convinced of their error and apologise. The Warders beg they won't mention it. Tableau of reconciliation. But JACK SNIPE, *the Comic Convict, and* ROBERT ARNOLD, *the Serious Convict, have escaped.*

ACT III. SCENE 1. *Bhurtpoor. (Ten years have elapsed.) Ladies and Gentlemen discovered. Enter* JOHNSON.

LADIES AND GENTLEMEN.–Wherever we go this mystic one follows us! What *can* he want?

JOHNSON *(to himself).*–All well, so far–but I am premature!
            [Exit, bowing apologetically to Ladies and Gents.

Enter MISS ALICE ARMITAGE (*the child who was dying of fever in the first act.*)

MISS. A. *(in high animal spirits).*–I hear there is going to be a mutiny. Oh, I *should* so like to see it!

SCENE 2.–*Interior of somebody's Bungalow.*

Enter JACK SNIPE *and* TRIGGS, *a Comic Person.*
(Great comic scene between JACK SNIPE *and* TRIGGS, *apropos of that lark, the Indian Mutiny, which is going on outside. But there is no ballet, my lord.)*

SCENE 3.–*A deserted Battle Field.*

Enter a CAPTAIN WILLOUGHBY, *meeting* JOHNSON.

CAPT. W.–This man again! It is too much.   *[Commits suicide.*

JOHNSON *(to himself).*–Poor fellow. But it was necessary to my scheme. Still I am sorry for him.
            [Bows apologetically to corpse and exit.

Enter SILAS.

SILAS.–Ha, a corpse! Strange, he is wonderfully like me! I will assume his clothes, and pass myself off as somebody else.
            [Does so, modestly, behind a plantain leaf.

Enter the BRITISH ARMY.

THE B. A. *(to* SILAS*).*–Hail, Captain Willoughby!
            [They salute him.

ACT IV.–*Oakfield Grange, near Southampton.*

SILAS JARRETT *discovered. Enter* JOHNSON.
SOME OF THE AUDIENCE.–Hiss!
SILAS.–Take him away, and chain him at the wing.

[They seize him.

JOHNSON *(to himself).*–Ha! Baulked! Then my scheme must
needs ripen without me! *[Exit, in custody.*

Enter MISS ALICE ARMITAGE.

MISS A.–I can never love you–for your eyes have changed
colour. They were blue, now they are mauve.

SILAS *(aside).*–Ha! Discovered!

MISS A.–Besides, I prefer Mr. Arnold. *[Enter* MR. ARNOLD.

Enter several escaped Convicts, headed by JACK SNIPE *and
Policemen.*

SNIPE. This is Silas Jarrett, the escaped burglar.

[They seize him.

SILAS *(aside).*–Thunder and lightning! *(Aloud)* This is
Snipe, an escaped convict. Seize *him*! *[They seize* SNIPE.

MR. ST. C.–Not so. Here is a free pardon for him for his
amusing behaviour in the verandah during the Indian Mutiny!

[General joy.

CURTAIN.–*Loud call for everybody. Everybody appears
except* JOHNSON. *Rattling of chains heard behind, as if a
manacled one were endeavouring to burst his bonds.*

OURSELVES.–An unsatisfactory, "sprawling" piece, without
beginning, middle, or end. Dialogue very poor. Most of the
characters have little to do with the story, and the part of
Johnson is impertinent to the piece, in every sense of the word.
That the piece is poorly played is not so much the fault of the
actors as of the author, who has given them very little chance
of distinguishing themselves. The scenery, however, is cleverly
constructed throughout, and in parts cleverly painted. This
"New piece, by MR. WATTS PHILLIPS", is a clumsy adaptation of
Le Comte de St. Helene.

Gilbert used *Not Guilty,* not only to satirise Phillips and Johnson,
but to tease the Lord Chamberlain, who had very recently banned
short ballet skirts. Comic periodicals were making a point of refer-
ring to this fiat, and Gilbert at this stage in his career was decidedly irreverent toward the censorship, anticipating his burlesque

The Happy Land (1873), in which Gladstone and two of his ministers are parodied. This incurred the wrath of the Lord Chamberlain (whom Gilbert later satirized as 'The Lord High Disinfectant') and of his reader of plays.

8 Improbabilities and a Touch of Prussic Acid

At times Gilbert represented characters behaving in a way diametrically opposed to their presumed purpose or interests, especially if they are officers of the law. For instance, Javert, after four acts and ten years of pursuing Jean Valjean in Henry Neville's adaptation, *The Yellow Passport* (*Fun*, 21 November 1868), discovers he has absent-mindedly been carrying Valjean's pardon in his pocket for all these years. In Boucicault's *The Long Strike* (*Fun*, 29 September 1866) a policeman addresses Noah Learoyd:

> Noah, you are going to burn down Manchester, but you mustn't. Mr. Radley has laid information, and I have come to tell you that you may escape. It's wrong of me; but I generally go wrong. I attribute it partly to my being the only policeman in Manchester who is allowed to speak a line, and partly to the confusing effect of having XLI on one collar and LIX on the other. *Am* I forty-one or fifty-nine?
>
> NOAH.–You look fifty-nine.
>
> . . . . .
>
> POLICEMAN.–The best way to detect a murderer is to let every one go whom you suspect.
> *[Lets every one go whom he suspects. Tableau.*

An 'idiot detective' in Charles Reade's and Dion Boucicault's *Foul Play* tells Arthur Wardlaw to escape (*Fun*, 20 June 1868):

> I always like everything smooth and regular, so escape while there is yet time. *(Aside.)* Not a common Scotland-yard detective. *He* would apply for a warrant for Arthur's apprehension. *I* like everything smooth and regular, so I connive at his escape.
>
> . . . . .
>
> Escaped? Ha! ha! A good joke! I like things smooth and regular. How they will enjoy this in Scotland Yard.
>
> . . . . .
>
> . . . I waited until the principal villain had escaped before I revealed myself. It is my customary plan. They call me the "Felon's Friend", in Scotland-yard. And well they may!

But what does it matter? After all, their law is only what Gilbert called 'stage law' and is not limited to idiot detectives. In one of his last parodies, for example, H. J. Byron's *Wait and Hope* (Gaiety, 1 March 1871), Lockwood announces (*Fun*, 18 March 1871):

> I have come to foreclose. The process is simple. If a mortgage debt is not paid the day it becomes due, the mortgagee has only to walk into the mortgaged premises, without any warning, and turn out the debtor by the moral influence of his presence.

Fortunately for the debtor in this case, Lockwood is accosted by a rude child: 'How sweetly she prattles,' he exclaims. 'This innocent child reminds me that I once heard a clock strike ten in my infancy. *I* was innocent then! By Heaven I'll be innocent now! (*Reforms*.)' And tears up the mortgage.

In other plays, probability was equally or further 'set at defiance' as Gilbert wrote of *Wait and Hope*. Victor, in *A Hero of Romance*, played by E. A. Sothern at the Haymarket Theatre, is accidentally locked in the ruined tower of Elfen with Blanche. Lest he compromise her he gallantly leaps into 'a sheer fall of at least twelve thousand feet' (*Fun*, 4 April 1868), appearing in the next act to tell the audience aside, 'Saved by a miracle! Not so much as a scratch!' On stage his fall was broken by projecting ivy. The *Tomahawk*'s review (28 March 1868) also in the form of a playlet, contented itself with alternating scenes burlesquing the adaptor, Westland Marston (working from *Ivy Hall*, an 1859 version by Oxenford), and scenes invented by the reviewer. In the *Tomahawk*, Victor jumps merely a couple of hundred feet after telling Blanche, 'Nay, start not; among my many accomplishments I number athletics!'

When a beggar woman faints in Lord Newry's drama, *Ecarté* (which appeared at the Globe Theatre for only one night, 3 December 1870), a Naval Lieutenant sings to her to revive her. Gilbert inserts an assurance: '(*And positively and actually he does sing to her, and positively and actually it does revive her . . .)*'. Robert Reece in 'Unrehearsed Effects' corroborated Gilbert and reported an exchange between the leading lady and the unruly audience, which Gilbert had bracketed in his parody and written down as 'Fact!!!':

Enter Frolicsome Young Lady
FROLICSOME YOUNG LADY.–I'm the jolliest girl that's out!
AUDIENCE.–Hiss-s-s-s!

FROLICSOME YOUNG LADY *(to audience).*–When you've quite done I'll go on.

AUDIENCE.–Shame! shame! Off! off! off!

FROLICSOME YOUNG LADY *(to audience).*–I can wait! (Does so.)

AUDIENCE.–Go home! Hiss! hiss!! hiss!!!

FROLICSOME YOUNG LADY *(curtseying rather too deeply).*–Thank you very much!

Clement Scott described her as drunk on the champagne quaffed in a picnic during the preceding act. This lady, according to Reece, wore a white satin slipper on one foot and a green satin boot on the other;[33] Gilbert summed up *Ecarté* (*Fun*, 17 December 1870) as

> probably the very worst piece in the world. It has no story, no development of character, no incident. Its dialogue is utterly contemptible, and its situations ridiculous in the extreme. Miss ALLEYNE's performance of the heroine was a piece of outrageous assurance, and her demeanour in the third act was loudly hissed by a most indulgent audience . . . .

The *Athenaeum* (10 December 1870) agreed: '*Ecarté* is commonplace in dialogue, old in story, clumsy in construction, and void of any form of dramatic merit.' Any chance it had was ruined by the acting since Miss Alleyne and others ranted lamentably and over-acted. The *Graphic* (10 December 1870) called it 'a dramatic failure more disastrous' than any for some time, ending with 'a burst of disapprobation from all parts of the house . . .'.

Very likely the greatest improbability, however, was that which provided the sensation of Tom Taylor and Augustus Dubourg's failure, *A Sister's Penance* at the Adelphi, opening 26 November 1866. There, Ammedoolah, originally an educated Hindu whom Gilbert turned into a minstrel show Bones, secretly poisons Markham's tonic in order to dispose of a rival for the love of Alice. She faints and is given the lethal glass to revive her. Fortunately her faithful maid has thrown out the tonic and replaced it with water. This in itself sounds as if it were a parody, but Gilbert took it further in his *Fun* review (15 December):

> ALICE.–How excessively strong it tastes of prussic acid.
>
> . . . . .
>
> ALICE.–Poisoned? Oh agony!   *[Writhes in great agony.*

Enter DR. HANDYSIDE.

DR. HANDYSIDE.–Alice poisoned–let me taste the medicine! *(Tastes it:–a fact!)* So it is. It is poisoned with prussic acid!

Enter PAMELA.

PAMELA.–Not so; I diluted the poison, and it is half water.

. . . . .

DR. HANDYSIDE.–Then you have only swallowed a quarter instead of half a tumbler of prussic acid, and all will yet be well.

Not even Kate Terry's performance could save Alice although Gilbert praised her, and the *Daily Telegraph* enthusiastically acclaimed her true pathos (27 November 1866). Gilbert re-used non-fatal prussic acid in *Philomel* (*Fun*, 26 February 1870) by Henry Thornton Craven, which had opened at the Globe on 10 February.

PHILOMEL

ACT I.–SCENE 1. *Old* ADDERLEY'S *Surgery at St. Heliers. Old* ADDERLEY *discovered making up prescriptions.*

ADDERLEY.–Another pint of prussic acid, and a tablespoon of strychnine ought to do the job, I think! Poor girl–poor girl!
                    [*Exit with soothing draught.*

Enter DR. ERNEST, *his son, and* DOROTHEE, *a housekeeper.*

DOROTHEE.–Well, Master Ernest, your pa will be surprised at your unexpected return from England. Whatever made you come?

DR. ERNEST.–I was warned in a dream that I had better return, so I came. I am always guided by my dreams. But my patients must not know this, or they might lose confidence in my prescriptions.

DOROTHEE.–They might. Your father has gone to prescribe for your old flame Philomel, whose marriage with St. Aubin embittered the remainder of your existence.

ERNEST.–So it did. I remember now you mention it. Is she ill?

DOROTHEE.–She is dying!

ERNEST.–Horror!

Enter Old ADDERLEY, JUDAH LAZARUS, *and* DU BOULAY, *in fancy dress.*

ADDERLEY.–My son? This is awkward!

ERNEST.–It was in consequence of a dream–

ADDERLEY.–Bosh. Leave me.

ERNEST.–But, sir–

DU BOULAY.–Get out. *(Ernest is kicked out.)*

ADDERLEY.–Now, what do you want with me?

DU BOULAY.–When Philomel dies, I inherit twenty thousand pounds.

JUDAH.–Oh! Moses!

ADDERLEY.–I know.

DU BOULAY.–When do you think she will die *(hoarsely)*?

ADDERLEY *(hoarsely)*.–I think it is very likely she will die to-night!

SCENE 2. *Boudoir in* MADAME DE ST. AUBIN'S *house. Old* ADDERLEY *discovered attending* PHILOMEL, *who is poorly.*

ADDERLEY.–A pint and a half to be taken three times a day as usual.   *[Exit.*

PHILOMEL.–Oh, it gives me such pains.

Enter ERNEST.

ERNEST.–Philomel!

PHILOMEL.–Ernest! I have been so ill!

ERNEST.–What has my father prescribed for you? *(Opens medicine bottle, and tastes.)* Prussic acid and strychnine! *(Aside.)* What could he have been about? If she drinks much of this it may injure her. They may well call him an irregular practitioner in the bill. I will drop it and break the bottle by accident. *(Does so.)* Oh, I have broken it.

PHILOMEL.–No matter. I will take a pint of champagne instead. Indeed, I prefer it.

(Grand charivari of three or four Comic Servants at intervals through this act.)

ACT II.–ADDERLEY'S *Parlour. Enter Old* ADDERLEY *and* DU

BOULAY.

DU BOULAY.–Is the girl dead yet?

ADDERLEY.–No doubt–I gave her a settler last night.

DU BOULAY.–Good. Then I will go and take possession.

[Exit.

SCENE 2. *The Boudoir. Enter* ERNEST, *meeting* PHILOMEL *looking a hundred per cent. better.*

ERNEST.–I am so glad you are well again! For I love you, sweet one!

PHILOMEL.–Bless you! *[Exeunt kissing.*

Enter Old ADDERLEY.

ADDERLEY.–Eh! What? Philomel not dead yet? The girl has the constitution of an audience! Ha! Here is some curious old sherry with a head. An ounce of arsenic in a wineglassful of this, and– *(Pours out glass of curious sherry, and puts an ounce of arsenic in it.)*

Enter ERNEST.

ERNEST.–Ha, papa, what are you doing with that wine?

ADDERLEY.–I–a–nothing.

ERNEST.–I will taste it. *(Is about to do so.)*

ADDERLEY.–Hi! stop. It's poisoned!

ERNEST.–Eh!

ADDERLEY.–That is–there is so much arsenic about just now– in the green paper hangings, you know– *(Aside.)* Oh, lor!

ERNEST.–Villain!

ADDERLEY *(proudly).*–Sir?

ERNEST.–Avaunt, or I denounce you!

ADDERLEY.–Do you insist on my avaunting?

ERNEST.–I do.

ADDERLEY.–Despair! *[Exit.*

Grand charivari of four or five Comic Servants at intervals through this act.

ACT III.–*Garden and terrace of the Chateau.*
Enter DU BOULAY.

DU BOULAY.–Two months are supposed to have elapsed, and yet Philomel is not dead. Ha! some one comes! *(Conceals himself.)*

Enter LUCILLE, *a young woman, and* ERNEST.

LUCILLE.–Yes; indeed you are not his son–you are the son of my father and mother. In other words, you are my–ha! ha!–brother!

ERNEST.–My sister!

LUCILLE.–Come with me to Noirmont Point at dead of night, and there you shall have the proof of this!

Enter PHILOMEL.

PHILOMEL.–Ernest going with a young woman to Noirmont Point at dead of night! I will follow them!

Du BOULAY *(coming forward)*.–Philomel going to follow Ernest and a young woman to Noirmont Point at dead of night! I will follow them! *[Exit.*

ADDERLEY *(entering)*.–Du Boulay going to follow Philomel who is going to follow Ernest and a young woman to Noirmont Point at the dead of night! I will follow them!

JUDAH *(entering)*.–Old Adderley going to follow Du Boulay, who is going to follow Philomel, who is going to follow Ernest and a young woman to Noirmont Point at dead of night! I will follow them, s'help me!

ALL THE COMIC SERVANTS *(entering)*.–Judah (s'help him) going to follow Old Adderley, who is going to follow Du Boulay, who is going to follow Philomel, who is going to follow Ernest and a young woman to Noirmont Point at dead of night! We will follow them! *[Exeunt.*

SCENE 2. *Near the Bay. Enter* ERNEST, *the Young Woman, followed by* PHILOMEL, *followed by* DU BOULAY, *followed by Old* ADDERLEY, *followed by* JUDAH *(s'help him), followed by all the Comic Servants, on their way to Noirmont Point at dead of night.*

SCENE 3.–*Noirmont Point, a precipice overlooking the sea.*

Enter DU BOULAY.

133

DU BOULAY.–There is Ernest with the young woman! One shot and– *(Draws pistol.)*

Enter PHILOMEL.

PHILOMEL.–Hold, monster! *(Stops him.)*

DU BOULAY.–Ha! Foiled! *(Aside.)* Philomel, marry me!

PHILOMEL.–Scarcely.

DU BOULAY.–Then die! *(Is about to throw her over the precipice when–*

Enter DR. ADDERLEY.

ADDERLEY.–Hold! *(They struggle.)*

Enter JUDAH.

JUDAH.–S'help me! *(All three struggle. Eventually* DU BOULAY *and* ADDERLEY *fall over Cliff; as they fall they catch at* JUDAH'S *coat-tails which are torn off,* JUDAH *holding on to a tree.)*

JUDAH.–S'help me, they're gone! *(Looks over Cliff.)* Here's a lark, they are smashed into little bits! *(Great and comic joy of* JUDAH *at awful death of two human beings.)*

Enter EVERYBODY.

PHILOMEL.–Are they dead?

ALL.–As mutton!

PHILOMEL.–Joy! But the young woman?

ERNEST.–Is–my sister!

PHILOMEL.–Then you are, indeed, my own. *(They embrace.)* *Grand charivari of six or seven Comic Servants over mutilated remains of* ADDERLEY *and* DU BOULAY.

CURTAIN.

OURSELVES.–A most unpleasant piece–well written in parts, but abominably constructed. The first two acts possess considerable literary merit–the last act is contemptible and disgraceful. MR. CRAVEN should bear in mind that the sudden death of two scoundrels is no lark. Even MR. CALCRAFT will bear us out in this opinion. It is excellently acted by MISS FOOTE, MR. NEVILLE, and MR. CLARKE. MR. PARSELLE plays a repulsive part very artistically. MISS AMY FAWSITT plays a broken English part very prettily indeed. Scenery fair. MR. GORDON deserves our thanks for having resisted a loud call.*

Obviously what Gilbert wanted above all was clarity, found infrequently in the plays he reviewed. As he said, writing of F. C. Burnand's *The Turn of the Tide* in the *Illustrated Times* (5 June 1869), 'English dramatists seem quite to ignore the golden rule of dramatic construction:–"Tell what you have to tell as briefly and as concisely as you can consistently with the proper development of your characters."' And later, in *Cassell's Saturday Journal*, he added, 'Everything that is said or done on the stage should have immediate effect, not require long reflection to be understood, otherwise many in the audience would be perplexed and wrapped in study instead of enjoying themselves. . . . To perplex an auditor is more than enough to irritate him.'

For example, 'The plot of this piece is not quite clear,' Gilbert wrote in *Fun*, burlesquing Sefton Parry's *The Odds* (15 October 1870). His dialogue and parenthetical remarks searched out the easily findable obscurities. For instance, when Tom Shuttle is not sure whether he or Withers has forged a bill to someone, Withers tells him, 'My dear Tom if you are going to distress yourself about everything that is not quite clear, you have an anxious evening before you.' From then on, 'not quite clear' becomes a litany:

> But how that is to avert a charge of forgery is not quite clear
> . . . . Why this is so, is not quite clear . . . . there is one obscure
> point which I should like cleared up . . . . It is not quite clear . . . .
> *Why this happens is not quite clear . . . . A great deal takes place*
> *in this scene, but how it affects the action of the piece is not*
> *quite clear . . . . The bearing of this scene upon the piece is not*
> *quite clear . . . . how this is ascertained is not quite clear . . . . For*
> *an ambiguous reason he suppresses a telegram directed by*
> *some one–whose identity is not quite clear . . . . what kind of an*
> *avowal is not quite clear . . . . why it is called* the *landing (for*
> *there are many landings in this bitter world) is not quite clear*
> . . . . *But why not, is not quite clear* . . . .

Moreover, two officers wearing cavalry uniforms try to decide if they are cavalry or infantry since they wear no spurs and several of their troupe cannot ride.

---

*Gordon was William Gordon, the scenic artist. Gilbert had, as we know, been conducting a campaign against designers who rushed on stage to acknowledge any applause for the set. Calcraft was the public executioner.

It is no wonder, then, that the *Graphic* (8 October 1870) found *The Odds* 'a weak, jerky, unlife-like drama of the bad old school...filled with a set of characters in whom it is impossible to feel any interest'. Reviewers, including Gilbert, commented on Parry's indebtedness to Boucicault's *Flying Scud* for a sensation steeple chase, the confusion of which Gilbert described:

> *(A crowd of utterly impossible people with that curious look of being dressed in dead men's clothes that usually characterizes a stage crowd. A bell rings. Some jerky wooden horses appear in the far distance, they cross from L to R, trotting over a wide river and clearing fields at a bound. They then cross from R to L, leaping high into the air when on flat ground, and trotting smoothly over the river as before. One conscientious horse leaps the river, and then, feeling that he has done wrong, goes back and trots over it. Eventually the horses amble on and take a terrific obstacle, eighteen inches high. It is announced that Jack-in-the-Box has won–but how this is ascertained is not quite clear.)*

Even more confused was *The Fast Family* by the younger Benjamin Webster, which opened at the Adelphi on 5 May 1866 and which Gilbert reviewed on 26 May for *Fun*. Here the parodistic characters possessed a dual identity *qua* actor and *qua* role, a device Gilbert would experiment with in *Our Island Home* at the Gallery of Illustration in 1870. Of course, other Victorian playwrights such as J. R. Planché and G. H. Lewes had put actors (like Buckstone) into fictitious plots, but Gilbert not only kept the players' names, but invented new personalities for them, often conflicting with or diverging from their real ones. He was also apt in these burlesque reviews generally to drop in an actor's or actress's name, with a remark that might suddenly end the suspension of disbelief, if it existed. This produced a jarringly comic effect, manipulating the tension and its breaking to emphasise the artificial, which, in its interplay with supposed 'true' reality, struck his own particular note. In the foregoing examples of burlesque plays reproduced here, this has been done frequently, but in *The Fast Family* it is done constantly; a single act will suffice to show the actors' disparity.

THE FAST FAMILY

ACT I.–*Interior of* MISS SIMMS'S *House.* MISS SIMMS *discovered buying lace of a very haberdashing young man.*

MISS SIMMS.–How much?

HABERD. Y. M.–Millions of francs per inch.

MISS SIMMS.–Then I will have it all. Have you anything else that is expensive? If so, I will buy it.

Enter MISS GODSALL *and* MISS SEAMAN *in ballet dresses.*

MISS GODSALL.–Miss Simms, what relation am I to you?

MISS SIMMS.–I don't know: they only give the Christian names in the bill.

MISS SEAMAN.–Oh, somebody pray tell us whose relations we all are.

Enter MR. EBURNE.

MISS GODSALL.–Oh, Mr. Eburne, are you my brother? If not, *what* are you?

MR. EBURNE.–Well, I don't think I am your brother; because I have to run away with you in the third act.

MISS SEAMAN.–Then perhaps you are *my* brother?

MR. EBURNE.–Well, but ain't you Miss Godsall's sister?

MISS SEAMAN.–Goodness only knows! But here comes Mr. Bedford, with a peculiar wig; perhaps he can enlighten us.

Enter MR. BEDFORD, *with a peculiar wig, and* MR. TOOLE.

MISS GODSALL.–Oh, Mr. Bedford, *who* are we? Are you my father?

MR. BEDFORD.–No, dear boy, dear boy*–I mean dear girl–not yet, but I shall be soon, for my son Toole is going to marry you, dear girl. Where is Ben Hoyton?

Enter PHILLIPS.

PHILLIPS.–Ah, Toole! Want my daughter, eh?

TOOLE.–Well, how much with her, if I take the whole of her?

PHILLIPS.–Millions of francs. I forgot how many.

TOOLE.–Let's see *(calculates).* Twice one's two–twice two's

---

*'Dear boy' and 'I believe you, my boy' were Paul Bedford's famous catch-phrases.

four, twice three's six–twice four's eight–twice five's ten–twice six is twelve, twice seven's fourteen.

OURSELVES.–Oh, hang it. I knew that years ago.

[Exit for some beer.
An interval of twenty minutes. Re-enter OURSELVES.

TOOLE.–Twice seven thousand and two's fourteen thousand, and four–twice seven thousand and four's fourteen thousand and eight,–twice seven thousand and eight's fourteen thousand and sixteen. Ha, very good;–then I'll have her.

Enter MRS. MELLON.

MRS. MELLON.–How extravagant everybody is!

Enter MR. BILLINGTON.

MR. BILLINGTON.–*Will* somebody tell me who I am?

MISS SIMMS.–You are my husband. By kind permission of B. Webster, Esq.

MR. BILLINGTON.–But who else? A fellow's something more than his wife's husband, I hope.

MISS SIMMS.–Oh no he isn't.

MR. TOOLE *(for some reason best known to himself).*–HA! I HAVE MISSED ANOTHER POST!   *[Exit* MR. TOOLE.

The Misses Sims, Godsall and Seaman were all performers of the period, as were the male characters. Paul Bedford had been for years an Adelphi low-comedian, often in alliance with Edward Wright in J. M. Morton's farces. These included *A Most Unwarrantable Intrusion Committed by Mr. Wright to the Annoyance of Mr. Paul Bedford* (1849). J. L. Toole was perhaps the greatest low-comedian of his day, husky-voiced and twinkling-eyed. In 1875 he was to play himself in Robert Reece's *Toole at Sea,* a farce depicting his imaginary sea-going adventures in a dream. Mrs. Alfred Mellon (Sarah Woolgar) played burlesque, comedy, and serious roles in works by Taylor, Phillips, Boucicault and others, mostly at the Adelphi. The *Athenaeum* (12 May 1866) thought the success of *The Fast Family* was owing to her vigorous performance.

These burlesques allowed Gilbert room to make failures in staging noticeable. For instance, shortly after the opening of act three of *The Long Strike:*

A big property pump, that has been forgotten in setting the scene, is at this moment shoved into the middle of the stage by peccant carpenter. General joy of audience. Then enter NOAH *looking benignly at pump.*

In the fence's cellar of Leicester Buckingham's drama *Love's Martyr* (*Fun*, 12 May 1866), Trevelyan measures diamonds in a quart pot, while two others fight for a will; one of them snaps a pistol which misses fire and another somebody falls mortally wounded. The names for the characters in this play are taken from annuals and sentimental novels published by the Minerva Press (early 1800s), as the characters themselves are well aware.

LOVE'S MARTYR

Prologue.–Apartment in Lady Belmour's Mansion.

Enter TREVELYAN *and* EDITH.

TREVELYAN.–Edith, you are my daughter!

EDITH.–And you my fond papa!   (*They weep.*)

TREVELYAN.–Notwithstanding the magnificence of my name, which was selected at an early age, from the Minerva Press, I am but Lady Belmour's steward!

EDITH.–And I, notwithstanding the ditto of my ditto, which was dittoed at an early ditto, from the ditto ditto, am but her companion!

Enter MRS. SPRIGGINS.

MRS SPRIGGINS.–Which my Lady is a kickin' of her bucket, as the sayin' is; and hours is the word, so I will keep me awake, make some coffee, as is a drink I holds with, and keeps one's eyes open, as crowbars is a fool to.

(*Prepares coffee.*)

Enter LADY FLORA VERNON *and* MARION.

LADY FLORA (*muses*).–My name was taken from a "Friendship's Offerings".

MARION (*her daughter*).–And mine from an "Affectionate Tribute!"

EDITH.–Lady Flora! Marion! I love you both, and would be on intimate terms with you.

LADY F.–Really, Miss Trevelyan! You are only Lady Belmour's steward's daughter; and though we respect you, we cannot yield our affection on demand.

EDITH.–Oh, how cruel! *(Weeps.)*

Enter REDGRAVE, *a Solicitor.*

REDGRAVE *(muses).*–To a "Devotion's Sacrifice" I am indebted for my appellation. But no matter. I have come to say that Lady Belmour has made a will, leaving everything to Marion Vernon–disinheriting her nephew, Paul Ryland, who is her heir-at-law. *(At least it wasn't quite this, but this will do.)*

(Exeunt Omnes.)

Enter TREVELYAN.

TREVELYAN.–Ha! Paul Ryland disinherited. And he owes me twenty thousand! Quick! the laudanum! *(Pours laudanum into coffee-pot.)* This will cause Mrs. Spriggins (whose name was certainly *not* selected from the "Minerva Press") to sleep soundly, so that I can obtain access to Lady Belmour's room, murder her, and secure the will.

(Exit, like a bad man, as he is.)

Enter MRS. SPRIGGINS.

MRS. S.–Now for my coffee, as is a drink I holds with.

(Drinks it, and falls asleep.)

Enter EDITH.

EDITH.–Mrs. Spriggins asleep! Then I will keep awake.

(Takes coffee and falls asleep.)

Enter TREVELYAN *(like a bad man, as he is.)*
(Edith *wakes, and sees him enter Lady Belmour's room.)*

EDITH.–Ha! my papa! Gracious goodness me, how awful!

(Screams heard from Lady B's room.)

Enter the Household, in dressing-gowns.

THE HOUSEHOLD.–We heard screams!

Enter SOMEBODY.

SOMEBODY.–Lady Belmour is murdered!

EVERY ONE *(except* EDITH*).*–Then you are the murderess!

(Exit EDITH, *very quickly. Tableau of every one,
except Edith.)*

ACT I.–*Evelyn's Studio at Hampstead.*

*(*PAUL RYLAND, REDGRAVE, *and many others, discovered,
having their portraits painted by* FRANK MORDAUNT.*)*

MORDAUNT.–Ryland, has it ever struck you as remarkable
that all our friends–Arthur, Evelyn, yourself, myself, Sir
Charles Ormond, and Redgrave, should have been christened
from a silk-bound annual of thirty years ago?

RYLAND *(mildly)*.–Never.

MORDAUNT *(aside)*.–Supercilious puppy!

RYLAND.–Where is Evelyn's wife?

MORDAUNT.–She never appears. She never leaves the
boudoir of the artist's wife, which will form the scene of the
third act.

RYLAND.–Then I will remain until the third act.

MORDAUNT.–Courageous creature! You over-estimate your
powers of endurance.

Enter MRS. MORDAUNT.

MRS. M.–Pickles. All serene. No flies. Walker. Also Slap-
bang. Likewise Over-the-left. And How's-your-poor-feet?

Enter SIR CHARLES ORMOND.

SIR. C.–Come, all of you, to Lady Ormond's ball to-night.

ALL.–We will.   *(They do.)*

ACT II.–*Drawing-room at Sir Charles Ormond's.*

Enter LADY ORMOND *(née* MARION VERNON.*)*

LADY O.–Sir Charles not yet returned? Then he *must* be
with a rival!

Enter MRS. SPRIGGINS.

MRS. S.–Which my daughter has run away with a artist
chap, as is no better than they ought to be, as the sayin' is, as
is parties as I don't hold with, through bein' that free in their
ways, as the sayin' is.

LADY O.–Good soul, two artist chaps are coming here to-night; I don't know anything of them, but one of them is doubtless the man you seek. There are only about three artists in the world.

Enter MORDAUNT.

MRS. S.–Wherever have you put my daughter, young man?

MORDAUNT.–Oh! I suppose you are my mother-in-law. Well, she's at home.

MRS. S.–All right, as the sayin' is. *(Exeunt.)*

(You see, a piece MUST *have an underplot!)*

Enter ARTHUR EVELYN.

ARTHUR E.–I am told that my wife knows something of Paul Ryland. Then she *must* have been his mistress! Oh, agony!

ACT III.–*Boudoir of the Artist's Wife.*

Enter the ARTIST'S WIFE.

(You see, she is EDITH TREVELYAN, *who is supposed to have committed suicide immediately after the murder in the first act.)*

ARTIST'S WIFE.–Oh, how I adore my husband!

(Exit Artist's Wife.)

Enter PAUL RYLAND *and* SERVANT.

RYLAND.–Send the artist's wife here. I have a message from her husband.

Enter the ARTIST'S WIFE.

ARTIST'S WIFE.–Ha! you are Paul Ryland, the man who instigated my excellent father to murder Lady Belmour!

RYLAND.–And you are the Edith Trevelyan who is accused of the murder! *(Exit* PAUL RYLAND. *Artist's Wife faints.)*

Enter EVELYN.

EVELYN.–Ha! Paul Ryland with my wife!

(Artist's Wife revives.)

ARTIST'S WIFE.–Yes!

EVELYN.–What was he doing here?

ARTIST'S WIFE.–I shall not tell you. Do not ask me. You

142

promised me you would never ask me to tell you anything about anybody.

EVELYN.–True; but I *should* like to know something about my wife's previous history. The first time I saw you, you were wandering in a wood, contemplating suicide, and I thought that the best I could do was to marry you on the spot.

ARTIST'S WIFE.–It was obviously the wisest course you could have pursued.

EVELYN.–But why were you contemplating suicide?

ARTIST'S WIFE.–Because I was pure, virtuous, excellent–in every way too good for this life.

EVELYN.–Oh! I see. That is quite satisfactory.

(They embrace.)

Enter LADY FLORA VERNON, SIR CHARLES *and* LADY ORMOND, *and guests from the Ball.*

ALL.–Edith Trevelyan, you are the murderess of the late Lady Belmour, whose name was taken, as we all know, from the "Devotion's Ecstasy" for 1836!

ARTIST'S WIFE.–Wow!

ARTIST.–I also remark, Wow!

ACT. IV.–*The Fence's Cellar.*

(Lights down. TREVELYAN *discovered, measuring diamonds in a quart pot.)*

TEVELYAN.–I am a Fence, and a Fence it is extremely difficult to get over. *(Knock.)*

Enter WINWOOD *and* SIR CHARLES ORMOND.

WINWOOD.–Give up the will, and Sir Charles will give you five thousand pounds.

TREVELYAN.–Never!

Enter PAUL RYLAND.

RYLAND.–Give it to me, and I will give you ten thousand.

SIR. C.–So will I.

RYLAND.–Ha! Then we will all fight for it! *(Pulls out pistols.)*

SOMEBODY.–Never!

SOMEBODY ELSE.–It shall be so!

SOMEBODY.–It shall *not!*

(They all take up weapons, and proceed to fight for the will. SOMEBODY snaps a pistol, which, of course, misses fire, and SOMBODY ELSE falls mortally wounded. At this moment, who should come into the cellar but ALL THE CHARACTERS, *with a candle.)*

ALL THE CHARACTERS.–We see it all. The old Fence was Edith's father, who murdered Lady Belmour, that the property might go to her nephew, who owed TREVELYAN twenty thousand pounds! Edith is innocent, and circumstantial evidence is again at fault.

TREVELYAN *(dying).*–More than this, Edith is Lady Belmour's child!

SIR CHARLES ORMOND.–*(Only I don't see how this is, myself.)* Then she is my sister!

(General Rapture, Final Chorus, and Comic Dance,
by ALL THE CHARACTERS.*)*

CURTAIN.

9 Making Comedy of Errors

No errors in costume, make-up, props, or scenery escaped Gilbert's rigorous eye. Other reviewers might comment on some, but none so watchful as he. Duck-fingered Joe of Tom Taylor's Holborn Theatre failure, *The Antipodes* (*Fun*, 22 June 1867), was admonished to remember that he *was* duck-fingered, that is his first and second fingers were joined by a web. (Other critics noticed his forgetfulness too.) In H. J. Byron's *Blow for Blow*, Dr. Grace hunts in fishing boots (*Fun*, 26 September 1868). Sir Ralph of *Maud's Peril* always hunts with a full band: 'It amuses the fox.' The Macronalds' kilts are stiffened out with crinoline and wire and are worn over worsted tights (Westland Marston's *Life for Life* [*Fun*, 20 March 1869]). Men whose occupations require them to be clean-shaven wear moustaches in play after play. Captain Gautier in Gilbert's parody of *Rouge et Noir* (*Fun*, 26 January 1867) remarks, in a play set in 1809: 'I will write a note to Pauline, and send it in an adhesive envelope—thus anticipating that useful invention by half a century.' In the same play, Gaspar enters Pauline's bedchamber through the window, explaining: 'I have come to carry off Pauline, and have climbed up here by means of a rope-ladder two and a half feet long.' The domed ceiling into which Edith is catapulted in *The Great City* turns up again in Boucicault's *Formosa* (1869).

On the dusty sea of H. J. Byron's *The Lancashire Lass* (*Fun*, 15 August 1868), a boat enters 'unfolding itself telescopically as it advances'; after two passengers land, it 'shuts itself up and backs off.' According to the *Athenaeum* (1 August 1868), hisses were mixed with applause for the boat and for the entire play, only one scene of which 'rises even to mediocrity.' Gilbert's judgement was not quite so harsh, and he praised the acting. The villain was played by Henry Irving, whom in these early days Gilbert admired, but, like Tennyson, chiefly when he played villains.[34]

Farmer Allen in Reade's *Dora*, adapted from Tennyson's poem, elicited a roar of laughter when he described 'eighteen pennyworth of straw' as 'the finest crop of straw I've seen this fifty year!' (*Fun*, 15 June 1867). The setting sun in this piece is 'shy, and goes out, but eventually returns, and sets very fast—a deputation of raspberry jam and pink coral advancing to meet it'. Victorian stage suns were, in fact, not very clear in their behaviour. One flooded light in the morning into the same room where it had set the night before. Moons were more stable, except for the three moons which illuminated Calais sands in *The Flying Scud* (*Fun*, 20 October 1866), Dion Boucicault's 'sensation' horse-race drama, opening at the Holborn Theatre on 6 October 1866 for a run of 207 performances. The race itself was shown by small profile horses in the background, but Nat appeared on a real horse.

THE FLYING SCUD

ACT I. SCENE 1. *Love Lane, near Doncaster.*

Enter TOM MEREDITH.

TOM.–Indeed, it was so! *(Weeps.)*

SCENE 2.–*The Gates of Nobbley Park.*

Enter JULIA LATTIMER *and* LORD WOODBIE.

LORD W.–I am fourteen, and I love you!

JULIA.–Fie, my lord! You are too young.

LORD W.–Oh, bother!

JULIA.–If you love me, discontinue that awful habit of swearing.　　　*[Discontinues awful habit of swearing. R.*

LORD W.–Will you wed me?

JULIA.–Not until you are old enough to go to Eton.

[Tableau.

SCENE 3.–*Flying Scud's Stable.*

Enter BOB, *the stable-boy, and* NAT GOSLING.

BOB.–I am getting stout.

NAT.–That's because you're always getting beer.　　*[Exeunt.*

Enter KATIE RIDEOUT *and* CAPT. GRINDLEY GOODGE.

CAPT. G.–Katie, you can guess why I have brought you to this stable. It is to propose to you. I love you.

KATIE.–Never!

CAPT. G.–Ha! scorned? Then I will lock you up with Flying Scud!　　*[Shoves her into a loose box and locks the door.*

[Exit GOODGE.

Enter TOM MEREDITH.

TOM.–I love Katie, and she is here! *(Hears screams from* KATIE *in loose box.)* Ha! My Katie in a loose box! Then she is ar–guilty! *[Exit insensible.*

SCENE 4.–*The Library in Nobbley Hall. Preparations for reading the Squire's Will.*

LAWYER.–This is the Squire's Will. I give everything to–including Flying Scud–Tom Meredith.

CAPT. G.–Ha! disinherited!

TOM.–Capt. Goodge, as everything is mine now; and notwithstanding that the will has not yet been proved, and although I am not one of the deceased's executors, hand me over the key of Flying Scud's stable.

CAPT. G.–As everything is, &c., and notwithstanding that, &c., and although you are not, &c., here is the key–but I will be avenged.

TOM.–Nat Gosling, I loved your granddaughter, Katie; but I have discovered her in a loose box, and after that, of course, I can't marry her. *[Tableau.*

ACT II.–*Hyde Park, Cumberland Gate. Enter* NAT.

NAT.–This is our family rendezvous. We conduct all our business here, just inside the park, by Cumberland Gate, and opposite the curds-and-whey shop. It's so quiet and retired.

Enter KATIE.

KATIE.–Ha! Grandfather! *[They hug.*

Enter BOB.

BOB.–Flying Scud is the favourite for the Derby!

NAT.–It's five-and-twenty year since I rode in a race! *[They weep.*

Tableau.

SCENE 2.–COL. MULLIGAN'S *rooms in Piccadilly.* COL. MULLIGAN, MO' DAVIS, *and* CHOUSER *breakfasting in a corner. The usual foils and boxing-gloves to indicate* MULLIGAN'S *downward career.*

COL. M.–We will doctor Flying Scud.

ALL.–We will! [*Exeunt.*

Enter JULIA LATTIMER *and* LORD WOODBIE.

LORD W.–Still I love you!

JULIA.–Still you are too young. Retire and grow older!

[*Retires up and grows older.*

SCENE 3. NAT'S *Lodging. Enter* CAPT. GOODGE.

CAPT. G.–This is Nat's lodging; and lo, he comes.

Enter NAT.

CAPT. G.–Sell me the key of Flying Scud's stable, and here are two thousand pounds!

NAT.–Done. (*Aside to audience.*) Wait a bit, you'll see–it'll be all right. (*Aloud.*) Here is the key.

GOODGE.–'Tis a-very well! [*Exeunt. Tableau.*

SCENE 4.–*The Pigskin Club. Jockeys discovered in full colours, and all standing in the third position, with right hands on their hips, and combs in their back hair. Enter* NAT.

NAT.–I have sold Flying Scud!

ALL.–Shame!

NAT.–But listen. I know a horse that is own brother to Flying Scud. They are, in fact, twins. I will substitute one for the other. Here are two thousand pounds, divide them among ye.

ALL.–Good! We will express our joy in a jockey hornpipe.

[*Express their joy in a jockey hornpipe, whatever that may be.*

SCENE 5.–*The straw yard. Flying Scud's twin brother discovered looking out of a first-floor window.*

Enter CAPT. GOODGE, *disguised apparently as a Pilgrim.*

PILGRIM.–I have come to doctor Flying Scud.

Enter NAT.

NAT.–All right. (*Exit* PILGRIM.) It's the wrong 'un!

SCENE 6.–*The Derby Day. (Opposite the Grand Stand.)*

Enter BOB BUCKSKIN *and* NAT GOSLING.

BOB.–The jockey that was to have ridden Flying Scud has been hocussed!

NAT.–Then I will ride for him!

[Rides and wins easily by a jerk. Joy of wooden crowd.

Enter NAT *on the winner.*

NAT.–I haven't yet been weighed, but no matter. I will just trot Flying Scud through the carriages in front of the Grand Stand–it'll do him good.   *[General joy. Tableau.*

ACT III. SCENE 1.–MO' DAVIS *at home.*

COL. M.–We will cheat Tom Meredith at cards, and forge an I O U in Lord Woodbie's name, and raise money on it. for an I O U is always a good negotiable security.

[They forge an I O U and exeunt.

SCENE 2.–*No matter.*

SCENE 3.–*The Tattenham Club.* GOODGE *and* MULLIGAN *playing at cards with* MEREDITH. MO' DAVIS *telegraphing contents of* MEREDITH'S *hand in a most unmistakable manner.*

MEREDITH.–I will play you–ar–for–ar–everything I–ar–possess–ar.

Enter LORD WOODBIE.

GOODGE.–'Tis well. *[Wins everything* MEREDITH *possesses.*
LORD W.–Goodge, I saw you cheating!
GOODGE.–Ha! Presumptuous boy!   *[Knocks him down.*
LORD W.–We will fight at Calais!   *[Tableau.*

SCENE 4.–*No matter.*

SCENE 5.–*No matter.*

SCENE 6.–*Calais Sands, illuminated by three moons.*

Enter MULLIGAN *and* GOODGE *with a riding-whip to show*

that he has just trotted over.

GOODGE.–This is the place where I was to meet Lord Woodbie.

Enter MEREDITH.

MEREDITH.–Lord Woodbie cannot come! I will fight you instead!

Enter JULIA LATTIMER *disguised as* LORD WOODBIE.

JULIA.–I am here. Let us fight

> [*They fight.* JULIA *is wounded.*

JULIA.–I am Julia. I would not let Lord Woodbie fight until he was old enough to go to Eton. So I came instead.

> [*Tableau.*

ACT IV. SCENE 1.–*No matter.*

SCENE 2.–LORD WOODBIE'S *room.*

Enter LADY WOODBIE, JULIA, *and* LORD WOODBIE.

LADY WOODBIE.–You are worthy to be the wife of a lord, although you are the scheming sister of an acknowledged blackleg. Take him!   [*Takes him.*

Enter TOM MEREDITH.

TOM.–Now to knock down the villains!

SCENE 3.–MO DAVIS'S *garret.*

MO' DAVIS.–I will take all the money that belongs to Goodge and bolt.   [*Takes money and hides under table.*

Enter GOODGE.

GOODGE.–Now to get my money and bolt. Ha! it is gone! That villain Mulligan's got it.

Enter MULLIGAN.

MULLIGAN.–Now to get Goodge's money and flee. Ha! it is gone! That villain Goodge has got it!

GOODGE.–Mulligan, we will fight.

MULLIGAN.–We will.

> [*They fight and upset the table, discovering* MO' DAVIS.

Enter EVERYBODY.

EVERYBODY.–Ha!

LORD W.–Goodge, you have forged an I O U for £2,000. Confess that Katie got into the loose box against her will, and you are free.

GOODGE.–I will confess anything you like if you will let me go.

MEREDITH.–This is most satisfactory. A more disinterested admission I never heard. Katie, come to my arms.

[They love each other.

NAT.–And if our Flying Scud will signify its approbation, there won't be a happier party in England than

Our Friends in Front!

CURTAIN.

Gilbert's Pigskin Club with its jockey hornpipe danced by a chorus of girls seems to be his own amusing invention, but it was really danced in *The Flying Scud* (although the set which Boucicault specified was the stable rather than the Club). This 'Terpischorean intrusion' was, according to *The Times* (8 October 1866), 'highly relished by the spectators'. The racecourse scene was full of the 'minute realities' of Frith's famous picture, and the race itself caused extreme excitement, pit, boxes and gallery, *The Times* said, shouting their approval. The set for Calais was, however over-mooned, considered beautiful.

A lurid moon shed its light over F. C. Burnand's sensation drama, *Deadman's Point; or The Lighthouse on the Carn Ruth*, at the Adelphi Theatre (4 February 1871). This melodrama gave Gilbert the material for his funniest review (*Fun*, 18 February 1871)–and his most comprehensive, for it contains ridiculous stage effects, anachronistic costumes, mistaken moustaches, and a guttural villain (he guggles):

DEADMAN'S POINT;
OR, ALL FEES ARE REVIVED AT THE ADELPHI THEATRE

ACT I. SCENE 1.–*Riverdale House, Twickenham.* SIR PHILIP COURTENAY *and* MAJOR PEARSON *discovered playing billiards.*

SIR PHILIP.–The action of the first act is anterior to the date of the Crimean war, when the infantry were not allowed to grow moustachios. But I wear a pair because I am a baronet.

MAJOR PEARSON.–*I* wear a moustache and a beard–but then (as my forage cap will show when I'm out in the Crimea in the third act) I am an officer of yeomanry cavalry, and in the yeomanry regulations are not strictly enforced.

SIR PHILIP.–I love Janet Trefel, the lighthouse-keeper's daughter.

Enter LADY COURTENAY (SIR PHILIP'S *mother), and a comic house-agent.*

LADY COURTENAY.–I want to go to the seaside!

COMIC HOUSE AGENT.–You shall!

ACT II.–SCENE: *Interior of a Coastguard Cottage, Cornwall.*

Enter MARY POLDEN, JANET TREFEL, *and* TOM POLDEN, *a coast-guard.*

TOM POLDEN.–Marry, ' tis a gruesome night, and the devil will work his worst round Deadman's Point to-night. The *Curlew* is in the offing, labouring heavily.

JANET.–The *Curlew*! And Sir Philip is on board! Let me go and save him!

TOM.–I'll run down to the beach and bear a hand–the gale rages furiously.

(Goes down to the beach in a very broad-brimmed tarpaulin hat, which is perched on his back hair–the very hat of all others for a gale of wind.)

[*Exit with* MARY POLDEN.

Enter STEVE HARGAR, *a guttural person, with rolling eyes, flashing teeth, and eyebrows like doormats.*

STEVE *(to Janet)*.–Now, pretty one, I have thee alone *(he gasps)*. Nay,'tis useless to resist *(he guggles)*.

JANET.–Unhand me, ruffian!

STEVE.–Never! *(he chokes)*.

Enter MARY.

MARY.–Unhand her, monster!

(There is something in MARY'S *eye that quells even this outra-geous scoundrel, and he slinks away abashed. But we do not see why one of* JANET'S *eyes should not have had the same effect.)*

SCENE 2: *Deadman's Point.*

The sea is raging tempestuously, and the demons of the storm are seen in the act of shaking it violently at the wings. Clouds of dust arise–the heavens are full of phenomena. The moon shines luridly, and the air is filled with flocks of transparent kidneys–fiery volcanoes spurt from the sea. It is indeed an awful and unusual sight. Presently, SIR PHILIP *is seen battling with the waves. He appears to be bound, stomach downwards, to an eccentric wheel, which revolves violently. The sea is tied tightly round his throat, and the irrestible machinery by which he is worked carries the ocean along with him. Being a baronet, he is dressed in a flowing garb of blue muslin. This has a very pretty and natural effect, and amuses the audience very much.–Then comes* JANET. *She leans over a rock and hands him onto dry ground. All laugh.*

[An interval of half an hour, to enable SIR PHILIP *to recover from the effects of his eccentric wheel.]*

ACT III.–*Exterior of Coastguard Cottage.*

Enter MARTIN GURDER *(a soldier of the 95th), and* MARY POLDEN.

MARTIN.–The date of this piece is 1854–that is why I wear a tunic (single-breasted, date 1859) and an artilleryman's forage cap. But where is my love, Janet?

MARY.–She has run away with Sir Philip–and perhaps is married to him.

MARTIN.–If he has deceived her I'll shoot him!

SCENE 2: *Zwan Kelly. The Fallen Cave.* JANET *and* SIR PHILIP *discovered making love,* MARTIN *listening, unperceived, in an uncomfortable attitude, and in an ungentlemanly manner.*

SIR PHILIP.–Janet, I love you!

JANET.–My sweet pet!

SIR PHILIP.–My dear love!

Enter MAJOR PEARSON.

MAJOR PEARSON *(significantly)*.–Come! *(He goes.)*

MARTIN.–If he has deceived her I'll kill him!

ACT IV.–SCENE: *In the Crimea–dead bodies about. Enter an obtrusive scene-painter. (We thought we had stopped this sort of thing.)* [*He bows and retires with mingled feelings.*

MARTIN GURDER *(desperately wounded)* revives.

MARTIN.–There is Sir Philip also desperately wounded–I will kill him! *(Is about to do so, when enter a Russian, who prepares to stab* SIR PHILIP.*) Ha! an enemy! (Shoots the Russian.)* I have saved my adversary's life!

Enter MARY *and* JANET *as nurses.*

MARY (goes to MARTIN).–Why it's Martin!

JANET *(goes to* SIR PHILIP*)*.–Why it's Sir Philip! *(Transports.)*

ACT V.–SCENE: *Pass of the Carn Dhu.*

Enter STEVE *and an Idiot.*

STEVE.–You say that the lighthouse-keeper has gold in the lighthouse!

IDIOT.–I do!–I've seen it!

STEVE.–Good! *(He rolls his eyes.)* You say that he is in the habit of leaving the lighthouse (in defiance of all regulations) to the care of Mary and Janet.

IDIOT.–I do!–I've seen 'em!

STEVE.–Then we will go and rob him of his go-o-o-o-ould! *(He works his eyebrows.)*

SCENE 2: *A room.*

Enter MARY *and* JANET–*then* LADY COURTENAY.

LADY COURTENAY.–Woman, who are you?

JANET.–I am your son's wife.

LADY COURTENAY.–But you should not have married him–he is above you in rank.

JANET.–True, but I loved him.

LADY COURTENAY.–Oh, I understand. Then come to my arms. My daughter! *(They embrace.)*

Scene the Last. Half a lighthouse, presenting sectional view, and showing two apartments, one over the other. MARY *and* JANET *in upper half. Enter from a boat,* STEVE *and* Idiot. *They descend into lower apartment, to rob the miser of his go-o-o-o-ould.*

JANET AND MARY.–We will escape by the boat and leave them here to starve! *(But the boat has drifted off,–very careless of* STEVE.*)*

JANET.–Happily there is another boat always alongside the lighthouse! *(But what would happen to this other boat always alongside the lighthouse, if a storm arose?)*

MARY.–Ha! *That* boat has drifted away, alas! *(Very careless of the lighthouse-keeper.* STEVE *and Idiot chevy the two ladies round and round the rock at the base of lighthouse.)*

STEVE.–Curses! *(He gnashes his teeth, rolls his eyeballs, works his eyebrows, scowls, glares, and tears his hair, for he is in a fit.)*

Enter MARTIN GURDER *and* SIR PHILIP *in a boat.*

MARY AND JANET.–Saved! Saved! Saved!

CURTAIN.

OURSELVES.–A very amusing little skit on the absurdities of the Modern Sensation Drama. The piece would have been perfectly successful if some of the audience had not persisted in looking at the burlesque situations from a serious point of view. MISS FURTADO and MRS. BILLINGTON played their parts with a mock-heroic earnestness which proved that both actresses thoroughly understood that the essence of true burlesque acting consists in an apparent belief in the sapience of inflated dialogue and extravagant "situations." MR.

BURNAND has been ably seconded by MR. LLOYD, the scenic artist, who thoroughly entered into the spirit of the thing. His "Comic Storm at Sea" is an admirable caricature. The management, imbued, no doubt, with some of MR. BURNAND'S infectious drollery, revived the system of box-keeping brigandage, which has long been in abeyance at this house, and succeeded in taking the audience completely by surprise. They seemed to enjoy the joke very much. Altogether, the burlesque is undoubtedly MR. BURNAND'S best.

Burnand had intended *Deadman's Point* to be taken seriously, but 'Ourselves' was so persuasive that one reviewer accepted it as a burlesque. That the shipwreck was as absurd as Gilbert made it out to be is corroborated by the *London Figaro*'s review, which found it 'a huge jest':

> What are supposed to be fleecy clouds scud along the sky, and across the silver moon, but the scudding clouds are, for all the world, like pictures of legs and stockings–legs of every imaginable deformity, and stockings of all imaginable shapes. This new cloud effect was treated with the derision it deserved. Then came Miss Furtado, on a slippery rock, in the centre of the stage, who appeared to be flinging coils of rope to a dark blue alligator. On came the alligator from the O. P. side, probably struggling, on his stomach, with a most uncomfortable barrel. Meanwhile, the dusty and most unwatery waves powdered and choked the audience. The dark-blue alligator, to the surprise of the audience, turned out to be a man–the lover of Miss Furtado, in fact, who, what with the obstinate barrel and the coils of blue muslin, what with the dust and confusion, looked a most pitiable object. I suppose the gentleman in the blue muslin dressing-gown was saved; but I honestly own that I never saw a worse shipwreck or yachtwreck, on the stage, in the whole course of my life.[35]

Although a run of two years had been prophesied for *Deadman's Point* before it opened on 4 February, its last twelve nights were announced on 11 March.

10 Satirising the Sounds of Drama

Almost the only defect Gilbert did not satirise in his review of Burnand's *Deadman's Point* was its music–if it had any. The insistence on musical accompaniment was one of Gilbert's greatest detestations, as shown in his Theatrical Lounger reviews for the *Illustrated Times*. For example, reviewing Andrew Halliday's *Daddy Gray* (8 February 1868), he objected that 'The incidental music is a horrible nuisance, and ought to be ruthlessly expunged . . . . Some musical minds are so curiously constituted that they cannot resist playing a fiddle whenever they see a young lady in tears.' And he thought that the incidental music of Colonel Alfred Richards's *The Prisoner of Toulon* (7 March 1868) 'should be carefully revised. I may be wrong; but I do not think that the "British Grenadiers" is the kind of air that one would be likely to hear from the band of a French regiment in the days of the Republic.'

A review of *The Poor Nobleman* (*Fun*, 16 May 1868) found Gilbert definitely annoyed: ' . . . "slow music" as an accompaniment to slow action or as a supplement to the entrance of an afflicted hero or heroine is a ridiculous impertinence'. The parody of *Oliver Twist* (9 May 1868) opens with the exhausted Oliver announcing

> How weary I am! That dreadful slow music is killing me. *(To conductor)* I ask you, *am* I the old lady of Banbury Cross? Very well then! I will dismiss my private band, and lay me down and go to sleep in the middle of the road, for who–who would run over a poor parish boy?

After giving Byron's *Wait and Hope* a new subtitle, 'The Builder's Private Band', Gilbert introduced it in a stage direction:

> . . . *(A full band, such as usually accompanies working builders on all occasions, is heard, and* JOHN LOCKWOOD *enters amid the clashing of cymbals and the bray of silver clarions.)*
> LOCKWOOD *(to his band outside).*–Remain without, but within ear-shot, and whenever I open my mouth, play soft music. *(Apologetically to audience.)* It is always thus with builders.

Melodramatic action and characters obviously necessitated melodramatic language, of which curses, as we have seen, were an important part. Perhaps Gilbert's most dire imprecation is uttered by Lockwood:

> LOCKWOOD.–Then *(working himself into a terrible state of mind)* my curses–my bitterest curses on you, Tarleton. I will blight your life! I will interfere with all your arrangements! I will inconvenience you dreadfully! I will confound your politics! I will pray for rain! I will run you up a semi-detached villa! I will increase the rate of discount at the Bank! I will send my private band to play under your windows! Thus–thus I devote myself to the destruction of the man who dared to be loved by John Lockwood's fancy! Ha! ha! ha!

'Ha!'s', single or multiple, were also popular, as the foregoing plays attest.

Irish and Scottish accents were variable after the usual fashion in mid-Victorian comic stages and pages. French was never pronounced accurately. 'Gendarmes' are almost invariably 'Jongdarmes', and in *Narcisse* (7 March 1868) La Pompadour soliloquizes: 'I am evidently not popular with the people . . . . Even the Queen is jealous of me! But I could forgive them all this if people wouldn't persist in calling me the "Pumpeydoor".'[36]

The best of Gilbert's dialect parodies was that of Watts Phillips's *Lost in London* (Adelphi Theatre, 16 March 1867), although Phillips allegedly studied the dialect of Lancashire. In a letter to John Coleman, published by Phillips's son, the dramatist wrote that *Lost in London* had been annouced repeatedly over the last five years, but was always put off because Webster told Phillips he dreamt he would die while acting Job. In the event, Job was played by Henry Neville, famous for his northern dialect roles.

LOST IN LONDON

ACT I.–SCENE 1. JOB ARMROYD'S *Cottage. Enter* NELLY.

NELLY.–I am Job Armroyd's wife. Ah, me!

Enter JOB ARMROYD.

JOB.–Ay, lass, thee be. It be just thoct t'baccle nicht that Job Armroyd slacks t'ould mine to tak cammie thackle!

[They embrace.

Enter TIDDY DRAGGLETHORPE.

TIDDY.–Eh, Job! Bock t'waite claken taggle?

NELLIE *(scornfully)*–Yes, Tiddy. *(Aside.)* I am the only person in these parts who is intelligible, except Sir Gilbert Featherstone. Can my emotion at his presence be attributable to that fact? It may be!   *[Sighs.*

SCENE 2.–*Bleakmoor. Enter* BENJAMIN BLINKER *(a tiger) and* TIDDY.

BLINKER.–Tiddy, have you got a biceps?

TIDDY.–Ah, lad!   *[Bonnets him.*

BLINKER.–True!   *[Exit, thoughtfully.*

Enter NELLY *and* SIR GILBERT.

NELLIE.–Ah, me! Sir Gilbert, would you tear me from my home?

SIR GILBERT.–I would.   *[Tears her from her home.*

TIDDY.–Eh? T'wold thockerfull dack t'bain clackie. I'll just gang tell Job!   *[Exit.*

SCENE 3.–*A coal mine. Ten thousand additional lamps. Red fire, Harmonic meeting apparently going on.* MR. P. BEDFORD *in the chair. Chorus of convivial miners.*

JOB *(reproachfully).*–Ah, tockle, thockle.
                          [They all shake their heads.

Enter TIDDY *down the shaft.*

TIDDY.–Job, t'woife gangt awa' wi' t'wockle Baronet!

JOB.–Eh? That were wrang o' Nellie!   *[All swoon.*

ACT II. SCENE 1.–*Regent's Park. Interior of Ferns Villa. Room garnished with profusion of roses; smiling corn-fields in distance.*

Enter NELLIE, *shivering.*

NELLIE.–How it is snowing without! I almost wish I hadn't run away with Sir Gilbert. I really feel some remorse at having left poor Job–and I express it by fainting over the furniture every quarter of an hour. But his dialect was so very provincial, that I could *not* stand him. At all events, I can understand Sir Gilbert perfectly.

Enter SIR GILBERT.

SIR GILBERT *(with his hat on)*.–I have invited crowds of distinguished guests to a ball this evening.

NELLIE *(with some show of reason)*.–Really, Sir Gilbert, you should have told me–there is nothing but cold mutton in the house. *[Faints over a sofa.*

SIR GILBERT.–Ha! Again! *[Carries her out.*

Enter TIDDY *and* MR. EBURNE *in a pair of pantomine whiskers.*

TIDDY.–Ah, lad. Oi be come t'seek sitivation.

MR. EBURNE.–Haw! *[Exit* MR. EBURNE, *with pomp.*

Enter NELLIE.

TIDDY.–Eh? It be our Nellie. Oh! thockt, thockt (quoting good old saying), "T'bockle wrackle maks thwockt pockle!"

NELLIE *(hysterically)*.–Tiddy–iddy–iddy–iddy!

[Faints over ottoman.

SCENE 2.–*Exterior of Ferns Villa by night. Snow.*

Enter BLINKER.

BLINKER.–Oh, what a biceps she have got! *[Writhes. Exit.*

Enter JOB, *broken.*

JOB.–Eh? Ah! T'waite pack 'taks t'ould thortle!

Adelphi guests arrive all at once at Ferns Villa, in ball dresses, trudging through the snow. Enter BLINKER.

BLINKER *(contemplating Ferns Villa)*.–Oh, dear me, who would have thought that the magnificent saloons of Ferns Villa, with their corridors, ball-rooms, ante-chambers, and so forth, could have been crammed into such a very ordinary-looking cottage! It never occurred to me before. *(Changing the subject)*–Oh, *what* a biceps she have got!

[Exit, writhing in great agony.

SCENE 3.–*Ante-room at Ferns Villa. Enter all the* SERVANTS.

BLINKER.–As there's a large party going on in the drawing-room, what is more natural than that the servants should embrace the opportunity of singing comic songs with choruses in the adjoining apartment?

ALL.–Nothing!

[They sing comic songs for half-an-hour.

SCENE 4.–*Ball room. Adelphi guests, in Berlin gloves, frock coats, fancy waistcoats, and affable manners, discovered dancing. They expatiate to their partners on the liberality of the entertainment. Ladies in pink net, made skimping, and no gloves, express their delight in the "usual manner" – that is to say, by holding up their hands. General joy. All partake of apples, which are handed about in reckless profusion.*

Enter SIR GILBERT.

SIR GILBERT.–I took this house of Ethel; or, Only a Life; and it was in this drawing-room that she died! It is a splendid room, in Danson's best style. Quite the Danson cheese!

Enter NELLIE.

NELLIE.–Ah, I faint! *[Faints over easy chair.*

SIR GILBERT *(to attendant)*.–Do carry this tiresome woman away! *[They carry her away.*

Enter JOB.

SIR GILBERT.–Job Armroyd!

JOB.–Ay, lad! Thees't gotten moi woife, Thackle bonnie barkie.

SIR GILBERT.–Tut! *[All tut.*

SIR GILBERT *(hospitably to guests)*.–Oh, I wish you'd all go into some other room. I have business with this man.

[Guests bow, curtsey, and depart.

JOB.–Give me moi wife!

Enter NELLIE.

NELLIE.–Ha! Job! *[Faints over grand piano.*

JOB.–Nellie!

Enter all the guests as if they had been listening at the keyhole.

They all point NELLIE *out to* SIR GILBERT *after the manner of triumphant fiends.*

SIR GILBERT *(annoyed).*–All right! *I* see her!   *[Tableau.*

ACT III. *Interior of a cottage. Enter* TIDDY.

TIDDY.–Ah, twockle bockers canna twartle t'back!

Enter BLINKER.

BLINKER.–I loves yer for yer biceps!

TIDDY.–Oh!   *[Kisses him. Exit* BLINKER.

Enter NELLIE, *very ill.*

NELLIE.–I am sick unto death! I have left Sir Gilbert and have come to live with Tiddy.   *[Faints over coal-scuttle.*

TIDDY.–Eh! lass, t'best bork the bainst t'war!

      [Carries her out.

Enter JOB, *determined.*

JOB.–Sir Gilbert's comin' t'ould cottage to nicht. I'll wait.

Enter SIR GILBERT, *cautiously.*

JOB.–Thee villain! Die!

SIR GILBERT.–Nay–

JOB.–Thees't tacken moi woife's love fra' me.

SIR GILBERT.–Nay; she could not understand you!

JOB.–Die!   *[Is about to fire pistol, when enter* NELLIE.

NELLIE.–Do not shoot him!

JOB.–Ah!

NELLIE.–Wow!   *[Dies over three-legged stool.*

JOB.–Dead! Well, well moight this drama be called Lost in Lunnon!

(Tableau of everyone, all shaking their heads except NELLIE.*)*

CURTAIN.

OURSELVES.–Very bad piece, very well acted, and placed upon the stage in the usual Adelphi style.

Usual Adelphi style meant the same old set and the same old supers. Whether in calling it a bad piece, Gilbert referred to the writing or the morals we cannot tell, but in his own early problem play, *Charity* (performed in January 1874), he attacked the double sexual standard which killed Nellie. The *Illustrated London News* thought some bits of this dialogue very telling, and reported enthusiastic audience applause. But it reproved Miss Neilson for fainting so repeatedly—'the orthodox melodramatic swoon', as Henry Morley called it.[37]

Almost as comic was the language Gilbert gave Saunders in W. G. Wills's *The Man O'Airlie* (*Fun*, 3 August 1867), adapted from the German of Carl von Holtei and first performed at the Princess's Theatre on 20 July:

THE MAN O'AIRLIE

ACT I.–*Drawing-room in Lord Steelman's Country House.* MISS STEELMAN *and* GEORGE BRANDON *discovered.*

MISS S.–George Brandon, we are engaged. I always hated you, but for some reason or other, which isn't clearly made out, I am ordered to marry you.

GEO. B. *(aside).*–She is rich and will pay my debts! *(Aloud.)* Miss Steelman, you love Sir Gerald Hope!

MISS S.–Perhaps!

Enter LORD STEELMAN.

LORD S.–I wear brass buttons because I am a nobleman. Such are the vagaries of rank!

MISS S.–James Harebell, a local poet, has come to see you, to beg your name for his title page.

LORD S.–Oh, bother. Send him up, and have done with him.

Enter JAMES HAREBELL, *dressed like* BURNS.

JAMES H.–My lord, I will sing you a little thing of my own!

LORD S. *(alarmed.)*–Oh, don't trouble yourself.

JAMES H.–Nay, but it's nae trouble at a'!

[Sings a little thing of his own.

LORD S.–Thanks. Now go.

JAMES H.–Nay; but I'll just sing thee anither.

LORD S.–No. please don't.

JAMES H.–Then you will gi'e me your name for my title-page?

LORD S.–Yes. Anything for a quiet life.

JAMES H.–Then I relent. *(To* BRANDON.*)* Here are twa hundred pound in notes, and the manuscript of my songs. Get them published for me, and I promise never to sing to you again.

GEO. B. *(jumping at the bargain).*–Done, with you!

[Pockets notes.

(Exit HAREBELL, *humming a little thing of his own, followed by* LORD STEELMAN *and* MISS STEELMAN.*)*

Enter SIR GERALD HOPE.

SIR G.–Pay me the five hundred pounds you owe me, or I will denounce you to Lord Steelman as a beggar, and marry Miss Steelman myself. It would be a contemptibly mean thing to do, but no matter.

GEO. B. *(giving* HAREBELL'S *notes).*–Here are two hundred–you shall have the balance tomorrow!

SIR G. *(aside).*–Confusion! *[Staggers out.*

Enter HAREBELL.

GEO. B.–Harebell, lend me three hundred pounds.

JAMES H.–I am only a poor Highland cottager, but certainly. *[Writes him a cheque for the amount.*

ACT II.–*Harebell's Cottage.*

MRS. HAREBELL *discovered, with* SAUNDERS, *a servant.*

MRS. H.–A'weel, a'weel, a'weel! There's a muckle mickle, i' th' pockle pickle!

SAUNDERS.–Eh! t'gowerin' bairn a nicht wi' Burns gin a body auld lang syne cockaleekie haggis! *[Exeunt.*

Enter HAREBELL.

JAMES. H.–My book's nae published yet!

Enter BRANDON.

GEO. B.–Your three hundred pounds are lost!

JAMES H.–Eh, then I'm just ruined!

GEO. B.–Not so; I can offer you Lord Steelman's secretary-ship. Take it, and be happy!

Enter MRS. HAREBELL *and* SAUNDERS.

MRS. H.–A'weel, a'weel, a'weel!

SAUNDERS.–Eh, ilka lassie has a laddie o'er the hills to Gowrie. *(To* BRANDON.)–Cam' ye by Athol?

GEO. B.–No.

[Tableau.

ACT III.–*Library in Lord Steelman's House. Enter* HAREBELL.

JAMES H.–My wife is dead. I sang to her too much. The jury returned a verdict of "accidental death".

Enter LORD STEELMAN, MISS STEELMAN, *and* SIR GERALD
HOPE.

MISS S.–I will not marry Brandon, to-morrow.

LORD S.–Ha! You might have mentioned that before.

SIR G.–Brandon is an embezzler.

Enter BRANDON.

LORD S.–Brandon, is this true? Are you an embezzler?

GEO. B. *(guiltily).*–I am!

LORD S.–Then go! *[He goes.*

JAMES H.–My Brandon an embezzler! Then I will go mad!

Tableau–HAREBELL *going mad.*

ACT IV.–*View of Highland Loch. Statue to James Harebell,
covered up is seen. (Ever so many years have elapsed.)*

Enter SAUNDERS *and* CROWD.

SAUNDERS.–Scots wha hae wi' pae wi' wha, wi' Wallace bled in ta tapsalterrie Cotter's Saturday Nicht wi' eerie drone and eldritch croon the bonnie blink o' Mary's e'e!

ALL.–Perhaps!

[They intimate to each other that SAUNDERS *is breaking
rapidly.*

Enter LORD STEELMAN, SIR GERALD HOPE, LADY HOPE *(late*
MISS STEELMAN*), and* SHY FRIENDS.

LORD S. AND HIS FRIENDS.–We always wear lavender gloves, tall hats, and patent leather boots in the Wilds of the Western Highlands, because we are such aristocrats.

LORD S.–Say, wasn't James Harebell a great nuisance, with his infernal songs?

ALL.–He was!

LORD S.–Didn't he bore our life out with his confounded rhymes?

ALL.–He did!

LORD S.–Was he even worthy of a pension from the Civil List?

ALL.–He was not!

LORD S.–Then does it not serve him right to give him a statue?

ALL.–It is a just retribution!

LORD S.–Uncover it!

[They uncover the statue. Derisive cheer.

SIR G. *(with a good deal of proper feeling).*–Well, really, the poor man is dead and gone, and it's too bad to publish that caricature of the unfortunate old bore. It is indeed!

Enter JAMES HAREBELL, *an idiot, and altogether a good deal fallen off since the last act.*

JAMES H.–Eh! It's my statue!

ALL.–Ha! it is James Harebell, gone daft!

JAMES H.–Eh, yes, it's Jimmy Harebell, gone daft from reading his own poems.

SIR G. *(to* LORD STEELMAN*).*–If we keep his poems from him he may yet recover.

LORD S.–He may; nay *(re-assuringly to audience)*, he will!

JAMES H.–I am better already *(recovers his intellect by a violent effort)*, and if our friends in front will explain to us why this piece is called the "Man o' Airlie", a painful feeling of doubt will be removed from our minds, and there won't be a happier party in all Scotland than–

SIR G.–The lover,

LADY H.–The lady,

JAMES H.–and the lunatic.

CURTAIN.

OURSELVES.–It's a remarkably well written piece, rather clumsy in construction, much too long, and much too Scotch; but with a good deal of thinking in it; and, on the whole, immeasurably superior to the general run of modern dramas, original or adapted. Admirably played by MR. VEZIN and MISS MOORE, very well played by MR. FORRESTER and MR. MACLEAN.

The *Athenaeum*'s reviewer found the Scottish dialect occasionally an interference, but admitted that it was so carefully written and spoken that the audience understood it. Hermann Vezin, who later played the leading male role in Gilbert's own *Randall's Thumb* and *Dan'l Druce*, seems no longer to be remembered as one of the great Victorian actors, although George Bernard Shaw greatly preferred his Dr. Primrose (in Wills's *Olivia*) to Irving's. (Of course, G.B.S. was not wholly unprejudiced.) He was, however, praised by a variety of reviewers for his elocution, his absence of rant, his subtlety, and above all, for his intelligence. The audience at *The Man o'Airlie* roared its approval after his third act exit (*Spectator*, 27 July 1867).

Gilbert also admired Vezin in Charles Reade's adaptation from the French, *The Courier of Lyons*, revived at the Gaiety Theatre (July 1870), which had been one of Charles Kean's stock pieces in the 1850s and would, re-titled *The Lyons Mail*, be a favourite of Henry Irving's from the late 1870s onwards. The *Examiner* (9 July 1870) described Vezin's performance of the dual role, Dubosc and Lesurques, as 'equally powerful, pathetic, and pleasing'. He played both the cold-blooded villain and his gentlemanly look-alike. Gilbert's parody, with its mispronounced French, appeared in *Fun* on 16 July 1870.

THE COURIER OF LYONS;
OR, THE CONFUSING CRIMINAL,
AND THE COMMISSARY-AND-A-HALF

ACT I.—*Public Room in a Paris Cafe.* CHOPPARD *and* FOUINARD *discovered carousing.*

CHOPPARD.—Curriol should be here.

FOUINARD.—He should. How amused he will be to see that I have reddened my nose, chalked my face, and blacked my nostrils. These effects combined with my fascinating knack of turning my lips inside out, will, I think, prove entertaining.

CHOPPARD.–By way of giving local colour to this scene I may state that my father bred a celebrated racehorse with the thoroughly French name "Daddy Long Legs."

Enter CURRIOL.

CURRIOL.–Has Dubosc, our captain, arrived yet?

CHOPPARD.–He has not. But my father bred, &c.

Enter LESURQUES, *with some aristocratic friends.*

LESURQUES.–Let us be happy, for we are good.

HIS FRIENDS.–*You* are good.

LESURQUES.–I rather think I am.   *[Exeunt to carouse.*

CURRIOL.–Lesurques is an old schoolfellow of mine.

Enter DUBOSC *(who is exactly like* LESURQUES, *only dirtier.)*

DUBOSC.–You are here? 'Tis well. To-night I have planned to stop the mail from Lyons, which carries untold gold. You will assist me?

ALL.–We will!   *[Exeunt.*

DUBOSC.–Now I am alone.

Enter JANETTE.

JANETTE.–Dubosc!

DUBOSC.–Ha! My wife!

JANETTE.–Give me money!

DUBOSC.–Never!

JANETTE.–Then beware!

SCENE 2.–*Exterior of the Lion Inn at Lieursaint, kept by* LESURQUES' *father. Enter* LESURQUES' *father and* JOLIQUET.

LESURQUES' FATHER.–I am starving. It is eleven o'clock p. m., so I will go and sell my inn by auction. *(Does so.)*

JOLIQUET.–Oh, my eye, I'm so frightened of being left alone!

Enter LESURQUES.

LESURQUES.–I am a wealthy man and my father is starving. So I have adopted a rather involved and unnecessarily intricate method of relieving him. I will leave a few Napoleons in his room and depart.   *[He does so, and exit.*

Enter DUBOSC *and his wicked pals.*

DUBOSC.–Boy, some wine!

JOLIQUET *(coming from cellar and believing the speaker to be* LESURQUES).–Here it is! Oh my! There are four of 'em!
                    (They take wine and lock the boy in the cellar.)

DUBOSC.–Here comes the mail. Look out.

*The Mail which has evidently had a very rough and dislocating
    journey from Lyons, enters, drawn by two perfectly fresh horses.*
[NOTE FOR THE MANAGEMENT.–*If the horses had been carefully
    wiped down with a sponge dipped in warm water before
    they appeared on the stage, they would have steamed in
    a natural and effective manner.]*

DUBOSC.–Ha! ha!

*All fire at everybody. A Courier is killed. The Mail is robbed
    of gold, which is carried loose in a deal box. Enter*
LESURQUES' *father;* DUBOSC *fires at him and hits him
    in the shoulder.*

LESURQUES' *father (who is not a wise father, and who
consequently believes* DUBOSC *to be his son).*–Ha! ha! My son!
                    [Falls insensible.

ACT II.–*Library in the House of* M. LESURQUES, *PARIS.*–
LESURQUES *discovered with his daughter* JOOLY, DIDIER
    (her young man), DORVAL *(a beak), and others. Also*
    LESURQUES' *father and* CURRIOL.

DORVAL.–Well I will say this–you are the very best man in
the world.

LESURQUES.–No, no.

DORVAL.–But I say, yes.

LESURQUES.–Well, well, perhaps I am.

*Enter a very long Commissary of Police, with a very tall cocked
    hat put on for some diplomatic reason wrong side before.
    Oh, everybody, do go and see this Commissary of Police.*

COMMISSARY.–Moosoo Lesook, the Jongdarmes tell me that
Dumong the Courier of Lyons was murdered last night at the
Leeong Inn at Loorsong. Ha! ha! *(Goes mad.)*

LESURQUES' FATHER *(looking sternly at his son).*–It is a-too terrue! I was there and saw it all!

DORVAL *(who sees at a glance the value of this old gentleman's evidence).*–Then we will have your testimony.

Enter Jongdarmes with CHOPPARD.

CHOPPARD.–I saw it all. *(Sees* LESURQUES *and thinks it is* DUBOSC.*) (Aside.)* Hallo! Dubosc collared!

DORVAL *(who is no fool).*–Then your evidence also will be valuable.

Enter Jongdarmes with JOLIQUET.

JOLIQUET.–I was present and saw the murder committed.

DORVAL *(with singular keenness of perception).*–Then we will examine you too.

JOLIQUET *(sees* LESURQUES *and thinks it is* DUBOSC*).*–Hallo! There he his! That's the man!

DORVAL.–Oh, impossible. That is the best man in the world!

LESURQUES.–Quite so.

JOLIQUET.–I don't care–he did it; and there's another! *(pointing to* CURRIOL*).* And there is a third *(pointing to* CHOPPARD*).*

LESURQUES.–Oh, ridiculous.

JOLIQUET.–But my master saw it all–didn't you? *(To* FATHER LESURQUES*).*

FATHER LESURQUES.–I did *(Struggles with his emotion.)*

DORVAL.–Did your son commit the murder?

FATHER LESURQUES.–He did! *(Aside.)* I'll teach my son to let me starve at Lieursaint while he lives like a fighting cock at Paris.

DORVAL *(like lightning).*–Then he had better be secured. *The Commissary immediately—but, oh, do go and see what the Commissary does! They secure him. Tableau.*

ACT III.–*Chamber overlooking Garden. Night.* JANETTE *and* JOOLY *discovered.*

JANETTE.–I am certain your father is innocent. At the moment of the murder he was at Choppard's stables. Here is Madame Choppard's day-book, and here is the entry that proves it. As this is a document of inestimable value, I will leave it here by the open window. *(Does so.)*

Enter DUBOSC, *by window.*

DUBOSC.–That page will prove my death. I will abstract it.

[Does so and exit.

SCENE 2.–*Here we have the Commissary again. He must be seen to be believed. Truth is stranger than fiction.*

SCENE 3.–*First floor of Cabaret, overlooking place of execution, which is evidently (on this occasion) somewhere on the Rue de la Paix. At all events the west front of Notre Dame is seen in the distance.*

DUBOSC *discovered.*

DUBOSC.–The crowd has assembled. Hark to the murmur. *(He harks R. Murmur ascends from L.)* Here is the condemned man. He *is* like me. Ha! ha! In another minute he will have perished. Eh! What's this? The crowd points to this window, and rushes this way! Gracious, they are going to arrest me! *(Shuts the door and draws a knife.)*

(Peculiar noise, as of gigantic lucifer match being struck. The door is broken down, and many Jongdarmes enter, with a clean crowd.)

SOMEBODY.–There he is! Seize him!

General scuffle. The Jongdarmes seize DUBOSC.

DORVAL.–Then you really didn't commit the murder?

LESURQUES *(irritated).*–Of course I didn't.

DORVAL.–I always said you were the best man in the world!

Tableau. Curtain.

OURSELVES.–a very striking play, excellently acted by MR. VEZIN, MR. ATKINS, MR. MACLEAN and MR. SOUTAR. MISS FARREN is admirable as JOLIQUET. MRS. LEIGH (an admirable actress, who has not yet taken her legitimate place on the stage) plays Janette extremely well. But the Commissary of Police is worth all the money.

Occasionally Gilbert used elaborate 'flowers of rhetoric', such as we have seen in *Ethel; or, Only a Life;* more often he played with parts of speech, giving them new meanings or new uses. For example, when Mrs. Montgomery in *Ethel* tells someone to avaunt, he avaunts. In *The Siren* (11 December 1869) Caspar exclaims, 'She has eloped with the tenor. I will after them! *(He afters them.).*' In the same review Sartorius announces, 'I am a great composer. *(Composes himself.)*'. Nellie of *Nellie's Trials* (20 January 1866) fulfils a stage direction: *Exit, affecting to be dead.*' Told to go away, Bob Gassitt in *Dearer than Life* (25 January 1868) ruefully says, 'I away! *(Aways.).*' After doctors give Sprawley an electric shock by mistake, there is a tableau of 'SPRAWLEY *dressed in somebody else's electric shock*'.

Gilbert had a quick ear for the slightest failure in enuciation, not only in his dramatic criticism, but, as we know, in the performance of his own plays and libretti. In *Barnaby Rudge* (24 November 1866), a collaboration between Phillips and Vining at the Princess's, A PARTY WITH FIGS IN HIS MOUTH appears in the first act to say, 'Chow chow. Popchip chock chow chobbles', to which a Stranger answers, 'Terroo. The young a-man says a-well.' The Party with Figs remarks, 'Cockchop chow Cogglechipchow.' Later he adds, 'Catchow cockchaw chop bow wow chick.' All this is accepted by the other characters as clear utterance. A character in the anonymous *Helen Douglas* runs all his words together as in 'Thencomeandstaywithusaslongasyoulike' and 'Howcanheprosecutehisplans *(gulp)* unlessIaskhimin?' 'My incoherent own!' cries Helen as he guggles at her (*Fun*, 30 July 1870). This five act tragedy was performed at the Haymarket in the summer of 1870 when Buckstone's season was over and the theatre was let to 'scratch' companies. 'Ourselves' described it as 'Perhaps the silliest piece since the palmy days of the drama.' *The Times* (21 July 1870) found it mild and harmless, 'a respectable specimen of the sort of melodrama that was considered interesting when George III was King'.

Lady Isabel in John Oxenford's version of Mrs Henry Wood's enormously popular novel *East Lynne* at the Surrey Theatre (5 February 1866) was played not by a 'scratch actress', but by Avonia Jones. She was generally unintelligible in Gilbert's review (*Fun*, 17 February 1866); nor was he alone in complaining about her voice:

EAST LYNNE

ACT I.–*Drawing-room in East Lynne.*

Enter LADY ISABEL CARLYLE.

LADY I.–Though I am the wife of a mere country mumble, yet I am the daughter of an Earl. Mumble, mumble, mumble. My husband is wealthy and mumble, and I love him mumbly; but I am jealous of him. I fear he loves Barbara Hare. Mumble.

Enter MR. CARLYLE.

MR. C.–My Isabel   *[They fondle.*

LADY I.–You love Barbara.

MR. C.–Oh dear no.

LADY I.–Then I will sing you a song.

MR C.–No, please don't.

LADY I.–Yes, but I insist.

SONG.–LADY ISABEL.

"Oh, my name is Isabella, with a gingham umberella,
And my father keeps a barber's shop in Islington."

MR. C. *(Aside).*–That's over!

LADY I.–Shall I mumble it once more?

MR. C.–Thank you, not any more.

LADY I.–Then I go. Mumble, mumble.   *[Exit* LADY ISABEL.

Enter BARBARA HARE.

BARB. H.–Mr. Carlyle, meet me, for some unexplained reason, in yonder forest at midnight.

MR. C.–I will.   *[Exit* BARBARA.

Enter LADY ISABEL.

LADY I.–Archibald Carlyle, whither away? Where are you mumbling to?

MR. C.–I cannot tell. It is a business secret.

Exit, to meet BARBARA, *for some unexplained reason, in yonder forest at midnight.*

LADY I. *(explaining to audience).*–It is nothing. He usually mumbles his clients for some unexplained mumble in yonder mumble at midnight. Mumble.

Enter CAPTAIN LEVISON.

CAPT. L.–Lady Isabel, fly with me!

LADY I.–No. 'Twere wrong. More than that, 'twere mumble.

CAPT. L.–Nay. Your husband is keeping an appointment with Barbara Hare, for some unexplained cause in yonder forest at midnight.

LADY I.–Ha! But I will not believe it. He uses yonder forest as his professional consulting room.

CAPT. L.–But see; here is a sixpenny telescope of extraordinary powers. It is achromatic, with two eye-pieces, portable metal tripod with jointed claw feet, will distinguish Venus's belts and Saturn's moons, the features of a person at fifty miles, and the time by a church clock in the next hemisphere.

LADY I. *(looking through telescope).*–Ha! It is too true! Then I will fly with you! But first let me write a letter to my husband. *(Writes.)* 'I am running away with Captain Levison. *He* does not meet his mumbles, for unexplained mumbles, in yonder mumble at mumble.'

[Exeunt LADY ISABEL *and* CAPTAIN LEVISON.

ENTER MR. CARLYLE *and* ATTACHED DEPENDANT.

MR. C.–Ha! a paper! From Isabel.

ATT. DEP.–Has she written to say that she is dead?*

MR. C.–No. But she has written to say that she has fled! I will not run after her, for I might catch her as she has only been gone a few minutes, and that would spoil the plot. I will simply tear my hair.   *[Simply tears his hair.*

TABLEAU.

ACT II.–*Isabel's abode in Grenoble.*

ISABEL *discovered in white dressing-gown.*

LADY I.–Mumble, mumble, mumble! Why does not Captain Mumble return?

---

*Fact. [WSG]

Enter CAPTAIN LEVISON.

CAPT. L.–Ha! My Isabel!

LADY I.–*(scornfully)*.–Mumbler! I am the daughter of an Earl.

CAPT. L.–Nay; my Isabel is harsh!

LADY I.–Mumble, mumble!

CAPT. L.–Nay, say not so!

LADY I.–Mumble, mumble, mumble. The daughter of an Earl is no mumbler!

CAPT. L.–What? Leave you for ever?

LADY I.–Mumble.

CAPT. L.–Then we are enemies!

LADY I.–Mumble. The daughter of an Earl—

CAPT. L.–'Tis well. I go.

[Puts on two great coats, some comforters, goloshes, your papa's friend, a flannel waistcoat, a hot-water bottle, and a respirator. Then exit.

LADY I.–He is gone!

Enter EARL MOUNT SEVERN, *her Huncle.*

EARL M. S.–Oi am yer huncle. Whoi have yer thus disghrached yer family?

LADY I.–Are ye come to tarnt me? Remember I am the daughter of an Earl!

EARL M. S.–Nay. Oi am coom to give ye a cheque for fower hondred a year! *[Gives her a cheque for fower hondred a year.*

LADY I.–'Tis well.   *[Exit* EARL MOUNT SEVERN.

ACT III. SCENE 1.–*Drawing-room in East Lynne.*

MR. C.–My late wife was killed in a railway accident. So I have married Barbara Hare.

Enter BARBARA HARE.

BARB. H.–And *I* have married Archibald Carlyle! Shall I sing you a song?

MR. C.–Nay–

BARB. H.–But I will–

MR. C.–No, don't. Where is the new governess, Madame Vine?

175

BARB. H.–She will be here anon. *(Sings.)*
"Her name is Isabella, with a gingham umberella,
And her father keeps a barber's shop in Islington."

Enter LADY ISABEL *disguised as a governess and looking like a compromise between the late Mrs. Elizabeth Fry and a Pantaloon.*
BARB. H.–Madame Vine, be seated.
LADY I.–Nay, for am I not a widow?
BARB. H.–True, I had forgot.

Enter Lady Isabel's child, WILLIAM.
LADY I.–Ha! *(clutches at the child.)* Ha! ha! Mumble! It is my own Mumble!
BARB. H. *(aside).*–What a singular governess!
LADY I.–Pardon me, but I am a widow!   *[Goes into a fit.*
BARB. H.–True, I had forgot. That accounts for everything.
MR. C.–I am going to stand for Lynne at the next election.

Enter MR. JUSTICE HARE.
MR. JUSTICE H.–Yes, and so is Captain Levison. *[Tableau.*

SCENE 2.–*William's bedroom.* WILLIAM *discovered in bed, dying, and* ISABEL *watching him.*

LADY I.–My mumble!
WILLIAM.–I have no recollection of my real mother.
LADY I.–Ha! my own boy!   *[Clutches at the dying child.*
WILLIAM.–Oh, Miss Jones, don't–you hurt me!
LADY I.–Nay, it is in the part.
WILLIAM.–Oh that I could see my own mother! I have no recollection of her, and she is dead, but still I should like to see her.
LADY I.–You would? Ha! ha! Behold!
                    [Pulls off her wig and spectacles.
WILLIAM.–Ha!   *[Dies in great agony.*

Enter ATTACHED DOMESTIC.
ATT. DOM.–You ought to be ashamed of yourself, to frighten a dying child with your stage-play tricks. The fright has killed him, and you deserve to be tried for manslaughter.*

---

*This is what the ATTACHED DOMESTIC *ought* to have said. [WSG]

ACT IV.–*Lady Isabel's bedroom.* LADY ISABEL *and* ATTACHED DOMESTIC *discovered.*

LADY I.–I am dying.

ATT. DOM.–Nay, say not so.

LADY I.–Send for my Mumble.

ATT. DOM.–I will. But he will be surprised to find that the new governess is only his old wife in disguise.

[*Exit* ATTACHED DOMESTIC.

LADY I.–Oh, I am mumbling, I am mumbling!

Enter MR. CARLYLE.

MR. C.–Madame Vine!

LADY I.–I am Isabel!

MR. C.–Isabel? But you are dead.

LADY I.–No, indeed!

MR. C.–But I say yes.

LADY I.–No. The rumour was unfounded.

MR. C.–Oh!

CURTAIN.–This is getting awkward. The family arrangements are becoming so extremely complicated, that I think I had better come down.

CURTAIN FALLS.

Dance by all the characters, blue fire, green fire, red fire, plaid fire, grand transformation scene, and rhymed tags, all unavoidably omitted.

11 Gilbert Satirises Gilbert

Three of Gilbert's parodistic reviews have closer personal associations with him than *The Yellow Passport* or *Formosa* which were the usual grist to his satiric mill. These three are Tom Taylor's *Mary Warner; or, Tried in the Fire*, which opened at the Haymarket on 21 June 1869 and proved to be a great success; Gilbert's own comedy-drama, *An Old Score*, at the Gaiety, which he reviewed on 7 August 1869, and his *Randall's Thumb*, reviewed on 11 February 1871.

For *Mary Warner*, in which Miss Bateman played the highly emotional heroine, Taylor had made the mistake of adapting a novel, *Margaret Meadows: A Tale for the Pharisees*, by William Gilbert, W. S. Gilbert's father. According to the *Athenaeum* (26 June 1869), Taylor had even borrowed some of the novel's dialogue, while the *Era*, *The Times*, the *Sunday Times* and other periodicals also noticed points of resemblance, although Taylor had changed the self-sacrificing mother in Gilbert's plot to a wife. Despite Taylor's variety of assertions that Dr. Gilbert's name had been omitted because of a misunderstanding, that he had earlier read the novel but did not re-read when writing the play, and that Dr. Gilbert himself had suggested the subject to him, the question of unacknowledged adaptation proceeded to arbitration, which awarded the novelist £200 and the right to have his name appear with Taylor's, a right he chose not to exercise. His son's review, perhaps designedly, appeared in *Fun* on 10 July, the last day of the Haymarket's season. As a review it is short and seems perfunctory; five of the twelve scenes are dismissed with variations of '*This scene has nothing to do with the plot.*' Gilbert also pointed out, but did not enlarge upon, Taylor's indebtedness.

MARY WARNER

ACT I. SCENE 1.–*Office and Works of* DUTTON AND DOWNES, *Mechanical Engineers. Enter* MR. DUTTON.

MR. D.–I am not only an engineer, but a mechanical engineer, which is curious.

Enter BOB LEVITT.

BOB L.–Here is a piece of mechanical engineering which I have just finished.

MR. D.–It is not good from a mechanical engineering point of view, so consider yourself dismissed.   *[Exit* LEVITT.

Enter GEORGE WARNER.

GEO. W.–Sir, you have benefited largely by my inventions, which you have appropriated. Give me, therefore, a round sum to enable me to emigrate.

MR. D.–Never!   *[Exeunt, angry, and in opposite directions.*

Enter BOB LEVITT.

BOB L.–Now to bone the cash-box, which is always kept in an open drawer.   *[Bones it, and exit.*

Enter MR. DUTTON *and* POLICEMAN.

MR. D.–Ha! the cash-box is gone!

POLICEMAN.–Then Warner must have taken it!

SCENE 2.–*Front Scene, between* BOB LEVITT *and* MILLY RIGG, *his sweetheart. It has nothing to do with the story.*

SCENE 3.–GEORGE WARNER'S *Lodging.*

Enter BOB LEVITT, *meeting* MARY WARNER.

BOB L.–My Mary!

MARY W.–Bob!   *[They embrace–yes, they du!*

Enter MR. DUTTON *and* POLICEMAN.

MR. D.–Warner, you have stolen my cash-box.

GEO. W.–Nay, good sir–you err.

MARY W.–My Bob a thief! Never!

MR. D.–It is, alas, too true!

MARY W.–Not so. I did it myself! I did, indeed! *(Aside)* Thus–thus will I save him!

GEO. W.–You, Mary! That was wrong.

MARY W.–Perhaps!

ALL.–Astonishing!   *[They seize her.*

ACT II. SCENE 1.–MILLY RIGG'S *Room. (This scene is immaterial to the story.)*

SCENE 2.–*Visiting Cell, Brixton Prison. (This scene has nothing to do with the plot.)*

ACT III. SCENE 1.–*Garret in Plumtree-court.*

MARY WARNER.–Five years penal servitude, and for my husband's crime!

Enter POLICEMAN

POLICEMAN.–Mary, you've been at it again. A gentleman has lost money, and you are suspected of having stolen it.

MARY W.–Good sir, you are mistaken–I have not left the house this night!

POLICEMAN.–Then leave it now. Come, my Mary, we want thee.   *[Exeunt* MARY, *in custody.*

SCENE 2.–*Magistrate's Room.*
(This scene does not bear in any way on the story.)

SCENE 3.–*Police Court in Westminster.* MARY WARNER *in dock,* GEORGE WARNER *on Bench. He is sworn.*

GEO. W.–That woman stole my property!

MAGISTRATE.–Heavens, how awful! Committed!
                              *[*MARY WARNER *shows her face.*

GEO. W. *(aside).*–Ha! that face! *(Aloud)* On second thoughts she did not steal my property.

MAGISTRATE.–Heavens, how satisfactory! Discharged!

ACT IV. SCENE 1.–*Plumtree-court, Westminster. (This scene does not matter.)*

SCENE 2.–*Garret in Plumtree-court.* BOB LEVITT *and* MILLY RIGG *discovered.*

BOB L.–Milly, Mary Warner never stole the cash-box. *I* took it!

MILLY R. *(with decision).*–Gracious!

SCENE 3.–*Passage in* GEORGE WARNER'S *House.*
(This scene is irrelevant).

SCENE 4.–*Drawing-room in the same. Enter* MARY WARNER.

MARY W.–I have come here to get work.

Enter GEORGE WARNER.

GEO. W.–Mary!

MARY W.–George!

GEO. W.–You are a thief, naughty Mary!

MARY W.–Oh, George, how can *you* say that?

Enter BOB LEVITT *and* MILLY RIGG.

BOB L.–Hold! *I* stole the cash-box!

ALL.–You did?

BOB L.–I did!

GEO. W.–Then Mary is innocent?

ALL.–She is!

GEO. W.–Rapture! *[They embrace.*

CURTAIN.

OURSELVES.–This "new and original" piece turns out to be an adaptation of MR. W. GILBERT'S novel, *Margaret Meadows: A Tale for the Pharisees*. In construction it is loose and slovenly, and the dialogue is not remarkable. It may be suggested that Bob Levitt's favourite observation, that he will tell "the truth, the whole truth, and nothing but the truth, so help him Bob", is just such an irreverence as the LORD CHAMBERLAIN is specially employed to prevent. MISS BATEMAN shows some power as the devoted Mary Warner, but her hard, inflexible voice, and monotonous utterance, are serious drawbacks to her complete success. MISS HILL played Milly Rigg very charmingly indeed, and received a bouquet for her pains–which bouquet was most rudely snatched from her hands by MR. HOWE and handed to MISS BATEMAN. MR. KENDAl and MR. HOWE played Bob Levitt and George Warner very satisfactorily. The piece was well-received.

(In Act I, scene 3, Gilbert–or the printer–seems to have confused Bob Levitt and George Warner; there is no reference to Bob's being present or accused. Mary, however, has rejected him before the play begins. Gilbert omits Mary's child, who has a touching scene with her unrecognised mother.)

Revived in 1870, 1877, 1878, 1881, and later, *Mary Warner* proved to be one of the most successful vehicles in Miss Bateman's career, popular both in England and the United States and second only to *Leah*. The *Graphic* (28 May 1870), however, reviewing the earliest of these performances, endorsed Gilbert's strictures. Its critic found her 'wanting in light and shade' and the plot 'a long monotonous tale of misery'.

Gilbert's reviews of his own plays are longer, a full page each, and are more fleshed out; but neither is remarkable in any sense. *An Old Score* was his first comedy-drama to reach the stage. Critics treated it seriously and were impressed with the dialogue, which they found sometimes brilliant. They pointed out, however, that this was Gilbert's *first* comedy—a promising beginning, but he would do better in works to come. At least it was not taken from the French. But, as the *Sunday Times* (1 August 1869) said, all the male characters were in some respect unpleasant with overtones of the cad. At first well-received, *An Old Score* had a short run, and the first-night audience unfortunately laughed at the heroine's sudden shift in affection.

In parodying his own play, Gilbert depended on fewer comic devices than usual. He stripped down dialogue—Casby's last speech is simply a short version of his 'great speech' in the original. He reduced motivation, expanded and contracted sums of money, but there are only two really satiric passages in the parody: Harold's announcement in Act II that money is the prime motivation of all the characters in the play and his farewell to Mary at the conclusion of the same act.

But how does one parody comedy-drama, itself full of satiric thrusts such as Harold's description of how to review a play for the kind of journal he now edits:

> Everything has its ridiculous side— except Shakespeare. And no one alive is equal to anyone who's dead. Those are the two golden maxims of satirical criticism.
>
> . . . . .
>
> I am the editor of a satirical journal, and a new piece is played. Very good. Remember it is a satirical journal and its power of satire must be allowed full play. If the company is good I abuse the piece; if the piece is good I abuse the company. I've no alternative.

MARY. But if both are good?

HAROLD. The supposition's absurd–but if both are good I pitch into the degenerate audience. There I'm safe. From the satirist's point of view, the audience is always degenerate.[38]

There were no sensation scenes; no Adelphi guests; no interruptive music to make fun of, but Gilbert did what he could and even praised Sam Emery and Rosina Ranoe, both of whom were considered miscast by several other reviewers.

AN OLD SCORE

ACT I.–*Interior of* COLONEL CALTHORPE'S *Villa, at Teddington.* HAROLD CALTHORPE *and* ETHEL BARRINGTON, *his cousin, discovered.*

ETHEL.–Harold, once you loved me.

HAROLD.–Once.

ETHEL.–But now you don't. Oh, cruel.

HAROLD.–But you are engaged to James Casby.

ETHEL.–What a ridiculous objection! You know that my engagements mean nothing. I am always hopping about from lover to lover. Besides, I don't love James Casby; I only want to marry him for his money.

HAROLD.–He is a snob.

ETHEL *(hurt).*–That may be, dear Harold, but it isn't pretty to say so. Forgive me, dearest. I did not mean to wound you by the bitterness of my reproaches.

HAROLD.–Ethel, he is a snob, because having been taken from the streets, thirty years ago, by my father, and placed by him in the way of making the gigantic income that seems always to fall to the lot of people who begin with nothing, he declines to assist my father by advancing him the few millions he requires to place himself straight with his creditors.

[Exit Harold.

Enter CASBY.

CASBY.–Ethel, you are making a great sacrifice in marrying me.

ETHEL.–I am.

CASBY.–I am plain–awkward–matter-of-fact–

ETHEL.–You are–oh, you are.

CASBY.–I am not brilliant.

ETHEL.–You are not.

CASBY.–My birth is contemptible.

ETHEL.–It is.

CASBY.–I am not worthy of you, Ethel.

ETHEL.–You are not–oh, you are not!

CASBY.–My darling Ethel, we agree on every point.

[Exit ETHEL.

Enter COL. CALTHORPE *and* PARKLE, *an attorney.*

COL. C.–James Casby, I owe Parkle two thousand pounds. Lend me that sum.

CASBY.–Never!

COL. C.–Remember, I made you! All you have you owe to me.

CASBY.–Still I repeat–never! I will pay you all I owe you, but not in money. *[Exit* CASBY.

PARKLE.–Well, Calthorpe, I shall go and sell you up.

[Exit PARKLE.

Enter HAROLD CALTHORPE.

HAROLD.–Papa, I want money.

COL. C.–Nonsense; you had sixpence last year. Sixpence, judiciously expended, should provide all the little luxuries a young man of your age stands in need of.

[Exit COL. C. *buttoning his trousers' pocket.*

HAROLD.–And Manasseh, a highly flavoured Jew, requires fifty pounds of me immediately! Ah, me!

Enter MARY WATERS, *a nursery governess.*

MARY W.–Harold! *(Rushes to his arms.)*

HAROLD.–Mary! My own! Now to prosecute our secret intrigue. There is a verandah opening out into the lawn–and several doors to this room–there are half a dozen people in the house who are always popping in and out of this apartment; but, nevertheless, you shall sit at my feet, lay your head upon my bosom, and confide to me all your little sorrows in the most affectionate attitude you can conveniently assume! *[She does so. They get very affectionate.*

MARY.–Yes, dear.

MARY *(in her innocence)*.–Does your papa wear a cocked hat?

HAROLD *(with proper pride)*.–He does, Mary!

MARY.–Oh, how I should like to wear a cocked hat.

[Sobs on his bosom.

Enter ETHEL.

ETHEL.–Harold! Miss Waters! This is wrong.

HAROLD *(with quiet decision)*.–Now, look here, Ethel. It's no use your coming here to bully-rag me. Get out!

Enter COL. CALTHORPE *and* MANASSEH, *a bill discounter.*

COL. C.–You scoundrel, you owe Manasseh thousands!

HAROLD.–Too true.

Enter CASBY.

ETHEL.–Oh, Mr. Casby, pay this debt for Harold, and I will try and respect you, although I can never love you!

CASBY.–No; I owe Colonel Calthorpe a heavy debt, but I shan't pay it in money.

COL. .–Lost! lost! lost!

HAROLD.–By way of making matters pleasanter, I don't think I could select a more judicious moment, papa, in which to inform you that I intend to marry MARY WATERS, your nursery governess.

MARY *(in her simplicity)*.–And then I shall wear a cocked hat!

COL. C.–Leave my house, sir, and take that hussy with you. You are no son of mine. *[Dance and off.*

ACT II.–HAROLD CALTHORPE'S *Chambers in Gray's Inn.*
HAROLD *discovered, editing a scurrilous paper.*

HAROLD.–Alone in London with Mary and not a penny to bless ourselves with, I started a scurrilous paper which brings me in a thousand a year.

Enter MARY.

MARY.–My Harold! We are not yet married, but we are awfully proper, nevertheless, and my being in your chambers must not be misconstrued. You have been very ill, and I have been nursing you. Here are eggs and sausages (although it is

July). Eat them and be happy.   *[Exit* MARY.

Enter ETHEL *and* CASBY.

HAROLD.–Ethel, what does this mean?

ETHEL.–Come back to us and James Casby will pay all your debts! I have bullied him into this concession.

CASBY *(weakly)*.–Yes; I have consented to do that.

HAROLD.–Indeed! Then I will return with pleasure. I will do anything for money. Indeed, every one in the piece (as far as I can judge) would do anything for money. Come to the home of my ancestors.

Enter MARY.

ETHEL.–Oh, I quite forgot this young woman. Adieu, and for ever.

(They are about to leave HAROLD *to his fate when enter* COL. CALTHORPE.*)*

COL. C.–Stop! I have come into a peerage and Harold must return.   I   am   now   Lord   Ovington!

HAROLD.–Oh, indeed, certainly. Good bye, Mary. You have been very useful to me–it will always be a satisfaction to you to remember that.

MARY.–Ah, me! *(Faints.)*

TABLEAU.

ACT III.–*Ovington Grange. Enter* COL CALTHORPE *(now Lord* OVINGTON*) and* CASBY.

LORD O.–Mr. Casby, Ethel don't love you. She absolutely dislikes you.

CASBY.–Impossible!

LORD O.–Ah, you don't know her–she don't care for you–and I think you had better break off the match.

[Exit LORD O.

Enter ETHEL.

CASBY.–Ethel, let us cry off.

ETHEL.–Certainly, with pleasure.   *[Exit* CASBY.

ETHEL.–That's all right. Now to flop my affections on Harold once more.

Enter MARY WATERS.

MARY *(wildly).*–Give me my Harold!

ETHEL.–*Your* Harold?

MARY.–Yes, he loves me! I came here to see him and am told that he has just left.

ETHEL.–Harold gone! Oh, send for Mr. Casby, somebody, that I may square it up with him again! *(Weeps.)*

MARY.–Forgive me, I cannot bear to see you weep.

[They embrace.

Enter HAROLD.

ETHEL.–Harold, take her and be happy.

HAROLD *(rather taken aback).*–Oh, oh, yes–of course, if you wish it. *(Takes her and is happy.)*　　　　　*[Exit* ETHEL.

Enter CASBY, *meeting* LORD OVINGTON.

CASBY.–Lord Ovington, I am going to pay my debt to you. You took me from the streets thirty years ago, from interested motives, and you spent ten pounds upon me. I am now worth millions, and I owe my prosperity to you. *Per contra* you have forged my name for several thousand pounds. Please suppose that I have prosecuted you for this felony, and that you are now a convict. *(Burning forged bills in candle.)* I take you from prison and I restore you to your position in society. I take you from a lower depth than I ever descended to, and I place you on a much higher social pedestal than I can ever hope to reach, and we are quits.

Enter ETHEL.

ETHEL.–Stay, I have heard all. I can't resist this proof of your magnanimity. A man who can chuck away thousands in this manner *must* make a good husband. Besides, Harold has determined to marry Mary Waters, so there is now no obstacle to our union. Take me away and marry me as soon as you like. *(Slyly.)* You had better make haste, for Parkle and Manasseh are both bachelors, and I might change my mind.

[Tableau.

CURTAIN.

OURSELVES.–The piece, which has many serious drawbacks, particularly in the construction of the first and third acts, is, at all events, admirably played. The character of Mary Waters is impossibly ingenuous, and, except that he is a gentleman, James Casby bears too strong a resemblance to that arch-cad John Mildmay. MR. NEVILLE plays James Casby with self-contained power, particularly in the last act. MR. EMERY, as the humbugging Colonel, and MR. CLAYTON, as his dissipated son, shared, deservedly, MR. NEVILLE'S honours. MISS HENRADE did ample justice to a most ungrateful part, and MISS ROSINA RANOE gave promise of future excellence in her representation of the ridiculously innocent Mary Waters.

The *Tomahawk*, believing itself to be Harold's fictitious paper, the *Tormentor*, published a rather brutal 'novelised' version of Gilbert's 'straight' play. It includes a soliloquy by Harold:

> My old friend, Mr. W. S. Gilbert, is having a row with me. I am awfully sorry. He declares that I sell my friends at a guinea a piece. Too bad. I know it's a crime in the literary world for a young man to succeed, but then it's really too bad! It's just what that literary hack, Type Bourgeois, observed when I wouldn't let *him* write for my paper. It's what they all say when I won't employ them. But then Bourgeois and some of the rest don't contribute to a rival and more satirical paper (price one penny) as Mr. W. S. Gilbert does, and that may make all the difference. I wish he was good enough for us. His 'Bab Ballads' in *Fun* were not bad; I mean some of them. The *Spectator* said they were coarse; well, *I* like coarseness. However, my friend W. S. G. has been too severe; he shall see that he has wronged me. *If I ever write a comedy I will never be such AN UNUTTERABLE CAD as to put a man I have regarded from childhood as my friend, and with whom I have never had a quarrel, into it for all the town to stare at.* NO, NO–THAT WOULD BE TOO COWARDLY AND BLACKGUARD! Yes, W. S. G., you shall see that you have wronged me–wronged me deeply!

This 'novel' was entitled 'THE TORMENTOR UNMASKED! or, HOW TO PAY OFF AN OLD SCORE! A SUCCESS (?) IN THREE ACTS' and appeared on 7 August 1869. The author was the editor, Arthur William à Beckett, whose father, 'à Beckett of *Punch*', had been a friend of Dr. Gilbert. Two weeks later, the *Tomahawk* published an apology,

Gilbert having assured it that he did not intend the *Tormentor* to resemble the *Tomahawk* in any way. One wonders.

Gilbert's second self-review dealt with *Randall's Thumb*, which opened the new Court Theatre on 25 January 1871 and ran for 100 performances. It offered more scope for parody, although, as before, he objected to the construction and praised the cast–as well he might since it included his favourite actor, Hermann Vezin. Turning the romantic dialogue into rhyme was amusing enough and justified by the verses which ended the play itself. Once more Gilbert made use of self-conscious failures of clarity. Since his review was not published in *Fun* until 11 February, he did not include the ending altered after the first night in which Buckthorpe turns out to be a hitherto unknown son of the comic couple. He did, however, let 'Ourselves' remark that 'the end of the last act is almost farcical'.

RANDALL'S THUMB

ACT I–SCENE: *Exterior of a Seaside Hotel. Enter* RANDALL, *followed by* BUCKTHORPE.

RANDALL.–Here we are at Beachington.

BUCKTHORPE.–Now that you have got me here, what do you want with me?

RANDALL.–I want you to make love to a young woman here, in order to ascertain something which is not remarkably clear, about somebody whose identity is not definitely made out, but who left some money to a person to whom I will not particularly refer, but which money I (for reasons that I need not enter into) am entitled to.

BUCK.–And if I refuse.

RANDALL.–I give you into custody on a charge of murdering somebody (never mind who) although you only killed him in self-defence.

BUCK. *(apologetically to audience).*–I am under his thumb. *(Aloud)* Good. I consent. *[Exit* RANDALL.

BUCK.–It is one of the disadvantages of being under a man's thumb that you must always do what he wants you to do. If you don't he's annoyed, and then where are you? *(Enter*

EDITH TEMPLE.) Edith!

EDITH.–Mr. Buckthorpe! This is a strange meeting!

BUCK.–Once I loved you, loved you blindly. But your papa behaved unkindly. And gave poor Reginald his *congé*. One evening in the *salle-à-manger*.

(There is no earthly reason why young lovers should talk poetry to each other and Cockney rhymes in French don't count.)

EDITH.–Because he found you had been tricking. And up your heels you had been kicking. You often stopped out late at night, sir. 'Twas broken off and serve you right, sir.

BUCK.–But I've repented of it sore, and I won't do it any more. To pardon me I pray you deign And let the match be on again!

Enter RANDALL.

RANDALL.–Very good.

BUCK *(taken aback)*.–You should have hummed something as you came in. But what do you mean by very good?

RANDALL.–This is the young woman whose money you are to get for me!

Enter BANGLES *(an old Indian surgeon, marvellously made up and admirably played by* MR. RIGHTON*) and* MISS SPINN *(an elderly maiden equally well made up and equally well played by* MISS MAGGIE BRENNAN.*)*

MISS SPINN.–I'm getting up a picnic to the Clump Rocks this day week. *(To* RANDALL*)*. Will you go?

RANDALL.–I will–so will Buckthorpe.

BUCK.–No; I must leave for town to-day.

EDITH *(Aside to* BUCK*)*.–Oh, Mr. Buckthorpe, please to stay!

RANDALL.–If you go I'll inform against you for that murder which you didn't commit.

BUCK. *(Aside, with some irritation)*.–I am so under his thumb!

RANDALL.–Ladies and gentlemen, Mr. Buckthorpe will join your party.

(General delight of everybody at this concession on the part of a total stranger, who is the companion of a most manifest and seedy swindler.)

ACT II.–SCENE: *The Clump Rocks–by the sea. Everybody discovered picnic-ing, the luncheon being spread on two picturesque, but evidently damp and sea-weedy rocks. A general smell of anemones pervades this delightful spot, and as the ground is covered with small sharp rocks, and all the party wear their shoes, the joy is general. As the luncheon takes place about half an hour before sunset in August–that is to say, about eight o'clock p.m.–it may be presumed that the party were some time making up their minds to settle on this delightful spot.*

SOMEBODY.–As luncheon is finished, and as this agreeable retreat is swamped by the tide twice a day, and as the tide will be at its highest in half an hour, perhaps we'd better go.

SOMEBODY ELSE.–It won't be too damp for me–I like it squashy! *[But they all go.*

Enter EDITH *and* BUCKTHORPE *(who have been overlooked rather unkindly, by the rest of the party.* RANDALL *listens.*

BUCK.–They've finished, and we're just too late. Oh, Edith, Edith, you would wait!

        If we could find a glass and plate,
        We'd lunch alone en tête-à-tête.

EDITH.–And will you always love me, dear?

BUCK.–While this heart beats with life, I swear!

EDITH.–But why do you with Randall chum?

BUCK.–Because I'm under Randall's thumb!

EDITH.–But how?

BUCK.–   Why, once upon a time
        I killed a man–it was no crime!
        I killed him but in self-defence–
        Of that I have no evidence.
        He knows it, and he says that he
        Will give me up to justice–me!
        If I refuse with him to chum.

BOTH.– Ah, me!
       Ah, thee! The weight of Randall's thumb!

[Exit EDITH, *weeping bitterly.*

Enter RANDALL.

RANDALL.–You've blown upon me!

BUCK.–I have. *(He is not going to talk poetry to* RANDALL.*)*

RANDALL.–I will give you one more chance. Get me the information I require by this evening and you are spared–refuse, and I give you up to justice.   *[Exit.*

Enter EDITH.

EDITH *and* BUCKTHORPE *sit on the dampest and most sea-weedy of the two spiky rocks. What are new dresses to her, or lavender trousers to him? The tide rises, phenomenally, through three cracks in the ground. It creaks–but they don't care!*

BUCK.–This is true happiness, my love, I vow–
I fear no kind of danger, Edith, now!

Enter RANDALL *in a boat.*

RANDALL.–I've come to fetch you off!

BUCK.–We are quite safe–it's quite calm.

RANDALL *(with awful intensity)*.–But there's a storm brewing for you. If you want to escape it you must do as I tell you.

Tableau; BUCKTHORPE *doing as* RANDALL *tells him.*

ACT III.–SCENE: *Same as Act I.* BANGLES *discovered.*

Enter EDITH.

EDITH.–I'm going to be married to Mr. Buckthorpe!
     [Exit EDITH, *all smiles and blushes and confusion.*

Enter BUCKTHORPE.

BANGLES.–Sir, I congratulate you.

BUCKTHORPE.–Stop–it is only right that you should know that I am an adventurer. I am accused of a murder by Randall, who is a forger–but I am innocent.

BANGLES *(with military decision)*.–Don't expostulate. I have always made up my mind that, come what might, Edith should *not* murder a marriner–I should say marry a murderer.

BUCK.–But I am no murderer.

BANGLES.–I will satisfy myself on that point. Leave it to me. Go away.   *[Exit* BUCKTHORPE.

Enter RANDALL.

BANGLES.–You charge Buckthorpe with murder.

RANDALL.–I do.

BANGLES.–Then give him into custody, or I'll give *you* into custody as an accessory after the fact.

RANDALL.–Confusion!

BANGLES.–Write a note to the Superintendent of Police, saying that a notorious criminal is stopping here. *(*RANDALL *does so.)* Now you can go.   *[Exit* RANDALL.

Enter BUCKTHORPE *and everybody else.*

BUCKTHORPE *(musing).*–This was committed on the 14th of August, 1868.

BANGLES.–Eh?

BUCK *(in a general way).*–I killed this person–his name was Peters, and he was a bagman–on the 14th of August, 1868.

BANGLES.–You pitched him over Banton Cliff.

BUCK.–Yes.

BANGLES.–Having run him through the neck?

BUCK.–Yes.

BANGLES.–Just *here. (Showing his neck.)*

BUCK.–Yes–yes.

BANGLES.–And hang it sir, do you mean to say I'm dead?

BUCK.–*You?* It was Peters.

BANGLES.–Peters be hanged. It was I!

BUCK.–Joy!

RANDALL.–Confusion!

Enter POLICE.

POLICE.–John Randall–arrest you–charge of forgery.

RANDALL *(with decision).*–I repeat, Confusion! *(They take off his wig and whiskers.)*

BUCK.– With joy I'm almost stricken dumb.

Once more I'm free from Randall's Thumb!

CURTAIN.

OURSELVES.–A very loosely constructed and improbable play–the end of the last act is almost farcical. However, the admirable manner in which it was acted by MR. VEZIN, MR. BELFORD, MR. FRANK MATTHEWS, MISS MAGGIE BRENNAN, MR. RIGHTON, MRS. STEPHENS, and MISS KATE BISHOP appeared to blind the audience to the defects of the play, and indeed almost gave an air of probability to the most farcical incidents. MISS BISHOP is a charming *ingénue*, MR. RIGHTON a most valuable character-actor. MR. VEZIN'S modesty and self-denial in playing a moderate part is an example that should teach many pompous incapables a valuable lesson. MISS BUFTON and MR. ASTLEY gave full effect to two redundant parts. The scenery is extremely picturesque, and the new theatre is the prettiest and most complete in London.

After this Gilbert wrote only a few more parody reviews, not from failing power–after all *Deadman's Point* was among them–but because he was now becoming a busy dramatist. At last, he ceased in late May 1871. It was time to leave *Fun* and reviewing. He had been at his best when dealing with melodramas that were easily suscep-tible of attack. He had found scarcely a play without vulnerable construction, if not of the whole, then of some significant part; in review after review he dismissed unnecessary scenes and found improbable or impossible plots. Dialogue was oftener praised as were casts, although by no means invariably.

While Gilbert might dismiss ranting actors, over-exertive come-dians, and actresses who were artless in every sense of the word, it was clear that his favourites were well-worth his praise. In addition to Vezin, he especially liked E. A. Sothern, Kate Terry, Henry Neville, John Hare, Henry Irving as a villain, and H. J. Byron, who had become an actor as well as a playwright. His favourite acting company was that of Marie Wilton and her husband, Squire Bancroft, at the Prince of Wales's Theatre, and the dramatist he admired most was obviously Tom Robertson, even though Gilbert was not loathe to object when a Robertson play did not measure up to Robertsonian standards.

As a reviewer Gilbert had by no means been uniquely severe. The relatively staid *Athenaeum*, for instance, could be as scornful as he, at times more so, as, for example, 'inadequacy attained its limits' (Miss Fane's performance in *The Courier of Lyons*, 9 July 1870). At the other end of the scale, the *Tomahawk*, 'which scalps us all',[39] used its version of the trial-at-law to make the dramatists, whom the Judge almost invariably found guilty, condemn themselves uninten-tionally out of their own mouths.

But it was Gilbert's wit, his unquenchable sense of the absurdity inherent in the plays themselves, together with his eye (and a strong pair of opera glasses) for literal detail which he could rearrange to produce the laughter that made his criticism so apt and so cutting. His format made it unnecessary for him to tell the plot since he could simply strip it to its essentials and use them—and it is surprising how closely he adhered to the original outlines. By limiting direct comment on the dramatist under consideration to a few sentences, he avoided the *Tomahawk*'s bludgeoning tone while being keener on the real shortcomings of the play. The lapse of time between opening night and the publication of his parodies enabled him to sharpen them, although his reviews for the *Illustrated Times* and others did not give him this leeway, nor did they need to. Perhaps, however, he wrote the parodies immediately after seeing the first performance—we cannot tell. The occasional error which crept in may be the result of either hasty composition or a faint hazing of memory.

12 Post-Burlesques

Occasionally Gilbert still contributed short articles on the theatre to other periodicals, frequently to the *Era Almanack*, where in 'Old Plays and New Plays' (1873) he pointed out that of nearly 4,000 plays produced between 1700 and 1830, 3,950 were then unknown except perhaps by name. Of the remaining fifty, only thirty-five were still produced in the theatre of Gilbert's day, and only eleven of these could be considered classics. Why then do critics emphasize the superior virtues of the past, Gilbert asked. He asked it again in an allied piece, 'A Proposal for Elevating the Position of the Modern Drama' (*Era Almanack*, 1875); this contrasted 'the state of hysterical adulation' in which critics approached any Old Play with their contemptuous tone in treating modern ones.

Quoting from Percy Fitzgerald's *Principles of Comedy and Dramatic Effect* (1870), Gilbert pointed out the 'reckless reverence' with which Fitzgerald quoted and approved passages from past plays (which to the twentieth-century reader are not so funny after all). Gilbert suggested that the critic try to 'work himself up into a state of frothy enthusiasm' for a contemporary dramatist and 'determine beforehand to make the very best of everything–to respectfully attribute all obvious blunders to a knowledge of human nature far deeper than even his (Mr. Fitzgerald's) own' and he will be astonished to find how really excellent a modern dramatist, such as James Albery (for instance), may be. Or let him approach an old play he considers faultless 'in the cold, sneering, captious ready-made frame of mind in which he deals with a modern piece, and he will be annoyed to find how thoroughly farcical and impossible, how vapid, how utterly idiotic' the old comedy may be made to appear.

Three years later, 'An Appeal to the Press' (*Era Almanack and Annual*) explained that critics are too ready on first nights to believe they are seeing 'an accurate embodiment of the author's intention'. This, Gilbert argued, is untenable (especially since by the late 1870s fewer critics were also dramatists).

> . . . before a play is presented to the public the intellectual assistance of thirty or forty people is placed under contribution, and every one of these has it in his power to affect the

result in some appreciable degree. [The people include the manager, the leading player, the low comedian, the scenic artist, the leader of the orchestra, the prompter, the lime-light man, the costumier, the carpenters, the perruquier, the utility man, and the super.] . . . .

In point of fact, the play as it is represented on a first night, *never* represents the author's intention with unimpeachable accuracy. It always falls, more or less, short of it, and sometimes it does so to a degree which must be inconceivable to those who judge a play by its sum-total without taking into consideration the items of which that sum-total is composed . . . . It is quite true that most of these dangers might be avoided by the simple process of adequate rehearsing; but there are not three theatres in London in which pieces are adequately rehearsed . . . .

If a few of the leading dramatic critics would take the trouble to attend the reading of a new piece–if they would then come down to the preliminary rehearsal at which parts are compared–if they would then sit on the stage during the succeeding rehearsals until the piece is produced, their eyes would be opened to many circumstances which are now entirely beyond their ken. They would, perhaps, find that the author's intention is entirely misinterpreted by the representative of the central figure of the piece–they would possibly find that the leading and second lady are not 'on terms,' to the manifest detriment of the scenes in which they are jointly concerned–they would probably find that some unimportant part has to be 'written-up' for some one for whom that part, as it originally stood, was not good enough, and they would certainly find that some important part has to be 'cut down' for some one for whom the part, as it originally stood, was much too good. And here, let it not be supposed that I intend to reflect, directly or indirectly, on the good-will and cheerful co-operation of the body of artists of all classes who are concerned in the production of dramatic pieces. I have the best reason in the world to know that the vast majority of them are actuated by a sincere desire that the piece which they are rehearsing may be successful, and that they spare no trouble or fatigue to bring it to a satisfactory issue. But an artist with a recognised position is entitled to take his own view of the character he is playing, even when it clashes with the author's intention, and it is impossible for critics who are unacquainted with what has taken place at rehearsal to know whether such an actor has availed himself of this privilege or not.

Of course I do not seriously argue that critics should make a point of attending rehearsals, but many of them who are unfamiliar with the process by which a piece is placed upon the stage would do well to attend a rehearsal now and then. This would tend as much to the actor's interests as to those of the author; for if the critic discovered, on the one hand, how frequently an author suffers through the incompetence of an actor, so likewise would he learn, on the other hand, how much more frequently the actor has to bolster up the work of an incompetent author, and how constantly the author is indebted to his exponents for suggestions that largely contribute to such success as his piece may eventually achieve.

Contrary to one of the fallacious legends which have grown up around his name, Gilbert appreciated the work of accomplished performers as his notes and presentation inscriptions show. As to rehearsals, when he came into his own at the Savoy, he rehearsed so diligently that Sullivan complained his singers were tired out by repetition.

Another of Gilbert's frequent objections appeared in 'A Hornpipe in Fetters' (*Era Almanack*, 1879), which attacked the critical assumption that French plays were superior to English plays as a matter of course. Here he argued that English dramatists write tame plays because subject matter the French take for granted is denied them and they must dance in the fetters of the title. For example, an English audience does not like conjugal infidelity, nor can an English dramatist introduce a duel since it is no longer an English custom. Furthermore, many dramatic critics have recently discovered 'that satire and cynicism are misplaced in comedy, and that the propriety of repartee is to be estimated by the standard of conversation in a refined drawing-room'. How lucky for Sheridan that this ukase had not been pronounced at the time when he was writing. Gilbert ended by saying that he had no objections to restrictions against adultery, but that these and the other restrictions described above should be fully considered when critics pronounced English plays dull.

Two of the most interesting of Gilbert's non-*Era* articles are the long 'A Stage Play', which appeared in *Tom Hood's Comic Annual for 1873*, and 'Actors, Authors and Audiences' in the Christmas number of the *Illustrated Sporting and Dramatic News* in 1880. In his introduction to the 1915 reprint of the former, William Archer called it 'a serious exposition in a whimsical key'. Gilbert depicts a playwright, who is more or less himself, called Horace Facile, in the process of writing and staging a play, the 'motive' or theme of which is to be 'the unnecessary and unchristian antagonism existing between the Theatre and the Church . . .'. The representative of each will be a professional harlequin, who has taken holy orders and loves the daughter of the Archbishop of Canterbury, and the Archbishop of Canterbury himself. The latter is a determined enemy of the stage but is also the freeholder of the theatre at which the harlequin is employed and derives from it an income of £4,000 a year–a theme which, Archer pointed out, is essentially that of Shaw's later *Widower's Houses*. Gilbert described his own method of writing separate scenes first (in another article, he said he wrote the ending first) and then connecting them with dialogue.

At rehearsal, each member of the cast has only his own lines and a few cues to work from (which was not Gilbert's method). The author reads the play to the cast. Gilbert read very well although in 'A Stage Play' he insists that all authors read their own works abominably. After three weeks or less of rehearsal, one imperfect scene rehearsal and no dress rehearsal the piece goes before the public and after a fortnight is probably at its best. This, says Facile, is wrong: instead, every member of the cast should have a complete printed (not hand-written) copy of the play to work from and there should be at least thirty rehearsals for a three-act play. In ten of these the scene should be set, and in five the cast should be dressed and made-up as for a performance. This is the French system, and when Gilbert stage-managed the Savoy operas, his reviewers acknowledged that productions on the first night were as smooth as if the piece had been running for weeks.

Using the *Tomahawk*'s format of a trial at law for his second *Illustrated Sporting and Dramatic News* article, Gilbert postulated a comedy called 'Lead', which failed so miserably that its unnamed author is being tried for writing an impossibly dull play. Witnesses called for the prosecution begin with the theatre manager, who produced 'Lead' without reading it, simply because he suddenly and unexpectedly needed something to put on. Members of the audience, also called, included a journeyman plumber, who hissed as soon as he was bored, regardless of the effect on the actors; a Guardsman; a medical student engaged to one of the actresses, who wrongfully hissed when he supposed her character died in act one; a Home Office clerk who did not hiss even though he found some scenes untrue to human nature. When he does hiss indecency or grossly bad taste, he waits till the end of acts in order to avoid disconcerting the cast, but he does not know that imperfect rehearsals have affected the play or that scenes were either omitted or re-written against the author's will. Each of these witnesses says he has written a play himself, but it has not been performed. (In an interview given to the *Daily News* in 1885, Gilbert remarked that he had 'a firm belief that every person who sits in the front rows of the stalls believes that he, she, or it, could write a play, enact a part, and stage-manage the whole affair far better than the author. But they forget that every trade, including that of a playwright, must be learnt.')

The leading lady, the low comedian, and the singing chambermaid then testify severally, each asserting that 'The parts I have played have frequently been hissed. No one has ever hissed me.' The comedian says he did his best for the comedy by introducing much tried and true 'business' such as attempting 'to convert a guinea-pig into a rabbit by rubbing it with Mrs. Allen's Hair Restorer'. The chambermaid, playing a broken-hearted governess, has introduced a song, 'Father's pants will soon fit brother' and danced a 'breakdown'.

Finally the dramatist defends himself: his play was at least original, but was not performed as he had written it. It might be dull, but he had been punished enough by loss of income. The jury finds him guilty but recommends mercy. In short, 'Actors, Authors and Audiences' is a more satiric expansion of 'An Appeal to the Press'.

In March 1911 Gilbert revised 'Actors, Authors and Audiences', retitling it 'Trying a Dramatist', for possible production at the Academy of Dramatic Art, of whose council he was a member. It was, however, not produced. He then intended to include it in his fourth series of *Original Plays*, but died before reading proof; 'Trying a Dramatist' was therefore published in the *Century Magazine* for December 1911 with illustrations by Frederick Gardner. It was later included in *Original Plays*, series four, second edition, fortunately without the illustrations which are too literal for the satire.

Of course Gilbert discussed topics related to drama in the interviews which he gave throughout his writing career. When his collaboration with Sullivan was well under way, however, these were, for the most part, devoted to his methods of composing the libretti and of stage direction. They also often dealt at some length with the attractions of his houses at Harrington Gardens or Grim's Dyke. In a few, however, Gilbert discussed other theatre topics, one of the most important being the treatment of blank verse. *Fun* itself (11 November 1865) had objected to actors mispronouncing words, evidently deliberately, and to speaking Shakespearian lines as if they were 'a lesson in one syllable for little boys', such as 'Ere-to-black-Hec-cate's-summons . . .'. 'SHAKESPEARE should not be sliced up like a sausage,' insisted *Fun* and asked for reform. More than twenty years later, *Speech* (February 1890) commented on 'the lack of knowledge of the art of elocution apparent in many of our young actors . . . . no perfect representation of Shakespeare can be given where a knowledge of the art is wanting'. According to the same journal, 'several of our contemporaries' had drawn attention to this failure in delivering blank verse. The next year *Moonshine* (22 August 1891) doubted that Beerbohm Tree could find 'enough young actors, who can speak blank verse . . . to support him really well' as Hamlet, since 'The art of doing justice to Shakespearian dialogue is as good as lost. The critics would say so oftener than they do, were they not too young to know, or too old to remember.'

In Edinburgh, during October 1897, Gilbert gave an interview, arranged for publicity purposes of his non-musical play *The Fortune Hunter*. The reporter distorted some of Gilbert's comments, but the dramatist made an important critical point after being led into the subject of verse speaking (although *The Fortune Hunter* was a serious prose play). Actors habitually delivered blank verse in a monotone, Gilbert said: they kept to one note through the sentence and finished a semi-tone higher or lower. He considered iambs necessarily mechanical; so to counteract them he used as much variety as the meaning allowed. In short, he advocated a style of speaking blank verse more like that of the twentieth century than of the nineteenth. In fact, Edward Rose, the playwright, recalled Gilbert as beginning in his fairy plays to reform 'the atrocious system of speaking verse which obtained a generation ago . . .'.[40]

Gilbert told Bram Stoker in an interview for the *Daily Chronicle* (2 January 1908) that the tendency of the modern stage was 'Forward! Distinctly forward. In fact, from the very first, from the days of Thespis there has been a continual development of a better class of play. There have, of course, been periods of set-back . . . . but such variations occur in the development of every art'. Gilbert's comments in his diaries about the plays he saw in the early twentieth century were, however, frequently dismissive. *'Pièce banale'* seems to have been his response to many of them.

A longer, more serious discussion of the New Drama took place during an interview Gilbert gave in 1901 to William Archer, an advocate for the playwrights who were prominent in the 1890s. Gilbert, a selective admirer of these works, argued that plays were artificial in the best sense of the word. Even while admitting that there were classical precedents for anti-climax, he did not like the tendency he saw in the current theatre of putting a great effect in the penultimate rather than the final act. He preferred a neat conclusion. When Archer objected that life was rarely likely to have neat conclusions, Gilbert retorted that

> in real life no curtain descends to tell you that the story is at an end. In point of fact, in real life the story never does end.... But in constructing a play I hold that you are not justified in interesting your audiences in the adventures of a group of personages unless you are prepared to furnish those audiences with some information as to what becomes of that group....A good many recent plays, otherwise of great ability, seem to me to come to a helpless, makeshift, essentially feeble end. I cannot think that is sound art. I don't like to see a thing left at a loose end.[41]

Gilbert was even able to say a reminiscent good word about Tom Taylor and about Burnand's effervescent burlesques.

Nevertheless, Archer thought Gilbert took 'a very liberal view of the theatrical situation'. 'I know there has been progress', Gilbert answered rather sadly, 'by a very convincing proof–namely, that I find myself altogether left behind.'

'Whether you admit the dramatic revival or not,' Archer rejoined, 'you were one of the prime movers in it. You restored the literary self-respect of the English stage.'

Notes

1. William Archer, *Real Conversations* (London, 1904), p.245.
2. Tom Robertson was also the Theatrical Lounger for the *Illustrated Times*, and briefly as a holiday substitute for Gilbert so was Clement Scott. A Gilbert letter identifies some of Scott's reviews, but since no marked copies have yet been discovered, my attribution must be based on internal evidence.
3. T. Edgar Pemberton, *The Life and Writings of T. W. Robertson* (London, 1893), p.234.
4. Elizabeth Sewell, *The Field of Nonsense* (London, 1952), p.144.
5. Holograph letter in the Pierpont Morgan Library, New York; quoted by permission of the Royal Theatrical Fund, owner of the subsisting copyright in W. S. Gilbert's unpublished works.
6. Edmund Yates, *Fifty Years of London Life* (New York, 1885), p.203.
7. *Illustrated Sporting and Dramatic News* (28 March 1874), p.101. Tom Taylor was more rigorous when he filled in for Oxenford.
8. Thomas Purnell *Dramatists of the Present Day* (London, 1871), pp.77-79.
9. In November 1867 Emery was again a plaintiff in an action versus Sefton Parry, theatre manager and actor, and was non-suited. See 'An Actor in an Action at Law', *Tomahawk* (23 November 1867), p.297.
10. John Hollingshead in his essay 'Dramatic Critics Criticised' (*Broadway*, I, September 1867, 30-35) listed a number of currently active reviewers and indicated those who also wrote plays. There were fewer, perhaps, than one might expect, but the list was not absolutely accurate and Hollingshead omitted the critics for theatrical papers and comic weeklies, most of whom were playwrights.
11. [William Mackay], *Bohemian Days in Fleet Street by a Journalist* (London, 1913), p.57.
12. Holograph letter in the Theatre Museum, London.
13. John Hollingshead, *My Lifetime* (London, 1895), I, 180.
14. Clement Scott and Cecil Howard, eds., *The Life and Reminiscences of E. L. Blanchard with Notes from the Diary of Wm. Blanchard* (London, 1891), II, 442.

15. Mackay, *Bohemian Days*, p.87.
16. Charles E. Lauterbach, 'Taking Gilbert's Measure', *Huntington Library Quarterly*, XIX (February 1956), 198. See also marked copy of *Randall's Thumb* in the Huntington Library. If Gilbert did receive a salary in his last months with *Fun*, it was probably for his illustrated Babs, as a note to 'Old Paul and Old Tim' suggests.
17. In the absence of the earliest marked copies one cannot be sure if Gilbert contributed more theatre material; for instance,was his first theatrical piece 'A Moor Proper' (16 November 1861), which burlesqued *Othello*?
18. John Mildmay is the leading male character in Tom Taylor's *Still Waters Run Deep*, first performed in 1855 and revived thereafter. Evidently Gilbert disliked him. Two months after he published his continuation of the play, he wrote 'A Pantomime with a Purpose', the title of which was to be 'Harlequin John Mildmay; or, The Demon Galvanism and the Fairy of the Still Waters' (17 March 1866). It is fantastic but not very funny.
19. Edith Browne, *W. S. Gilbert*, 'Stars of the Stage' series (London, 1907), p.17.
20. James Ellis, ed., *The Bab Ballads* (Cambridge, MA, 1970), p.358. John Richardson was perhaps the originator of the portable booth theatre in the early nineteenth century. His show performed in the country and at London fairs, and continued after his death in 1836. Although cut-downs of serious drama might be given, 'Richardsonian' meant blood and thunder melodrama to Gilbert and his contemporaries.
21. Edward S. Lauterbach, '*Fun* and Its Contributors: The Literary History of a Victorian Humor Magazine', unpublished doctoral dissertation (University of Illinois, 1961), p.278.
22. There is a brief history of nineteenth-century burlesque dramas, including references to pre-Victorian treatments in Ted R. Ellis III, 'Burlesque Dramas in the Victorian Comic Magazines', *Victorian Periodicals Review*, XV (Winter 1982), 138-43.
23. William Best and Henry Bellingham were minor and not particularly notable playwrights who frequently collaborated. Gilbert satirized their hackneyed subjects and forced rhymes.
24. A *Fun* cartoon (13 September 1862), p.25, ridicules advertisements of this product.

25. *Solon Shingle*, the play which Gilbert re-titled *Draco Beach*, was a one-act comedy drama first performed in England at the Adelphi Theatre on 3 July 1865. Solon had little to do with the plot, but constantly mourns for his barrel of apple sauce. Owens was praised as an actor, but the play was damned. Evidently his company was an imported summer group.
26. Henry Morley, *The Journal of a London Playgoer from 1851 to 1866* (London, 1891), p.313.
27. Robert Reece, 'Unrehearsed Effects', *Theatre*, II NS (April 1879), 168.
28. Quoted by Percy Fitzgerald, *The Savoy Opera and the Savoyards* (London, 1899), p.14n.
29. 'From Our Stall', *Fun* (2 February 1867), p.215.
30. Robert Louis Brannan, ed., *Under the Management of Mr. Charles Dickens: His Production of 'The Frozen Deep'* (Ithaca, NY, 1966), pp.79-88. Brannan published the text of the 1857 *Frozen Deep* for the first time; Collins's 1866 revision was printed but not published. He eliminated the earlier Nurse Esther and gave Clara second sight instead.
31. Holograph letter dated 2 August 1864 in JWS collection.
32. Mrs. Wood's last exit, carried off in a tub with her legs sticking out, elicited intense hissing. An English-born American actress making her London debut, Mrs. Wood might have done well as a 'Yankee gal', but not as Miss Miggs, according to the *Illustrated Times* (17 November 1866), p.311.
33. Reece, 'Unrehearsed Effects', p.169. According to the *Graphic* (10 December 1870), one boot was black, not green; Clement Scott remembered one green, one red, when he wrote about her drunkenness (*Drama of Yesterday and To-day*, London, 1899, II, 289-90).
34. Frank Archer, *An Actor's Notebooks* (London, 1912) excerpted in J. C. Trewin, *The Pomping Folk in the Nineteenth Century Theatre* (London, 1968), p.225. Gilbert, reviewing *All for Money* in the *Illustrated Times* (17 July 1869), p.43, called Irving 'the very king of fashionable villains'.
35. This extract was published in *Musical World* (11 February 1871), p.87.
36. Tom Taylor adapted *Narcisse* from a play by Brachvogel with the same title; this, in turn, had been based on Goethe's translation

of Diderot's novel *Le Neveu de Rameau*. *Narcisse* was played for the first time in England at the Lyceum on 17 February 1868, although Bandmann had played Brachvogel's version in America. It was not very successful, but Gilbert liked Bandmann. Winton Tolles, *Tom Taylor and the Victorian Drama* (New York, 1940), p.214.

37. Morley, p.310.
38. Lacy's Acting Edition (London, [1869]), pp.23-24.
39. Undated letter to the editor of *Musical World*, signed C. C. C. (4 January 1868), p.11.
40. Edward Rose in Cyril Maude, *The Haymarket Theatre: Some Records & Reminiscences* (London, 1903), p.157.
41. Archer, *Real Conversations*, p.111

Bibliography

Manuscript Sources

The Henry E. Huntington Library contains the Proprietor's copies of *Fun* beginning in late May 1865. Tom Hood, who had just become editor, marked each issue with the names of contributors and the fees they were paid. Gilbert contributed nothing after 27 May 1871 until December 1874, when he published the three parts of *Rosencrantz and Guildenstern*, his burlesque of *Hamlet*.

Peter Joslin's Gilbert and Sullivan collection contains Gilbert's own marked copies of *Fun*, but they do not begin until 1862.

Works by W. S. Gilbert.

'Actors, Authors and Audiences', *Holly Leaves* (Christmas 1880); revised as 'Trying a Dramatist', *Century Magazine*, LXXXIII (December 1911), 179-89.

'An Appeal to the Press', *Era Almanack* (1878), 85-86.

The Bab Ballads by W. S. Gilbert, ed. James Ellis (Cambridge, MA: Harvard University Press, 1970).

'The British Playgoer, and All That Is Expected of Him', *Tinsley's Magazine*, III (January 1869), 634-40.

'A Hornpipe in Fetters', *Era Almanack* (1879), 91-92.

'Old Plays and New Plays', *Era Almanack* (1873), 76.

An Old Score, (London: Thomas Hailes Lacy, n. d. [1869]).

'A Proposal for Elevating the Position of the Modern Drama', *Era Almanack* (1875), 86-87.

Randall's Thumb. Original Plays, 4th Series (London: Chatto & Windus, 1911).

'A Stage Play', in William Archer, ed., *Papers on Playmaking*, 3rd series (New York: Dramatic Museum of Columbia University, 1913).

'Unappreciated Shakespeare', *Illustrated Sporting and Dramatic News* (Christmas number, 9 December 1882).

Secondary Sources

Archer, William. *Real Conversations* (London: William Heinemann, 1904).

Brannan, Robert Louis. *Under the Management of Mr. Charles Dickens: His Production of 'The Frozen Deep'* (Ithaca, NY: Cornell University Press, 1966).

Browne, Edith. *W. S. Gilbert* (Stars of the Stage series) (London: John Lane, 1907).

Ellis, Ted R. III, 'Burlesque Dramas in the Victorian Comic Magazines', *Victorian Periodicals Review*, XV (Winter 1982), 138-43.

Fitzgerald, Percy. *The Savoy Operas and the Savoyards* (London: Chatto & Windus, 1899).

Hollingshead, John, 'Dramatic Critics Criticised', *Broadway*, I (September 1867), 30-35.

——————————. *My Lifetime*. 2 vols. (London: Sampson Low, Marston & Company Ltd, 1895).

Jones, John Bush, 'W. S. Gilbert's Contributions to *Fun*, 1865-1874', *Bulletin of the New York Public Library*, LXXIII (April 1969), 253-66.

Kent, Christopher, 'Periodical Critics of Drama, Music, & Art, 1830-1914: A Preliminary List', *Victorian Periodicals Review*, XIII (Spring & Summer 1980), 31-54.

——————————, 'More Critics of Drama, Music, & Art', *Victorian Periodicals Review*, XIX (Fall 1986), 99-105.

Lauterbach, Charles E., 'Taking Gilbert's Measure', *Huntington Library Quarterly*, XIX (February 1956), 196-202.

Lauterbach, Edward S. *'Fun* and Its Contributors: The Literary History of a Victorian Humor Magazine'. Unpublished Ph.D dissertation (University of Illinois, 1961).

[Mackay, William]. *Bohemian Days in Fleet Street by a Journalist* (London: John Long Ltd, 1913).

Maude, Cyril. *The Haymarket Theatre: Some Records and Reminiscences* (London: Grant Richards, 1903).

Morley, Henry. *The Journal of a London Playgoer from 1851 to 1866.*

2nd edition (London: George Routledge and Sons, 1891).

Nicoll, Allardyce. *A History of English Drama 1660-1900, vol. 5, Late Nineteenth Century Drama 1850-1900*. 2nd edition (Cambridge: Cambridge University Press, 1962).

Pemberton, T. Edgar. *The Life and Writings of T. W. Robertson* (London: Richard Bentley and Son, 1893).

Phillips, E. Watts. *Watts Phillips: Artist and Playwright* (London: Cassell & Co. Ltd, 1891).

Purnell, Thomas ('Q'). *Dramatists of the Present Day. Reprinted from 'The Athenaeum'* (London: Chapman and Hall, 1871).

Reece, Robert, 'Unrehearsed Effects', *Theatre*, II NS (April 1879), 168-71.

Scott, Clement. *The Drama of Yesterday and To-day*. 2 vols. (London: Macmillan and Co. Ltd, 1899).

Scott, Clement, and Cecil Howard, eds. *The Life and Reminiscences of E. L. Blanchard with Notes from the Diary of Wm. Blanchard*. 2 vols. (London: Hutchinson & Co., 1891).

Sewell, Elizabeth. *The Field of Nonsense* (London: Chatto and Windus, 1952).

Stedman, Jane W. *W. S. Gilbert: A Classic Victorian and His Theatre* (Oxford: Oxford University Press, 1996).

Tolles, Winton. *Tom Taylor and the Victorian Drama* (New York: Columbia University Press, 1940).

Trewin, J. C., ed. *The Pomping Folk in the Nineteenth-Century Theatre* (London: J. M. Dent & Sons Ltd, 1968).

Yates, Edmund. *Fifty Years of London Life* (New York: Harper & Brothers, 1885).

Periodicals
Athenaeum, Era, Fun, Graphic, Illustrated London News, Illustrated Sporting and Dramatic News, Illustrated Times, London Society, Musical World, Punch, Theatre, The Times, Tinsley's Magazine, Tomahawk.

Index